This book examines the social, economic and cultural
evolution of the peasantry in France and its place in French
society since 1789. Within a chronological framework, Annie
Moulin analyses the changes experienced by the peasantry, as
a subsistence economy has been gradually replaced by a
commercial, capitalist farming system. From a position of
numerical dominance in French society prior to 1789, the
relative population level of the French rural sector has
declined dramatically, with corresponding political
implications. Cultural and social shifts in diet, housing and
education have combined to alter vastly the patterns of rural
life in France, and in this lucid account Annie Moulin explores
the problems and tensions that have beset the peasantry since
the Revolution.

Peasantry and Society in France since 1789 is intended for a
student readership, and will complement neatly successful
earlier works by Pierre Goubert and Peter Jones, dealing
respectively with the seventeenth-century and revolutionary
peasantries. Important undergraduate aids include a
chronology and bibliographies of both French and English
works, and these, together with the Clearys' expert translation,
should make Annie Moulin's the standard introductory
account of the post-revolutionary peasantry.

For Henri Bonnet,
winegrower
1866–1955

Published by the Press Syndicate of the University of Cambridge
The Pitt Building, Trumpington Street, Cambridge CB2 1RP
40 West 20th Street, New York, NY 10011-4211, USA
10 Stamford Road, Oakleigh, Melbourne 3166, Australia
and Editions de la Maison des Sciences de l'Homme
54 Boulevard Raspail, 75270 Paris Cedex 06

Originally published in French as *Les Paysans dans la société française*
by Editions du Seuil 1988
and © Editions du Seuil, 1988

First published in English by
Editions de la Maisons des Sciences de l'Homme
and Cambridge University Press 1991 as
Peasantry and Society in France since 1789
English translation © Maison des Sciences de l'Homme
and Cambridge University Press 1991

Printed in Great Britain at the University Press, Cambridge

British Library cataloguing in publication data

Peasantry and society in France since 1789.
1. France. Peasants. Social conditions, 1450–1660
I. Title II. [Paysans dans la société française. *English*]
305.563

Library of Congress cataloguing in publication data

Moulin, Annie.
[Paysans dans la société française. English]
Peasantry and society in France since 1789 / Annie Moulin:
translated from the French by M. C. and M. F. Cleary.
    p. cm.
Translation of: Les paysans dans la société française.
Includes bibliographical references and index.
ISBN 0 521 39534 8. – ISBN 0 521 39577 1 (paperback)
1. Peasantry – France – History. 2. France – Rural conditions.
I. Title.
HD1536.F8M6813 1991   90–22363
305.5'633'0944–dc20 CIP

ISBN 0 521 39534 8 hardback
ISBN 0 521 39577 1 paperback
ISBN 2 7351 0000 0 hardback (France only)
ISBN 2 7351 0000 0 paperback (France only)

WD

Peasantry and society in France since 1789

ANNIE MOULIN
University of Clermont-Ferrand

Translated from French by
M. C. and M. F. CLEARY

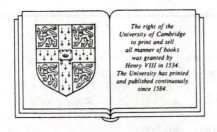

The right of the
University of Cambridge
to print and sell
all manner of books
was granted by
Henry VIII in 1534.
The University has printed
and published continuously
since 1584.

CAMBRIDGE UNIVERSITY PRESS
Cambridge
New York   Port Chester   Melbourne   Sydney

EDITIONS DE
LA MAISON DES SCIENCES DE L'HOMME
Paris

Peasantry and society in France since 1789

Contents

Maps and diagrams

Outline chronology

1789

March	Elections to Estates General
March–May	Agrarian troubles in Provence, Picardy, the Cambrésis and Quercy
15 July–6 August	The Great Fear
5–11 August	Seigneurial rights declared purchasable
2 November	Church property ceded to the nation

1790

January	Peasant uprisings in Quercy, Périgord, Brittany
16 March	Legislation allowing communal land to be divided in the preceding thirty years abolished
14 May	Procedure for sale of church lands agreed

1791

February	Formation of government-directed clergy
28 September	Rural Code established. Recognition of the right to enclose land

1792

February–March	Counter-revolutionary turmoil in Lozère and the Dauphiné
Spring–summer	Anti-seigneurial uprisings in Provence and Périgord
14 August	Division of communal land authorised. Application of the text quickly suspended
25 August	Requirement that seigneurs be allowed to repurchase their rights permitted only if they could prove exercise of such rights in the last thirty years
4 September	Cereals requisitioned and taxed to provide for the military
22 September	Troubles in the Beauce over cereal taxation

1793

24 February	Conscription of army of 300,000
11 March	Start of Vendée revolt
4 May	Price maxima set for grains and flour
3 June	Sale of *émigré* property in small lots
10 June	Division of communal lands authorised with agreement of community. Decree suspended in 1796
17 July	Abolition, without compensation, of all seigneurial rights
26 July	Decree of death sentence ordained for all profiteers
11 September	National price maxima set for cereals
29 September	National price maxima set for wages and foodstuffs

1794

24 September	Abolition of price maxima

1795

22 August	Constitution of year III suppresses municipal councils in communes with fewer than 5,000 inhabitants

1797

21 May	Communes forbidden to sell communal land

1799

28 December	Churches allowed to open on Sundays

1800

17 February	Law creating new administrative structures in France

1801

15 July	Signing of Concordat

1804

21 March	Civil Code established

1807

15 September	Work on the *cadastre* starts

1812

8 May	Taxes on cereals introduced

1813
20 March   Central *caisse* charged with selling off communal land

1816
28 April   Communes recover all land not yet sold. They are
                    allowed to let such land in blocks

1817
February   Agrarian troubles in Brie and Champagne
May–July   Agrarian troubles in the Auvergne, Brittany,
                    Bourgogne, the Limousin, the Orléanais

1825
27 April   *Emigré* indemnities agreed

1827
21 May   Forestry Code passed

1829
Spring   *Guerre des Demoiselles* in Ariège

1831
21 May   Law reestablishing election of municipal councils by
                    electoral body

1833
28 June   Guizot legislation on schooling

1836
21 May   Communes empowered to maintain local roads

1842
11 June   Legislation on railway construction

1844
30 May   Hunting permits instituted. Seen as a restriction on
                    free hunting established at the Revolution

1845   Publication of Balzac's *Les Paysans*

1846
Summer   Disastrous cereal harvest

1847
28 January   Legislation facilitating grain imports

1848
2 March   Universal male suffrage
16 March   '45 centimes' tax imposed
3 July   Decree allowing election of mayors in communes with
                     fewer than 6,000 people
3 October   Tourret law on agricultural education

1849
13 May   Legislative elections reveal a 'red' peasantry

1850
6 December   Law allowing individuals to initiate dismantling and
                     redistribution of communal land

1851
December   Rural resistance to *coup d'état* in south-east, northern
                     Massif Central, the south-west

1860
23 January   Commercial treaty with Great Britain
28 July   First law on mountain communal land. Communes
                     allowed to sell up to one-third of such land

1863   First evidence of phylloxera in Gard

1867   Creation of Société des agriculteurs de France

1868
11 July   Communes allowed to borrow funds to maintain local
                     roads

1871
16 April   Municipal law allowing election of mayors in
                     communes with less than 20,000 people

1872
27 July   Military law establishing principle of compulsory
                     military service

1875
14 December   Distillers granted special privileges

1878
May   Start of Freycinet Plan

1879
16 June   Establishment of departmental professors of
                   agriculture

1880   Gambetta founds Société nationale d'encouragement
                   à l'agriculture

1881
16 June   Free primary education established
14 November   Creation of post of Minister of Agriculture

1882
28 March   Law establishing obligatory education and non-
                   religious teaching staff
4 April   Restoration of communal land in upland areas

1884
24 March   Customs tariffs established on imported wheat
5 April   Law establishing system of municipal elections

1886   Creation of Union centrale des syndicats agricoles de
                   France

1887
2 December   Compulsory anti-phylloxera syndicates established.
                   Replanted vines exempted from property taxes.
                   Publication of Émile Zola's *La Terre*

1889
9 July   Common pasturing on cultivated lands abolished.
15 July   Three-year military service established.

1892
11 January   Méline tariffs, reinforcing customs duties on
                   agricultural imports

1894
30 March   Seigfried law on inheritance practices
6 November   Local credit *caisses* established

1897
29 March   New upper limit for customs barriers depending on
                domestic prices

1899
31 March   Creation of regional credit *caisses*
9 July   Right of common pasturing abolished.
                Eugène Le Roy's *Jacquou le Croquant* published.
                René Bazin's *La Terre qui meurt* published

1904
January   Strikes by agricultural workers in Hérault and Aude
4 July   Statutes of the *mutualité agricole* established

1905
January   Congrès de défense du Midi viticole held at Béziers
March   Military service reduced to two years
9 September   Law on Separation of Church and State

1907
June   Viticultural revolt in Midi
29 June   Laws regulating addition of sugar to wine
22 September Creation of Confédération générale des vignerons

1911
April   Demonstrations by viticulturalists in the Aube
16 September Office Central at Landernau founded

1914
2 August   Mobilisation of troops

1915
16 October   Control of wheat market introduced

1916
20 February   Legislation on cultivation of unused land
29 July   Taxes on cereals

1918
10 February   Price controls introduced
27 November   Chauveau law on *remembrement*

1919
July   Strikes by farm workers in the Paris Basin

1920
5 August   Creation of national Crédit agricole

1922
25 March   Programme for creating national electricity grid
                      drawn up
15 April   Legislation on accident insurance in farming

1924
3 January   Chambers of Agriculture established
March   Creation of Association générale des producteurs de
                      blé

1925
18 January   Worker-peasant syndicates regrouped into Conseil
                      paysan français

1928
December   Dorgères organises the first Comités de défense
                      paysanne

1929   Creation of JAC

1930
16 April   General revision of the *cadastre* begun

1931
4 July   Wine statute drawn up. Modified between 1933 and
                      1934

1933
13 February   Creation of Confédération nationale paysanne
10 July   Minimum wheat price fixed

1934
April   Creation of Front Paysan
24 December   Minimum wheat prices abandoned.
                    Law allowing distillation of surplus wine. Grants for
                    pulling up vines

1936
20 June   Paid holidays instituted
5 August   Extension of family allowances to farm labourers
15 August   Office nationale interprofessionnel du blé created

1937
July   Strikes by farm workers in the north and Paris Basin

1939
21 April   Law granting farm inheritors who continue working
                    on the farm to inherit without having to split the farm
29 July   Extension of family allowances to farmers

1940
21 November   Law to improve rural living conditions
2 December   Corporatist organisation of agriculture instituted

1941
9 February   Regulations to govern sowing and harvesting of crops
30 May   Grants available for those wishing to move into
                    farming
5 July   Measures to improve agricultural education
13 October   'Family gifts' system brought in

1942
16 December   Organisation of Corporation paysanne

1943
15 January   New legislation to prevent excessive division of farms
                    on inheritance
4 September   Rights of tenant-farmers reinforced

1944
26 July   Corporation paysanne suppressed
12 October   Creation of CGA

1946
13 March   Creation of FNSEA
13 April   New statutes for farmers and sharecroppers
18 May   Creation of INRA

1948
10 March   Limit of 2,400 working hours per year for salaried
                     farm workers

1950
11 February   Chambers of Agriculture reinstated

1951
15 February   Creation of Centre national des indépendants et
                     paysans

1952
10 July   Old-age insurance introduced for farmers

1953
28 July   Violent demonstrations by viticulturalists in the Midi
22 September   Comité de Guéret created
12 October   Road-blocks set up in central France
15 December   Creation of SIBEV and Interlait

1954
19 January   Statutes of CGA modified – much of its power lost

1955
1 May   Pierre Poujade's initiative created Union de défense
                     des agriculteurs de France
1957
25 March   Treaty of Rome
Summer   Series of peasant demonstrations
18 September   Agricultural prices indexed

1959
February   Abandonment of price indexing
7 April   Creation of MODEF. It becomes a syndicate in 1975

1960

February	Series of agricultural demonstrations
2 August	Law on agricultural education
5 August	Orientation Law established

1961

25 January	Sickness, disability and maternity provisions for farmers
June	Violent peasant demonstrations in Brittany
8 August	Complementary Orientation Law passed (Pisani Law). Creation of GAEC and IVD

1962

14 January	Start of Common Agricultural Policy

1967

1 July	Single EEC market for cereals comes into effect

1968

1 June	Agricultural workers granted right to minimum wage (SMIG – *salaire minimum garanti*)
10 December	Publication of Mansholt plan

1969

2 December	Creation of Fédération française de l'agriculture

1970

31 December	Groupements fonciers agricoles legalised

1973

13 July	Law regulating position of farm assistants (family members) drawn up

1976

6 February	Grants made available to young farmers
March	Violent peasant demonstrations

1980

4 July	New Orientation Law

1981

4 June   Creation of Confédération nationale des syndicats de travailleurs paysans

1982

23 March   Agricultural demonstrations in Paris at instigation of FNSEA

6 October   Creation of offices nationaux interprofessionnels d'intervention

1984

30–31 March   Establishment of milk-quota system in EEC

Abbreviations

CETA	Centre d'études agricoles
CGA	Confédération générale de l'agriculture
CNASEA	Centre national pour l'aménagement des structures des exploitations agricoles
CNJA	Cercle national des jeunes agriculteurs, later Centre national des jeunes agriculteurs
CNSTP	Confédération nationale des syndicats de travailleurs paysans
CUMA	Coopérative d'utilisation du matériel agricole
DJA	Dotation aux jeunes agriculteurs
FASASA	Fonds d'action sociale pour l'aménagement des structures des exploitations agricoles
FFA	Fédération française de l'agriculture
FNSEA	Fédération nationale des syndicats d'exploitants agricoles
FNSP	Fédération nationale des syndicats paysans
FORMA	Fonds d'orientation et de régularisation des marchés agricoles
GAEC	Groupement agricole d'exploitation en commun
GFA	Groupement foncier agricole
INRA	Institut national de la recherche agronomique
INSEE	Institut national de la statistique et des études économiques
IVD	Indemnité viagère de départ
JAC	Jeunesse agricole catholique
MODEF	Mouvement de défense des exploitants familiaux
ONIB	Office national interprofessionnel du blé. Became in 1940 ONIC: Office national interprofessionnel des céreales
PCF	Parti communiste français
POS	Plan d'occupation des sols
RBE	Revenu brut d'exploitation
RPR	Rassemblement pour la république
SAF	Société des agriculteurs de France
SAFER	Société d'aménagement foncier et d'établissement rural
SAU	Surface agricole utilisée

SFIO	Section Française de l'Internationale Ouvrière
SIBEV	Société interprofessionnelle du bétail et des viandes
SMIG	Salaire minimum interprofessionnel garanti
SNEA	Société nationale d'encouragement à l'agriculture
SNIPOT	Société nationale interprofessionnelle de la pomme de terre
UDF	Union pour la démocratie française
UTA	Unité de travail annuel
UTH	Unité de travail-homme

Introduction

It might be argued that, with the publication in 1975–6 of the four-volume *Histoire de la France rurale*, under the general editorship of Georges Duby and Armand Wallon, little more remains to be written on the subject of the French peasantry.[1] Nevertheless, some fifteen years later, there does seem some point to writing this current book, if only to attempt a synthesis of some of the recent ethnographic and historical theses which, in their infancy in the 1960s and early 1970s, have come to fruition today.

The current work focuses first and foremost on the peasantry, and the place it has occupied in French society. Because of that, it moves beyond a consideration of agriculture alone but, by the same token, is not able to include the totality of the rural world. Of course, the very term peasant is a notoriously difficult one to pin down.[2] In the eighteenth century, the peasant was, above all, a country-dweller, rooted deep in his native soil.[3] His skills were clear-cut and well defined: in the words of one of La Fontaine's characters: 'I am a peasant, no more nor less . . . I can sow seeds, plough the soil, graft the vine and that's all'.[4] Then, three-quarters of the population were peasants and agricultural activity dominated the rural economy. At the same time, the term peasant had undoubted pejorative connotations, which lasted throughout the nineteenth century. It was largely synonymous with a coarse, crude, uncultured person. It is hardly surprising, then, that politicians chose to use more neutral, perhaps more flattering, terms such as cultivator, in their speeches. Those landed gentry, passionate agronomists, much preferred to speak of themselves as farmers.

At the start of the twentieth century, however, the word peasant was rehabilitated thanks to agrarian thinkers. Agricultural organisations in the inter-war years consciously sought to use the word peasant as a rallying cry and source of pride. In the years after 1945, the era of the farmer-technician, the word again took on somewhat unfavourable connotations. Not that these lasted long. By the end of the 1960s, in a rural world in which the place of agriculture was increasingly marginalised,

1

the term peasant seemed, to town-dwellers at least, to represent stability
and a sense of belonging in a world that was rapidly changing. But, one
might ask, does the peasantry still exist? Does the term peasantry signify
a community of shared values and solidarity? Outside attitudes, sometimes hostile, at other times favourable, will determine, to a large extent,
the future use of the term.

The way in which the word peasant has shifted its meaning over time
is especially indicative of how the world at large has defined, identified
and recognised the peasant world. To what extent is that world now fully
integrated into the French nation? Maurice Agulhon has suggested that,
after centuries of resistance, especially fiscal, by the start of the Third
Republic it had become one of the chief anchors of the regime. Equally,
however, both Eugen Weber and Henri Mendras have painted a picture
of a peasantry which remained, in part at least, foreign to society at large.
For Mendras, peasants were, above all: 'people who live in a society with
a high degree of economic and political independence and autarchy
from society at large and who have their own, distinctive, patterns of
living'.[5] Perhaps in this sense, then, the 1960s saw the end of the
peasantry.

Equally controversial is the economic and social position of the
peasant. Is he a capitalist entrepreneur, owner of his means of production? Or is he rather exploited by a society which draws from him the
products it needs and pays him but poorly in return? The land, then,
cannot be simply regarded as but one more factor of production. The
evolution of the peasantry and the national and global economy cannot
be separated. The ways in which agriculture has changed have determined the relationship between the peasantry and the society that
surrounds it.

The current work, then, cannot escape such difficult questions. Over-
simplification is undoubtedly a real danger. The peasant world evolved
only slowly up until the early 1950s, but the rate of that evolution varied
from one region to the next. However, a full study of the regional cases
is especially difficult, simply because so many regional monographs
focus on 'problem peasantries' south of the Loire. The risk of over-
generalisation must, however, be tackled in order to identify long-term
secular trends. The Revolution marked a vitally important staging-post.
Even if it failed to bring about a massive modification of agricultural
structures, the abolition of seigneurial fines and taxes permitted the
peasantry to keep more of what it produced. From this fact flowed the
slow improvements in living conditions once demographic pressures had
begun to ease. The end of the Second Empire marked an important
turning-point. The long agricultural depression made land investment

less attractive for non-farmers, whilst improvements in communications accelerated urban influences in the countryside. The wars and the crisis of the 1930s which separated them brought many peasants face to face with the gap that separated their lives from those of their fellow citizens. That gap closed rapidly between 1950 and 1970. In under twenty years the peasantry was confronted by massive changes. Such changes were to call into question the very existence of the peasantry.

1

From the ancien régime to the Restoration: 1789–1815

The quarter of a century which separated the fall of the ancien régime and the Restoration was a decisive one for the French peasantry. In the space of a generation, the social structure and organisation of rural society was both challenged and changed. The rural population, more than three-quarters of the total, was far from indifferent to the tumultuous events in Paris; what is clear is that it is far from easy to determine its precise role in the break up of the old regime and the implementation of the new revolutionary politics. This debate continues apace. One need do no more than consult the impressive bibliographical material devoted to agrarian problems over the last ten years for evidence of this.[1]

Controversy has ranged over a number of key issues regarding the economic and social evolution of the countryside in the second half of the eighteenth century. Did agricultural production grow or stagnate in this period? The answer will to some extent determine the historian's interpretation of the economic crises and peasant unrest of the immediate pre-revolutionary period. There has also been much debate over the place of the peasantry in the revolutionary process itself. For at least the last forty years the interpretation of Georges Lefebvre, that the peasant revolution, both anti-feudal and anti-capitalist, existed and functioned independently of the bourgeois revolution has held sway. This view was challenged some ten years ago when Albert Soboul, following the work of the Russian historian, Anatolii Ado, argued that the peasant movements were a variant of, rather than distinct from, the bourgeois revolution. François Furet and Emmanuel Le Roy Ladurie have further argued for an autonomous type of peasant engagement in the revolutionary upheavals, which was essentially conservative and opposed to the technical innovations which bourgeois farmers were introducing. This basically conservative attitude on the part of the peasantry explains, they argue, the hidden areas of resistance to the Revolution, areas which have long preoccupied the historiographers of the Revolution. The continued polemic is, furthermore, greatly accentuated by the enormous diversity of local conditions and constraints which seem to render the search for generalisation illusory. Only the continued development of regionally based research can advance the debate.

1. A dominated and dependent peasantry

Ancien régime society was overwhelmingly rural in character. Of the 27 or 28 million people that made up the nation in 1789, at least 22 million were rural-dwellers whilst some 18 million – men, women, young and old – were engaged in agriculture. Almost three out of four French people were peasants. They comprised not one but a multitude of different peasantries living in a diverse kingdom in which regions and districts jealously guarded their differences and autonomy. Beyond this diversity, however, some points of convergence are clear. The peasant was not an isolated individual, and an apparently uniform set of economic, social and legal systems and practices helped to structure patterns of life in these diverse village communities.

Agricultural systems

The routines of peasant life, profoundly marked by conditions of work, were closely dependent on agricultural practices. Northern farming systems have perhaps received most attention. They were based primarily on a division of village territory into three parts, each distinct and with a different legal status, but together forming a complementary whole.

At the centre, in the village, were the houses and gardens (the latter not always directly adjacent to the former). These lay largely outside the collective constraints which structured the community. The garden area was subject to neither the property tax (*dime*) nor, as a rule, to the various seigneurial taxes. The peasant could use it as he wished; he tended, above all, to grow vegetables or the vine. Part of the land would perhaps be reserved for flax. In many regions, the limits of this personal garden area would be marked by some form of fence or, more simply, by a series of crosses or markers adjoining the pathways.

Beyond such boundaries stretched the cultivated land, given over primarily to cereals. This agricultural zone was subject to the twin constraints of heavy seigneurial taxation and the strong communal control which formed the base of most eighteenth-century peasant communities. The best-known such constraint was the right of common grazing (*vaine pâture*). After the harvest, the status of the land would change. The fields would become common property. The poor of the village had the right to glean those cereals that had escaped the harvesters and the animals of the village, herded together, were able to pasture on the newly harvested land. This right of common grazing was precious to the poorer peasants,

Table 1. *The three-field system*

Year	Field 1	Field 2	Field 3
1	Winter wheats	Spring wheats	Fallow
2	Spring wheats	Fallow	Winter wheats
3	Fallow	Winter wheats	Spring wheats

constrained as they usually were by a shortage of pasture land. Common grazing, however, also implied constraints on field rotations. Since individual boundaries were forbidden on these lands, individual farming practices were hardly practicable. The land would usually be divided into three parts or *soles* and a triennial rotation was the usual pattern (see table 1).

On each field, the cycle would commence with autumn cereals, most commonly wheat or rye, sown in October. The harvest would be taken fairly late in early August of the following year. The land would then be left as stubble for a few weeks, ploughed and worked once or twice between October and March, after which barley or oats, occasionally wheat or beans, would be sown. After harvesting in August and a period of liming, the field would be left fallow for a year until the following autumn. In that time it might be ploughed six or eight times, depending on the region. Only when the field was in stubble would common pasturing be allowed.

In addition to the gardens and cultivated land, the village community usually possessed a range of uncultivated lands – heaths, forest, marshland and waste areas. These constituted an invaluable resource for the village. They helped, for example, to provide animal litter, firewood and materials for building repairs and additional rough pasture for animals. But the extent of these communal lands showed marked regional variations. In the Artois they rarely exceeded 3 per cent to 4 per cent of agricultural land, whereas in the Massif Central up to half a community's land could be made up of these 'waste' areas.[2] In the second half of the eighteenth century, they were constantly under threat. As cereal prices rose, certain nobles sought to extend their territories here; a peasantry hard pressed by demographic expansion often sought to nibble away likewise at community land. The attitude of the authorities was usually circumspect for fear of arousing strong peasant reaction. In the north and east, as well as in the south-west, however, some divisions of communal land were authorised: one-third to the nobility, two-thirds to the village community. Thus, in the Artois, between 1770 and 1781, one-fifth of all communal land had been divided in this way. For both peasants and labourers without land the gains were immediate. But the opposition of some large farmers, conscious that they were losing pasture land, limited these operations.[3] Elsewhere there was opposition to the one-third share of the nobility. What is clear is that these land divisions exacerbated the divisions within many rural communities.

The three elements of the farming system – gardens, cultivated land and communal territory – showed marked variations from one region to another. In regions where cereal production was less dominant, a different division often operated. In Brittany and the centre-west, where pastoral farming was significant, communal areas were often vast and unencumbered by complex restrictions. Likewise, where cultivated land could be enclosed by high hedges, there were few limitations on individual farming practices. South of the Loire, climatic conditions and relatively infertile soils again meant a somewhat different farming system from that in the north. On the 'cold soils' of the Auvergne and Limousin. a biennial rotation was widespread. Here a year of fallow would succeed an autumn cereal, usually rye. It may be supposed that the triennial rotation represented an advance over the biennial. But in terms of productivity, this was not necessarily the case, for the March harvest often represented but half of what would be obtained from a good autumn sowing. In practice there was often little difference between a biennial rotation giving one harvest every second year, and a triennial which gave one and a half harvests every three. The principal advantage of the triennial rotation was that the period of preparation for the spring sowing fitted in well with a traditional 'dead' period in the agricultural calendar. Nonetheless, the triennial rotation was technologically limiting. The attempt to produce two successive crops from one field meant that the fallow had to be maintained, whereas it was possible, with a biennial rotation, to gain a catch crop of, say potatoes, during the lull in working the land.

Occasionally the land would be left fallow for a number of years, a system of farming known as *pâtis*. In Mediterranean France, farming systems were much more varied. Because the summer drought often prevented spring wheat from fully maturing, biennial rotations were the rule (often with fruit trees interplanted), except where irrigation was a possibility. If these trees gave variety they also limited the extent of common grazing. Animals were thus usually confined to the communal lands. In viticultural areas, the fallow often disappeared altogether. It should be clear that these farming categories are merely a pale reflection of the true diversity of the countryside, a diversity which defies the cartographer. Nonetheless, François Sigaut has attempted to map the varied farming systems in the late eighteenth and early nineteenth centuries and his map, whilst not exhaustive, serves admirably to emphasise the diversity of local situations and systems evident at the end of the ancien régime.[4]

Notwithstanding such diversity, it is possible to identify some common characteristics of these agrarian systems (see figure 1). Except in areas of viticulture, all of them give a clear priority to subsistence products, especially cereals. Antoine Lavoisier noted this fact in 1787: 'Agriculture in most French provinces . . . can be regarded as a producer of cereals above all else; animals serve merely as beasts of burden and providers of manure.'[5] It is above all the shortage of animals, and therefore of manure, that lies at the root of the poor yields. Whilst information on these is sparse, they can be crudely measured in terms of the number of grains harvested for grains sown. Averages seemed to oscillate between 4 and 6 to 1, a return which can be roughly equated to about 7 to 9 quintals per hectare. Only in the most fertile regions, such as Picardy, would returns of around 20 per hectare obtain. The provision of seed, therefore, represented a major drain on production. Between one-fifth and one-quarter of the harvest would therefore have to be reserved, perhaps even more in poor years. These poor yields meant that land devoted to animals was limited and therefore manure in short supply; this was the 'vicious circle' described by Marc Bloch. Cereals became a 'necessary evil' in the system.

Animals were present, however, in all systems. In the Paris region, the *viticulteurs* fed their cattle with the grass used to train the vines[6] and pastoral farming undoubtedly progressed in upland regions in the course of the eighteenth century. Overall, however, techniques remained poor and productivity low, with primitive tools and practices evident. For ploughing, the heavy plough (*charrue*) dominated in the north, the lighter (*araire*) in the south.[7] Human labour remained at the base of all farming systems, with large inputs required for only meagre returns. In such conditions then, what kind of progress was possible?

The taste for agronomic discourse might lead us to believe that progress did take place. From about 1750, under the impulse of Quesnay and the Physiocrats, the agronomists emphasised the importance of agriculture. For them, land and land alone was the ultimate source of productivity: 'The land is the unique source of wealth; only agriculture can secure and increase these riches.'[8] Modernisation of the economy, it was argued, depended on the modernisation of farming. A more dynamic agricultural system, based on the English model with the introduction of forage crops into new rotations and the expansion of animal

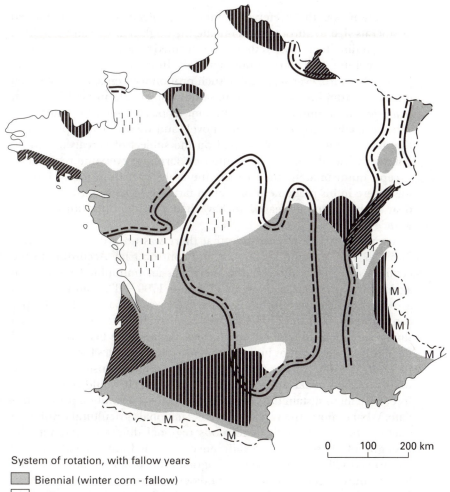

System of rotation, with fallow years

Biennial (winter corn - fallow)

Triennial (winter corn - spring cereals - fallow)

Quadrennial (three grain crops, then fallow)

System of rotation, without fallow

Two or three successive harvests of cereals + application of manure or long periods of waste

Flanders system (with industrial and forage crops)

Pasture (periods of waste interpolated with periods of rotation)

M   Mountain or upland cultivation

Figure 1 Systems of cultivation in France, c. 1800. (*Source:* F. Sigaut, 'Pour une cartographie des assolements en France au début du XIXe siècle', *Annales ESC*, May–June 1976, pp. 632f.)

production, was the preferred solution. Intellectuals and enlightened aristocrats vied to advocate and imitate the English model and sought to propagandise their views in their newly formed rural academies, societies of agriculture and agricultural journals In reality their impact was limited. Voltaire, ever sceptical of such pronouncements, many of which emanated from his rival Rousseau, sardonically noted in his *Dictionnaire philosophique*: 'around 1750, the nation, its palate jaded by a surfeit of verse, tragedies, comedies, opera, novels and theological disputes over the nature of grace, finally settled on the subject of cereals . . . Many eminently useful things were written on farming; everyone read them, except, unfortunately, the farmers themselves.' Arthur Young himself was severe in his judgement of French farming.[9] The English model, so dear to his heart, appeared to have had precious little influence in France.

Are we therefore to conclude that there was no progress in French farming? The question is complex and controversial. According to the economist Jean-Claude Toutain, there was an undoubted increase in agricultural production between 1700 and 1790.[10] The annual rate of growth of agricultural production may have reached as much as 1.4 per cent between 1750 and 1790. Michel Morineau, however, has questioned the methodological base on which these figures have been built,[11] and has emphasised the gaps in documentation and statistics for this period. In 1840, the date of the first national agricultural census, agriculture hardly seemed to have made dramatic progress. It would seem, there-fore, difficult to sustain the view of an agricultural revolution prior to this date. What is more, the very concept of a national agricultural revolution may be unreal, given the enormous regional differences. It was the strength of these regional differences that led Emmanuel Le Roy Ladurie to talk of 'small steps of agricultural progress' linked to the 'steady introduction of new technologies which took the place, in France, of an agricultural revolution on the English model'.[12] Thus, in Languedoc, yields rose only slowly from the 1730s but the rise noticeably quickened after 1750. These results were obtained by a combination of growth factors. Transport improvements and the intensification of man-power were the most important. The introduction of secondary crops, notably potatoes and maize, was also important. Patterns of demographic growth in the second half of the eighteenth century also appear to suggest an improvement in the availability of food. In most regions, birth rates remained high at around 35 to 37/1,000, birth limitations being achieved largely through late marriage. Death rates fell slightly to around 30/1,000. Advances in medicine and hygiene, barely perceptible in the countryside, can hardly explain such a fall. It seems clear that the demographic pressure which resulted acted as a catalyst for agricultural innovation.

Given the paucity of sources, a clear response to the question of an 'agricultural revolution' is difficult. Nonetheless, some points of agreement are possible. The term agricultural revolution must be regarded as singularly inappropriate in the French case, unless one can regard as revolutionary a process that took some two centuries to complete. What agricultural progress there was took place rather as an accumulation of small, unspectacular changes: piecemeal clearances of the heathlands, catch crops on the fallow, a steady intensification of labour. To be able to proceed much further, the notion of some sort of national transformation has to be abandoned, at least until the realities of regional changes are more fully understood.

Whether or not there was decisive progress in French farming in this period, it is at least clear that the agricultural economy was fragile and highly vulnerable to fluctuation. The root cause of food crises in the countryside remained climatic: a severe winter, sharp spring frosts or a damp summer all threatened the harvest. Patterns of peasant consumption showed dramatic variations because of both climatic events and the weight of feudal taxes. In addition, the need to provide seed for the next year created additional stress in the domestic larder. Agricultural prices often fluctuated wildly with severe social consequences. Internal customs barriers and archaic transport networks made the circulation of food products difficult and costly and amplified regional isolation. Many peasants were forced to buy food during periods of shortage and cut back on other purchases, a situation which exacerbated social tensions. Many peasants were forced to dip into their meagre savings or else borrow. For much of this period, then, agriculture dictated economic rhythms. Subsistence crises would, in their train, engender a crisis of under-consumption in the economy. Such crises served, above all else, to highlight the profound inequalities in rural society and the fragile social structures on which that society was based.

The burdens of the social order

At the end of the ancien régime, ownership of land was the pivot around which social hierarchies were organised. It is also important to note that many peasants did not own all the land they farmed. What is more, peasant ownership of the land was frequently hedged round with a multitude of limitations and requirements imposed by an aristocratic landlord.

The division of property ownership between the different social groups is poorly understood. Global estimates rarely seem to agree. In broad terms we can note that the nobility controlled some 20 per cent to 25 per cent of the land in 1789, the church between 10 per cent and 15 per cent, the bourgeoisie between 20 per cent and 30 per cent. The 'landowning classes' to use the expression of the Physiocrats, therefore possessed around half of all land whilst representing only some 5 per cent to 8 per cent of the population.[13] The peasantry owned at least one-third of the land, more likely around a half. This seems to be the most convincing hypothesis. By way of comparison, it is worth noting that both Arthur Young and Alexis de Tocqueville considered that peasant owner-ship of land was much more widespread in France than England. Where detailed studies have been undertaken, considerable variations in these figures are apparent, variations which reflect the relative accessibility of different regions, their proximity to major urban centres or the fertility of the soil. In upland Auvergne, for example, peasants owned some 75 per cent of the land. In the Béarn the figure was as high as 90 per cent. Close to towns, the figures were usually much lower. In the area around Chartres, for example, it was no higher than 40 per cent.[14] Similarly, where the church was powerful, peasant ownership was reduced. Thus in the Gâtine of Poitou, peasant ownership hovered between 10 per cent and 20 per cent. To the south-east of le Mans some 87 per cent of the land was in non-peasant hands.[15] The property market, largely dormant in the eighteenth century, provided little scope for most peasants to improve their position.

    Such property divisions meant that many peasants were obliged to work other people's lands. The average size of farms differed little from the average size of property blocks. Non-farming landowners would rarely let their land in a single block to farmers – the large tenant farms of the Paris Basin and the north were the exception in the eighteenth century. Their average size was over 50 hectares in the Artois.[16] But the bulk of the land owned by the nobility or bourgeoisie were divided into small sharecropping units of a few hectares. Thus, in the Gâtine of Poitou farms rarely exceeded 3 hectares.[17] The sharecroppers were controlled by owner-leasers who, in some regions, were able to profit from demo-graphic pressure in the second half of the eighteenth century by demanding stricter and stricter leases. Sharecroppers were frequently required to pay their leases in kind, money and work. Given the regional diversity of conditions, generalisation regarding the importance of rent payments in the agricultural economy is difficult. According to Paul Bois, a figure of between 25 per cent and 33 per cent of farm production may be a realistic figure for the department of Sarthe.[18] It was a high per-centage, particularly when the range of other, additional charges, is added.

The *seigneurie* comprised those lands over which seigneurial authority was exercised. Freehold land, over which there were no seigneurial rights was rare north of the Loire. The seigneurial system represented a type of ownership characterised by the payment of rents in kind or money, either fixed or in proportion to the size of the harvest. The manner in which these taxes were organised varied but, in almost all cases, the nobility would exercise a range of legal rights and controls over their lands which emphasised the subordinate position of the peasant. The real extent of the feudal impress is, however, not easy to determine. The study of the 50,000 or so seigneurial estates in the kingdom is hardly sufficiently advanced to enable a precise picture to be drawn for the end of the ancien régime.[19] What information is available, however, does at least allow us to pick out some of the major regional contrasts, for seigneurial charges varied greatly on both an inter- and intra-regional scale. It appears they were very heavy in Brittany, Bourgogne and the Auxois, as well as in the lower Auvergne. In the Midi, the demands appear to have been somewhat lighter. The juxtaposition of two proverbs sums up this contrast nicely: 'No land without a noble' applies above all to the north of the country in cases of dispute, whilst in the Midi 'No noble without a title' was preferred. In this region, peasants did not hesitate to resort to both the law and archives to defend themselves against what they considered excessive seigneurial demands.

Precise estimation of the weight of seigneurial charges is thus difficult. Most estimates have examined their importance relative to the gross or net revenue of the farm, after deduction of costs. Jean Nicolas has argued for a figure of between 8 per cent and 12 per cent in Savoie, broadly comparable to the 15 per cent figure that Jacques Godechot argued for in the Toulouse region. But the charges reached 20 per cent in the lower Auvergne and even as much as 25 per cent in the Brive region. Elsewhere, they were often much lower, as in the region around Lodève or at La Chapelle-Basse-Mer in the Vendée.[20] In addition to these charges, the place of the tithe payable to the church needs to be considered. Including seed for the next sowing, this was usually between 7 per cent and 9 per cent of the total harvest, occasionally 13 per cent, as in Gascony, but only rarely the 10 per cent of popular imagination. Such figures and estimates are frequently uncertain and often raise more questions than they answer. What is important, however, is to establish how they changed over time.

A central question concerns the evidence for a seigneurial reaction in the second half of the eighteenth century. A number of historians have argued that the level of these various charges, particularly those that were paid in money, became relatively less important as prices rose in the course of the century. Nonetheless, there are some signs of a tightening up of seigneurial demands from about 1760. After this date there is evidence that a number of seigneurs engaged surveyors and land-agents to revise and redraw their estates. A greater rigour in the tabulation and enforcement of seigneurial rights is also evident, especially amongst more-recent bourgeois purchasers of estates. This greater vigilance was undoubtedly a reflection of the need to justify the purchase of such estates. The increasing attention given to such matters is hardly surprising given that such revenues often accounted for a large proportion of seigneurial income (as much as 40 per cent or 50 per cent, for example, in Savoie and the Dauphiné).

In some regions, the seigneurial reaction took a different form. Some seigneurs sought to encourage agrarian individualism at the expense of collective customs and practices. Thus they attempted, for example, to limit common rights to collect wood in neighbouring forests or to encourage the division of the communal wood in order to be able to sell the wood at a high price themselves. In some instances, seigneurs sought to usurp control of entire communal areas – meeting, not surprisingly, the fierce opposition of villagers. The fact that many seigneurs were absent from their lands hardly improved their relationship with the peasantry. Frequently, their place was taken by entrepreneurs, in the role of bailiffs, money-gatherers and farm managers who, in exchange for a proportion of revenues, would ensure the strict enforcement of seigneurial rights. By the same token, many of the older, paternalistic duties of the seigneur, such as traditional gifts and services, were often neglected, accentuating the sense of grievance of many peasant communities against their seigneurs. As grievances increased, so did the number of legal actions brought against a seigneur by his community. In many regions, peasants appeared to be very much on the defensive.

'Royal' taxation and demands added a further burden to the demands of land rent and seigneurial rights. Because the peasantry was, to a large extent, self-sufficient, it was hardly affected by the range of indirect taxes that afflicted urban populations. But the tax on salt, the *gabelle*, was particularly resented, for salt was essential for making bread and soup. Direct taxation in particular was a major demand, notably the ever-increasing capitation tax and the French *taille*. They bore especially heavily on the peasantry because many towns were exempt and exemption privileges could frequently be bought and sold by better-off members of the community. The payment of the *taille* gave rise to numerous complaints. In those regions where a personal tax had to be paid, this was levied according to the taxpayer's means, which were estimated by collectors designated by the village community. In areas where the *taille réele* was customary, as in the Midi, this was levied on everyday goods. Overall, it is difficult to estimate the impact of these Royal taxes because not all provinces paid the same charges. Pierre de Saint-Jacob has argued for a figure of around 10 per cent to 15 per cent of farm revenue being paid in direct taxes. In the Auvergne, according to Abel Poitrineau, the amount paid varied from 12 per cent to 22 per cent of revenue. Undoubtedly, then, it was a heavy charge which had to be paid, good harvest or bad.[21] If we add up these various seigneurial rights and taxes together with the *taille*, we are looking at a loss of between one-quarter and one-half of the revenue of the peasant household. For the sharecropper, already committed to paying a proportion of revenue to the landowner, the position was even more serious. These revenues, then, were lost to agriculture. They served rather to finance some of the spectacular urban developments of the eighteenth century. For the peasantry, such developments were an irrelevance. The towns, then, were a veritable parasite, draining both money and cheap labour from the countryside and giving little in return.

The burden of these charges meant that complementary sources of income were required for most peasant families. Seasonal or temporary migration of part of the population was the preferred solution in areas of poor land, especially the uplands.[22] Several hundreds of thousands of men would leave the high mountains of the Massif Central, the Alps and the Pyrénées each year to work as labourers in the surrounding lowlands. In such regions as many as one-third of all adult males would be absent for upwards of half the year. They worked as stone masons, log-sawers, flax-combers, knife-grinders, rag-and-bone men, chimney-sweeps, door-to-door sellers, animal herders, and, on occasion, beggars. They would be forced to take risks both in their journeys and occupations in order to be able to return with some precious cash. Such funds would be used for the most pressing bills. What little remained would be saved in the hope, often, alas, a vain one, of buying a little land. Another solution to the cash shortage was working at home; this was an option especially in those rural areas close to industrialising towns. It was the domain, above all, of the textile industry. A manufacturer located in a nearby town would undertake to provide the necessary raw materials to peasant families who could produce more-than-adequate yarn or cloths at salaries much below urban rates. For a peasant society often facing over-population, such work provided an indispensable additional income. In this way, peasant society provided a useful reserve of manpower for urban activities. The exchange between town and country was thus hardly an equal one; perhaps it is not inappropriate to consider it as one of domination.

From the outside, the peasantry appeared to form a homogeneous and undifferentiated mass. It was a part of the 'vile populace', the dregs of society. Peasants were poorly dressed, stupid and hardly much above their animals . . . and yet, they were indispensable. Such was the popular image propounded by some examples of late-eighteenth-century literature. It was hardly a fair reflection of a society which was highly diverse and which recognised itself as such. *Le Paysan parvenu* of Marivaux or the *Paysan perverti* of Restif de la Bretonne were both subtler and no doubt closer to reality than many of their contemporaries. There was a rigid and complex system of hierarchies within the village which was clear when, for example, the tax-collector would take great pains to distinguish on the registers between the small farmer and share-cropper, or the day-labourer and the migrant worker. Such distinctions reflected both the legal and economic hierarchies in peasant society.

What we may term the dependent classes were in the majority; between two-thirds and three-quarters of all peasants in most villages fell into this category. At the bottom of the hierarchy were the day-labourers. Sometimes they owned a few meagre goods, perhaps a house or garden, but their poverty forced them into working for others to keep the family economy afloat. The mass of labourers who worked on a daily-rate basis were the essential manpower at times of seasonal work. The collective nature of much agricultural work at least gave them an assured place in seasonal work patterns. These people depended on two things – the economic conjuncture and the goodwill of their employers. Ultimately, only by turning their hands to all sorts of tasks could they assure their livelihood. At times of economic hardship, some family members would be forced into migration, ending up perhaps joining the mass of migrants making their way along the highways of the kingdom. These, to adopt the phrase of Albert Soboul were the 'peasant-proletariats', barely distinguishable from the peasant smallholders who sought to eke out a meagre living from smallholdings they owned or leased. In good years, such peasant families could survive, although payment of taxes would always pose difficulties. When times were bad many went to the wall, crushed by mounting debts and an emptying larder. For many, placing their children as workers on other, larger farms, was the sole solution to their difficulties.[23]

Where a peasant could count on some 4 to 10 hectares of land, a degree of economic independence was possible, although this depended in part on the region and the conditions under which that land was held. In the Gâtine of Poitou, for example, only 15 per cent of all rural inhabitants were fortunate enough to be in this group.[24] In the cereal-rich plains of the Paris Basin, numbers were even smaller. Even within this group, however, there was an intrinsic variety of socio-economic status, between the peasant who owned his tools and farmed a smallish plot of land, and the big farmer who dominated his parish. Some farmed both their own land and land they were able to lease, a position which, in the Beauvais region studied by Pierre Goubert, allowed them to farm as much as 100 hectares. Many such large farmers were able to use their control of property and the amalgam of rights surrounding landownership to great effect. At such a point, the line between independence and domination is crossed. These farmers could lend both money and goods, they were active participants in affirming their seigneurial rights and dues. Through marriage, they intermingled with the rural petty bourgeoisie, the millers, café-owners, many of whom were also seed-merchants and animal-sellers. Like them, these landed groups drew their power from their position as intermediaries between the peasant community and society at large.

Rural hierarchies, so complex and finely graded, can hardly be reduced to the simple contrast between day-labourers and peasant proprietors. It is evident, for example, that there were strong ties uniting these two, apparently opposed groups, which often overrode their differences.[25] Thus the labourer would perhaps borrow a plough-team from the landowner, or borrow seed in times of hardship. In exchange, he would work a set number of days on the farm. Such a system provided the larger farmers with a willing and docile workforce. This reciprocity, founded as it was on a basic inequality, ensured the preeminence of a small section of the peasantry. This pattern of economic dependency was reflected in complex systems of clientage in the village, reinforced by the cultural dominance exerted by those who could read or write, over the illiterate majority. It was perhaps only the freedom from such cultural, economic and social constraints which permitted the sometimes violent conflicts which broke out between large farmers and their migrant harvesters, coming from different regions, even from Paris, conflicts which the traditional system of clientage in the village tended to suppress.[26]

Solidarity and division in the village

At the base of all social organisation lay the family unit, the source of solidarity.[27] Around the family unit, daily life and work were structured. In the longer term, the family was the means by which property and social structures were passed from one generation to the next. Work, the winning of the daily bread, embraced all family members, young and old alike, for all were part of the social unit. Whilst the family was the basic organising pivot, there was a degree of occupational specialisation between family members, the field being the chief work-place of adult men, the farmyard that of adult women. Children were sent young to keep an eye on the animals. Those old people too enfeebled to work were not always kindly treated.[28] In a society in which family patrimony counted for everything individuals were of little regard.

Marriage customs can be especially revealing about the place and perpetuation of the family unit. In general, peasants married late in the eighteenth century – anything between the ages of 25 and 27 for women, 27 and 30 for men. In order to marry, it was generally necessary to establish some sort of property and goods. Such requirements also constituted a way of limiting births. Endogamous marriages were very common. In some regions, between two-thirds and three-quarters of partners were from the same parish, despite the strict religious taboos on marriage between close relatives. Geographic proximity seems to have been the guiding principle behind the choice of a partner – hardly surprising, given the narrow horizons of most country-dwellers. The same constraints applied to the social origins of partners. Thus, in Alsace, two-thirds of all farmers' sons married farmers' daughters, three-quarters of all sons of day-labourers married daughters of day-labourers.[29] Such close social constraints were also hardly surprising, given the primary importance of the family unit in most regions. North of the Loire, the conjugal family was most common and cohabitation between the married couple and their parents was relatively rare. On the death of the parents, partible inheritance was usual with the result that the farm would often be split up.[30] In other regions, notably Provence, the Auvergne, Limousin and the Pyrénées for example, a different system operated, with only one child inheriting. The inheritance would take place on his marriage, not on the death of his parents. In exchange he would be required to 'pay-off' the other children of the family with sums of money, furniture or clothing at a rate agreed with the local notary. In Provence, those children who did not receive the farm were well-compensated; elsewhere, in the south-west for example, the compensation was often scant.[31]

In the countryside, the local community, which frequently, though not always, coincided with the parish and commune was the basic structure of social life.[32] There were some 40,000 such communities and they provided the organisational framework within which village life was ordered. The most important organ of administration was the village assembly which would meet perhaps five or six times a year, usually on a Sunday following mass, in the village square if there was no *mairie*. All heads of households were regarded as members. In some areas, the meetings were also open to women. To debate and decide on important issues a quorum of two-thirds was required. What kinds of decisions were taken? At the meetings such issues as the date of harvesting, the use and management of communal property (the church and presbytery, the cemetery) would be debated. But the most important issue was taxation for, each year, the community would have to nominate its tax-collectors, responsible both for deciding a fair tax allocation within the community and organising its collection. The administrative powers usually sought the nomination of a single person, or *syndic*, who would serve as an intermediary between the community and the administration.[33]

The vitality of these rural communities varied greatly from one region to the next. In Flanders, the Artois and Hainault, for example, they were feeble, primarily because of the power of the local nobility and their representatives, who could impose their will with ease. On the other hand, in the Bourgogne and the urbanised countryside of Provence, these communities were very powerful. But one should not be deceived, for, in many villages, this apparent democracy was but a facade. The poorest villagers often played no part in such assemblies in the eighteenth century. Real power lay in the hands of the non-peasant rural bourgeoisie, whose careful manipulation of the client–patron system that was endemic ensured their preeminence. In some regions, this preeminence was even institutionalised in a much smaller assembly of restricted membership, comprising around a dozen people who would take the key decisions. Perhaps not surprisingly, members of the legal profession were especially influential. They were present in all but the smallest of villages and because, quite literally, their word was law, they wielded great power. They bore witness to most family and community activity. Other, more modest individuals could also mediate in certain ways between the village community and society at large. Thus, the innkeepers and café proprietors, even the barbers and wig-makers of the larger villages formed a kind of rural elite with a power based on both economic wealth and access to information from the outside world, either written or spoken, denied to so many other members of the community. This knowledge, based on the ability to read and write, represented a major source of power and control over a peasantry whose members were obliged to live their lives under the direction of legal documents which they could not read for themselves.

Frequently from a similar background, the priest was also able to exercise a mediating function, albeit in a rather different sense to the other groups.[34] Through taking control of the religious life of the community, through the catechism and liturgy, he could, quite literally, make what he taught into an unquestioned truth. His control of the sacraments meant he could intervene and guide all stages of the christian conduct of his flock. His task, however, should not be regarded simply as a spiritual or ideological one. Particularly in western France he played an important administrative, social and quasi-official role as representative of the state. It was his role at the end of mass to announce royal decrees or parliamentary statements. As well as these duties, registers of baptisms, marriages and burials were maintained by the priest; in addition it was the priest who would undertake to provide letters of reference to those who might need them, such as someone undertaking a journey. His word was final regarding the choice of a midwife or schoolteacher. In the enclosed *bocage* of western France the church represented the only central meeting place, the only crossroads which could draw together the members of an often scattered population. Here, then, the rural community cohered around the priest. In other regions, however, clerical preeminence was less marked, notably in the Midi. The important task of drawing up some sort of map of the influence of these various *notables*[35] in the countryside remains to be carried out.

Level of education as well as economic power would appear to be crucial determinants of status and power in the community. Unfortunately it is far from easy to establish the different levels of education in the rural community.[36] Rural schools taught, above all, the ability to read. Unfortunately this ability is far from easy to quantify from archival evidence. The only quantifiable data we can use relates to the ability to sign one's name. From the seventeenth century onwards, it was obligatory for marriage partners to sign their names (or leave a mark) in the parish registers; the historian thus has a useful, if imperfect data source. Such data can be used to gauge the level of instruction in the village. In the nineteenth century, these registers were used by Maggiolo, one-time rector of the Academy of Nancy, who was able to elicit this information from village teachers. The map which he drew up for the period 1789–90 shows a sharp division between two regions either side of an imaginary line connecting Saint-Malo and Annecy. To the north of this line, most men could sign their names, to the south, relatively few could do so. Thus in the Alps, where many village teachers deserted their schools in winter for the more amenable climes of upper Provence, few could sign their names. Likewise in the Auvergne and Limousin, fewer than 30 per cent of men were able to sign their names. Female rates throughout the country fell well below male ones. How can we explain such contrasts? Perhaps the view that in the south and west the importance of local dialects meant a rejection of the teaching of French warrants consideration.

Local differences should also not be ignored. Perhaps areas of higher literacy were linked to the presence of small, independent village schools. We know little about their geographical density; indeed, even the presence of a schoolmaster in a village tells us little about the viability of his school. Many had an ephemeral working life; most, in any case, would only operate on a seasonal basis. It appears that the level of resources available in the village was a key factor. Many communities would offer a fixed salary to the teacher provided that the poorest children would be educated free. Other parents would be required to pay the school for the education of their children; the sums required, often seemingly very low, were sometimes a major drain on scarce family resources. Other factors – local circumstances, the attitude of particular personalities – also influenced the activity of community schools. Thus, the attitude of inspectors or the local bishop could be important in speeding or slowing down local initiative. Some of the strongest correlations seem to relate to the geographical nature of the community. In valleys or along important routeways, schools were often numerous; by contrast, areas of difficult communications or forested zones frequently had few schools. Commercial activity brought in its train not only resources, but also contacts, and, perhaps a greater openness which encouraged parents to send their children to school.

The presence of a school did not make the spread of knowledge a certainty. As the church forbade mixed classes, often it was only boys who would be sent to school. Where historians have been able to calculate participation rates, these are pitifully low, sometimes fewer than one-tenth of eligible children. Between Easter and All Saints' Day, only the youngest children would be sent to school. In addition to the low level of attendance, the impoverished nature of the curriculum must be noted. In many schools, following clerical guidance, only reading ability would be taught. Writing and mathematics, introduced rather later, required a much longer exposure to school than was the case for many children, who would be required to join the workforce, full-time, by the age of twelve. The result was a great social disparity in levels of instruction. Because of their frequent contact with the outside world, many more viti-culturalists than peasants could sign their names. Day-labourers could rarely sign their names, whereas in Alsace books were often found in the homes of modest peasant farmers. Such works – almanacs showing the dates of agricultural fairs and the phases of the moon, saints' lives, works on primitive treatment of animal and human maladies reflected the essentially pragmatic literary requirements of the population. But we should not be blinded by the poverty of literacy in the village into thinking that any form of culture was absent. On the contrary, collective life in many villages, attested to a vital and vibrant popular culture in many communities.

Celebrations, in a society characterised above all by poverty and misery, helped to make the drudgery of a hard and grinding daily life more bearable.[37] Certainly there was plenty of opportunity for celebration. Evening gatherings, for example, often including little more than the immediate family, were frequently imbued with a sense of celebration. Under the pretext of carrying out certain group tasks, gatherings of lace-makers or spinners would take place. These provided occasions on which the young of both sexes could get together. Family celebrations, births and burials also provided an opportunity to meet. As well as Sundays, most dioceses had at least thirty or so holy days. Add to this the range of festivals linked to the various customs, both pagan and christian, the celebrations surrounding harvest and sowing times of the year. In Provence, the choice of two patron saints, one for summer, one for winter, served to increase the opportunity for celebration. The religious and profane were frequently intermingled with a variety of games and competitions, often lasting for several days.

The village festivals were usually organised by the groups of young men in the parish. These were the so-called *bachelleries* typical of the centre-west region studied by Nicole Pellegrin.[38] Whilst all levels of the village hierarchy were present in such groups, the very poorest were often especially important. The costs of these various festivals were usually financed by a sort of tax on marriages and, most especially, on remarriages. The *bachelleries* appeared in some way to police the morals of the community, with the authority to attack those who broke the rules and to reprimand those who deviated from the dominant sexual mores of the village. Thus, no husband should be beaten up by his wife and widowers were not supposed to marry young girls, a move which might deprive young men of their marriage prospects. Punishments were usually humorous rather than violent. The guilty party would frequently be tied to an ass, head facing the tail, and be paraded round the village, exposed to general ridicule. A hefty fine would have to be paid before he would be allowed to dismount. These *bachelleries* reveal two complementary aspects of the community. Their activities gave, firstly, the illusion of unity in the village – all the young men, of whatever social background, would play their part. But, secondly, they reveal how young adult males were in some ways set apart from the rest of the community. Such organisations allowed them to display their strength and virility which would normally be kept under control by the social pressures of the community, and this virility served, paradoxically, to reinforce the rules of tradition in the village and to chastise any deviants. But these events, especially with the addition of alcohol, could sometimes lead to scuffles by the end of the day. Thus, two villages would often fight each other, under the pretext of pastoral conflicts. The youth of the village would be required to manifest its solidarity in defending the honour of the community.

Village life was not without discord, however.[39] If criminal archives seem to indicate a greater degree of delinquence in the town than the countryside, this is probably because relatively few crimes in the country-side would even come to the notice of the authorities. Many would be settled before any police intervention by arrangements between villagers of a financial or other kind. The study of 'visible' crime in the rural community (crime, that is, which came to the attention of the judiciary) indicates a preponderance of offences in market-places, along the high-ways and in posting-houses, taverns and hotels. This concerned, in the main, young men. In Normandy, violence appeared to be declining in this period whilst thefts increased dramatically, but this pattern did not apply in Brittany or the Auvergne.[40] Can such trends be explained by economic changes?

It is important not to confuse violent criminal behaviour and general social unrest. Thus, peasant unrest could be expressed in a variety of traditional, non-violent ways such as tardiness in paying taxes and deliberate obstructiveness. At least some of this behaviour can be explained as a form of social protest opposing the rural community to society at large. At the most elementary level, one finds the smuggling of salt or the exploits of social bandits, of which Mandrin is the best example. The more spectacular form of peasant protest, the uprising against the state or its representatives, was much less common in this period than in the seventeenth century, perhaps because the real weight of royal fiscal demands was falling.[41] On the other hand, however, after 1740 a rash of anti-seigneurial activity can be detected, particularly from the Nord to Bourgogne. The peasantry here was especially opposed to the initiatives of reforming landowners, busily enclosing their land. But, all in all, relatively few rural communities were in open revolt. Can this be attributed to the lack of research and archival evidence of such popular uprisings, or rather, can it be argued that the diminishing weight of feudal and royal oppression was making such protest less and less necessary?[42] If this latter hypothesis holds, then the burst of popular anti-feudal discontent between 1789 and 1791 could be explained in terms of a sudden fierce reaction to the current predicament rather than as the climax of a long series of popular peasant unrest. Any study of the role of the peasantry in the Revolution cannot be divorced, then, from this broader context.

2. The peasantry and the Revolution

In 1789, for all its diversity, the French peasantry nonetheless shared a common feature: its extreme sensibility to the economic conjuncture which made the weight of the seigneurial system all the harder to bear. The destruction of this system constituted a prime reason for peasant involvement in the Revolution. But the steady disillusionment of the years between 1790 and 1792, to which were added the burdens of war, led to the breakdown of this apparent united resolve and, in some regions, the peasantry came to form the bulwark of the counter-revolution. In the space of some ten years the gap between those who wielded economic power and those who were dependent on it was widened.

The food shortage and its consequences

The crisis of 1788–89 was exceptionally severe, firstly, because it was preceded by a long period of agricultural stagnation. The work of Ernest Labrousse, based primarily on price–revenue ratios has helped to clarify the mechanisms of this crisis.[43] Whereas in earlier periods, crises had been largely regional in their impact, sparing some areas and some sectors of the agricultural economy, the latest crisis had ramifications throughout the kingdom. Thus, for several years viticultural regions had been hit by a slump in demand. Then, from 1788, cereal harvests in northern France were affected by storms and high rainfall. This was followed by an especially severe winter in the Midi, where olive trees were frozen over. As a consequence of these climatic events, in some areas the failure of the winter wheats meant that sowing had to be repeated in the spring, thereby depleting still further the precious stocks of cereal. Not surprisingly then, the usual spring shortages were, in 1789, particularly severe. As a consequence, there was open speculation and prices rose quickly. These rises were stimulated above all by those who possessed cereal surpluses, primarily the beneficiaries of seigneurial and ecclesiastical dues. Such crises, however, were not new in the kingdom. What was new, according to Ernest Labrousse, was that this food crisis not only developed rapidly into a general economic crisis, but also coincided with a crisis of the monarchy. Because it was at once a financial, institutional and moral crisis, its resolution had to involve a political dimension. The conflict was thus played out at a level in which direct peasant intervention was usually limited. In 1789, however, things were a little different, for the calling of the Estates General brought the peasantry directly into national political life.

The decision to try to defuse the impending political crisis was taken initially in August 1788.[44] The procedures adopted were complex, but in rural areas there was at least some element of democracy. Each community was required to convene a meeting of its inhabitants – or rather those inhabitants who met certain qualifications. Thus males aged at least twenty-five and paying some form of community contribution were invited to the convocation. These assemblies were required to draw up, under the guidance of a judge, or, failing that, a lawyer, an account of their grievances, the so-called *cahiers de doléances*, and to elect delegates to the larger assemblies, which would then send delegates to the Estates General at Versailles. Not that the peasantry was numerous at the palace; only one peasant deputy, a Breton, Gérard, achieved temporary notoriety by being elected. If the form of voting for deputies meant that there was little direct peasant representation nationally, this did not mean their input was minimal.

The *cahiers* constitute an immensely valuable source – some 40,000 of them in various states of preservation – and they are far from having been fully analysed. The task is an immensely complex one. It is difficult to interpret many of them outside the context of the lives of the particular community and the ways in which they were drawn up. The gaps in their content as well as the detail they contain are also significant. It is rare to find the full and open expression that one might expect from a village assembly. In some cases an urban *cahier* has simply been used as a model and transcribed for the village. Undoubtedly, it can be argued that those responsible for drawing up the documents – the judges, solicitors or office-holders – interpreted, perhaps even concealed, the real intentions of those tongue-tied and illiterate peasants who voiced their grievances. It is the voice of the lawyer, above all, that echoes from these documents of the past.

Given these limitations, then, what do these documents contain? They express above all what one would expect, grievances, complaints, injustices. A sad and moving catalogue of hurts which move the reader to pity. But beyond such stylisation, what else do they reveal? Above all else, they outline grievances against the feudal regime and, more particularly, the weight of seigneurial impositions. Freeing property from such onerous dues seems to mark the essential political and social aspirations of the bulk of the peasantry. Added to this demand is a vigorous defence of collective, communal rights with a large number of assemblies revealing an implacable hostility to the growth of agrarian individualism. The *cahiers* also reveal serious complaints about the way in which taxes were organised and show the unpopularity of royal taxation. But on one point they are clear – the rural assemblies expressed their loyalty to and confidence in Louis XVI. It is not the king who is at fault, they argue, but those who have advised him badly and who have failed to tell him of the real condition of the peasantry. The documents indicate, too, a sense of aspiration and the hope that changes were in the wind, a feeling increased by the nation-wide scale of the *cahiers*. In some regions, indeed, the drawing up of the documents was interpreted as a sign that the king was on the side of the peasantry against the rapacious seigneurie. It can hardly have been by coincidence that, in Provence, rioting against the nobility broke out on the very day that the *cahiers* were drawn up. Above all else, the effect of the calling of the estates General was to mobilise the peasantry. From that moment on it was on the march.

From March 1789 unrest spread through the countryside.[45] In some places – Provence, Quercy, Picardy and, a little later, Franche-Comté and the Mâconnais – châteaux were attacked and some of the symbolic instruments of economic repression destroyed. Weathervanes were pulled down, grain measures, used for calculating seigneurial dues were broken. Where they could find them the attackers eagerly destroyed property and tax documents. Violence towards seigneurial tax-farmers was also evident whilst those intermediaries with cereal stocks were a further obvious target. In other regions, wood-gathering expeditions were organised in forest lands belonging to the nobility and attackers were keen to settle scores with forest guards and agents.

At the same time, the food crisis swept numerous bands of beggars onto the roads of the kingdom demanding alms and sustenance, often with threats of violence. When they failed to get these threats of arson were usually forthcoming. As the harvest approached the sense of collective fear increased. How was this especially precious harvest to be protected? Added to this sense of unease was the disquiet at the turn of events in Paris and Versailles. The news of the taking of the Bastille and the apparent triumph of the Third Estate was decisive in spreading both hope and fear: hope, initiated by the sense that reforms were imminent; fear, brought on by the prospect of the power of those opposed to reform. The forces of the counter-revolution would not be slow in appealing for help abroad to provide troops to massacre the revolutionary patriots.

The combination of all these rumours and fears was to create what Georges Lefebvre, employing a contemporary expression, called the 'Great Fear'.[46] Between 15 July and 6 August rumour and counter-rumour spread through an excitable and disturbed populace; troops were seen destroying and burning crops and villages and pillaging the towns. Sometimes they were English, sometimes Germans, elsewhere from the Piedmont; the rumour could be varied to suit local conditions. In areas distant from frontiers, mere bands of brigands sufficed. The peasants formed resistance groups arming themselves with sickles, flails and, more rarely, firearms. The tocsin rang out the alarm from church steeple to church steeple. Analysis of the phenomenon has shown that the fear, originating in six locations, spread through most of the country. Only Brittany, Alsace and Lorraine resisted, most probably because of language differences.

Once the fear had passed, the peasants remained armed. From defence many passed to attack. Agrarian revolts broke out in Provence, Bourgogne and Dauphiné. Châteaux were pillaged as peasants sought to destroy all documents relating to the imposition of seigneurial rights. If they could not be found, the whole château would be razed to the ground to ensure the dreaded documents, mute testimony to so much repression, were destroyed. Not that such extreme action was everywhere the pattern. In many villages the peasants carried on with harvesting as usual but simply refused to hand over seigneurial dues. In doing this, however, it was not just the nobility that suffered, for an appreciable amount of seigneurial land was in the hands of the bourgeoisie. The Constituent Assembly thus saw the restoration of some sort of order in the countryside as an urgent priority.

Agrarian reforms

The peasant revolution, regardless of whether or not it is considered autonomous, occupied an important place in the unfolding of the Revolution itself. The peasants were not disinterested spectators of the events that rocked Paris between 1789 and 1795. Through a process of feedback they were able to impose or stiffen decisions taken by often-hesitant assemblies. The areas of peasant interest were clear enough – any debate on seigneurial rights or attack on communal practices or landownership would call into question the whole socio-economic system of the countryside.

At the beginning of August 1789, the Constituent Assembly faced a thorny problem. If it demanded that royal authority be reestablished in the countryside by military force, it ran the risk of seeing those same forces turn their attention to the ferment in Paris once the country was pacified. Equally, however, pacifying the peasantry by abolishing feudal rights would hurt the pockets of many deputies who drew a considerable part of their income from such rights. During the night of 4 August, these individual pecuniary concerns gave way to political expediency. The debates appeared planned in advance. A young nobleman without fortune, the Viscount of Noailles, proposed the abolition of feudalism. He was supported by the Duke of Aiguillon, one of the most powerful landlords of the kingdom. Their speeches threw the richer members of the assembly into disarray, whilst the more liberally inclined sought to emulate the two proposers. In a wave of enthusiasm, feudalism was abolished and the church's tithe abandoned. The ancien régime appeared to be over.

In the cold light of day, however, the opponents of change regrouped and the decrees passed between 5 and 11 August stealthily introduced subtle, but fundamental, restrictions into the legislation. All those feudal rights which were imposed by violence or were personally degrading were abolished. Thus, forms of forced labour, serfdom, hunting rights and the like disappeared. All those communal lands which had been appropriated by the nobility in the last thirty years were returned to the community. The suppression of the tithe was also confirmed; henceforth, other means of supporting the clergy would have to be devised. But the heavy dues which related to ownership and use of land were not abolished. Instead, it was argued that they could be removed only through purchase, because, it was argued, they depended on a contract between noble and peasant. The way in which repurchase was permitted further increased the sense of deception many peasants felt. The sum demanded was fixed at twenty times the annual value for dues paid in money and twenty-five times the annual value for those paid in kind. Not surprisingly, such figures were well beyond the means of most peasants. Furthermore, the only proof that nobles were required to show for the existence of such contracts was evidence that payments had been made in the last thirty years.

The sense of betrayal felt by many peasants was enormous. Few such dues were purchased by them; the majority was bought by rural merchants or urban landowners. In many regions the peasantry reacted by refusing outright to pay any such dues which they believed the Revolution had abolished. Where the weight of such dues was especially heavy, as in Brittany and Provence, there was open revolt. Armed peasants sacked local châteaux. Concern over food shortages also helped mobilise many country-dwellers into groups of armed gangs, often with municipal officers at their head, moving from one market to the next to ensure that profiteering did not take place.[47] Entire communities were in ferment, regrouping into large and dangerous armed bands. The poorer peasantry, equally alarmed by price rises, was not averse to sacking the occasional rich farmhouse that it came across.

In August 1792, this increasingly dangerous agitation, coupled with the fact that the country was now also at war, sparked the Legislative Assembly into action. It cancelled all reimpositions of feudal dues unless clear evidence of the ancient nature of such rights could be established. The move was prompted by events in Paris on 10 August 1792. Since many titles had already disappeared in flames since 1789, the measure effectively led to the disappearance of many seigneurial rights. Then, in the spring of 1793, a new political crisis settled the matter. On 17 July 1793 the Convention Montagnarde, wishing to establish authority over the countryside, definitively abolished all seigneurial rights. Not all of them disappeared, however. Thus, sharecropping contracts, for example, specified that the cropper, rather than the landowner, should continue to pay all those dues levied on the land. In the west and south-west, such dues survived in farm leases (often disguised as simple rent payments) well into the twentieth century.[48]

If peasant unrest sought and brought about the suppression of seigneurial rights, it had quite the opposite aim with regard to the reform of the agrarian system. Any initiatives taken by reforming deputies quickly met the implacable hostility of the peasantry, which effectively prevented the application of any legislation that was passed. At the heart of the Constituent Assembly, physiocratic ideas prevailed. The Agricultural Society of Paris dominated the agriculture and commerce committees, which had been charged with the task of reform, and they sought, through the elaboration of a new Rural Code, to destroy any obstacles to agricultural progress. From the autumn of 1789 the principle of individual liberty in the exercise of property rights was seen as integral to the Declaration of the Rights of Man. This principle marked the triumph, at least in theory, of agrarian individualism, underpinning the right to enclose, the abolition of communal pasturing and the ultimate division of communal lands. But, because of continued peasant unrest, the full discussion and elaboration of these principles was considered inopportune and continually put off. It was thus an abridged version which eventually appeared as the decree of 28 September 1791.[49] But the rights of common pasturing were considered sacrosanct if they were based on usage dating back to 'time immemorial'. Those rare studies which have examined the new Rural Code indicate that its application was limited. In the Velay, a region of small farms, enclosure proceeded but slowly. In Roussillon, those owners living in the plains adhered to the new legislation; in the neighbouring uplands, the inhabitants continued to resist enclosure and common pasturing was maintained.[50]

The question of dividing communal lands was never tackled in the new Rural Code, despite the efforts of the Agricultural Committee.[51] Because it was such a sensitive issue the Assembly took a prudent and cautious line. Those divisions that had occurred in the last thirty years were annulled on 16 March 1790; the lands which had been ceded to the nobles were returned to the community. A first law on division of the communal lands was voted on 14 August 1792 at a time of national crisis.

Ownership of communal land was formally vested in the community, which was permitted, if it so wished, to divide it amongst all its inhabitants. But the precise mechanisms of division were never elaborated and the following months saw great rural unrest. The Convention finished by rescinding the text of the law, to restore the peace.

A new law, passed on 10 June 1793, authorised the division of communal lands between all inhabitants of the community if one-third of the community sought such a change. In practice, because the law provoked such hostility, the Directory suspended its application in 1796. The chronic difficulties faced in resolving this issue testify to the complexity of interests involved. In some regions, the better-off peasants were keen on a division which would increase their cultivated land, whilst poorer peasants were anxious to continue to use the communal land. In pastoral regions, by contrast, it was often the larger peasants who were opposed to a division of the commons which would restrict their abilities to maintain large herds. Those peasants without land, however, regarded division as a means of gaining a precious first step on the ladder of landownership. What then, was the precise impact of these different measures? In the current state of research it is, unfortunately, impossible to say with any precision.

The sale of national lands was undertaken, not in order to free land for the peasantry, but rather to resolve the crisis in state finances. In a complex and audacious plan, the Constituent Assembly sought to simultaneously reduce the national debt and solve the problem of how the clergy was to be supported. Having decided on the night of 4 August 1789 that the tithe should be abolished, the National Assembly decreed that state support must be forthcoming for the clergy. In exchange, church possessions would be given over to the state and then sold to provide the necessary funds for this state support. From 1792, the amount of property to be sold was swollen by confiscated lands belonging to those nobles and non-nobles who had fled the country. The objective of these sales was clearly financial – to swell, as rapidly as possible, the coffers of the state. But such sales were difficult and time-consuming to organise, hence it was decided to create a system of credit-notes or *assignats*. Church property served as security for these notes, which would be withdrawn as and when the properties were sold.

Financial considerations were determinant in the system of sales. The law of 14 May 1790 decreed that purchases were to be made of single units, block by block. The arrangements were to be made in the main district towns. Such conditions inevitably meant that the poorer peasantry played little part in the sales. The only concession made to it was that it could avail itself of twelve-year loan terms at a 5 per cent interest rate. If, furthermore, the amount raised by splitting properties and lands exceeded the total anticipated for the single unit, property division was permitted. Grouping of monies to purchase lots did take place. Thus in the Gard, 16 peasants pooled their resources to buy a block of land at 525 pounds whilst another group of 106 paid 154,000 pounds for a large unit of land.[52] Such isolated examples serve to underline the real land hunger in the countryside. But, in April 1793, such group purchases were forbidden, ostensibly because they interfered with the free operation of the market. In fact, the main reason for the interdiction was to prevent the operations of the so-called 'black bands' – speculators who forced down prices for the lots they wished to purchase, often with the threat and exercise of force on other would-be purchasers. With the decline in the value of paper money, such purchases could represent an excellent investment. Speculators bought land using depreciating credit-notes before reselling the land in small plots to peasants. Gilbert Garrier has studied one such group in the Beaujolais. This band was led by a group of cloth merchants with sufficient financial resources and with a sufficiently detailed knowledge of the property market to be able to make a killing.[53]

The balance-sheet of national sales is not easy to draw up. The hardest task is to trace what happened to property after the first sale. It is, furthermore, well nigh impossible to identify the individuals behind the named purchasers. Was the land kept intact, amalgamated with other properties in the area, or split up and resold? We do not yet have any study on the national scale, which is hardly surprising given the mass of documents that would have to be analysed. It is evident, however, that there were sharp regional differences in the proportion of land put up for sale. In the country as a whole, perhaps 10 per cent of all land changed hands. But there were regional differences – from some 4 per cent in the Rhône to nearer 25 per cent in the Artois.[54] Any national estimates can be no more than mere approximations.

It would appear that the main beneficiaries of these sales were non-peasants, although it cannot be denied that the number of small landowners did increase following the sales. Again regional differences are important. Much depended on local conditions and on local factions. In the department of Nord, where Georges Lefebvre has studied the process, it is clear that by a mixture of menaces and even riots, the peasantry was able to restrict bourgeois purchases. Between 1789 and 1802 bourgeois ownership increased from 26 per cent to only 28 per cent, whilst that of the peasantry advanced from 30 per cent to 42 per cent.[55] In lower Alsace, up until 1793, sale of land in lots benefited the small purchaser. After that date, it is apparent that peasant indebtedness increased, and the amount of land put on the market outstripped the supply of peasant capital. But, in this region, the peasants benefited from the relative disdain of the bourgeoisie for investment in land. In other areas, the gains in peasant property were but minuscule, as in the Beaujolais, Côte d'Or or Paris region. In the Versailles district, for example, six-sevenths of the land sold was bought by the bourgeoisie or aristocracy, who continued to buy until 1792. Among the peasants, then, who were the biggest buyers? In the Nord, one-third of all purchasers were previously landless although this appears an exceptionally high proportion. In the Chartres region, the large farmers and rural aristocracy bought at about the same rate as the bourgeoisie of Chartres and Paris. In Dijon, most purchasers were already owner-occupiers. There is no doubt that the sales reinforced peasant landownership, but they benefited primarily those who already held land rather than those seeking, for the first time, to acquire property.

The peasantry divides

After 1792, with the nation at war, the peasantry was squeezed ever harder. It was obliged to feed both the towns and the army and these pressures brought about a widening gap between different groups and different interests. In some regions, the peasantry went so far as to take up arms against the republic; everywhere, the peasantry emerged from the revolutionary period profoundly divided.

The events of 1792 were decisive. The threat of war became real after April and, as military defeat followed military defeat, a second wave of revolutionary fervour swept through the capital during the summer. Political uncertainty was compounded by the economic crisis. Whilst harvests had been good since 1789, shortages nonetheless developed because the marketing of cereals slowed down. Those who had stocks preferred to hold on to them rather than sell them for devalued credit-notes. From 1793 a long series of government measures was instituted to cajole and coerce the peasantry into releasing grain. In July of that year, profiteering was declared a capital offence. In September, price controls were brought in and districts were required to organise a system of requisitions. After the fall of Robespierre, this coercive and often brutal system eased and, as a result, deliveries to the market once more slowed down. In 1795, the national guard had to be used in many villages to ensure that official requisitions were delivered.

Unrest in the countryside was not linked merely to the problem of devalued credit-notes. After 1793, many peasants expected little to come their way as a result of the Revolution. The abolition of seigneurial rights had, at a stroke, removed that which had previously cemented the peasantry together. Other more pressing interests, interests which differed from one group to the next, came to the fore. Thus, owner-occupiers now sought to safeguard their newly acquired lands, whilst the poorer members of the community pressed for a division of communal lands. This latter preoccupation led to the emergence of the 'splitters', the 'rural *sans-culottes*' as Albert Soboul has termed them.[56] Such aspirations were incomprehensible to a government fervently attached to the defence of private property and which had, in any case, other, far more pressing concerns on the military front.

It was the military difficulties which were the catalyst for a series of revolts in the southern Massif Central and the west in the spring of 1793. The revolts followed the decrees of 20 and 24 February, which sought the conscription of some 300,000 men. In many areas, the formation of the volunteer batttalions in 1791 and 1792 had largely exhausted both enthusiasm and willing bodies for the fight. The creation of additional contingents was organised through a kind of lottery, a return to a system of conscription which was so detested under the ancien régime and one which provoked widespread resistance. In the Massif, from the Haute-Loire to Aveyron, an uprising occurred.[57]At Lapanouse, near Severac-le-Château, Aveyron, the youth of the village refused to take part in the draw. This spark of revolt quickly spread to surrounding cantons and several hundred insurgents moved into Lozère to escape from the army. Then, under the leadership of a lawyer from Nasbinals called Charrier, an ex-deputy with *émigré* links, they marched on Marvejols and Mende, which fell without a fight. But, faced with an increased republican army and the unwillingness of his men to move too far from their native region, Charrier eventually gave the order to disperse. Betrayed, he was guillotined at Rodez on 17 July 1793. For a further year sporadic outbreaks of unrest continued in the region although attempts to link forces with federalist groups at Lyon failed.

In the west, at the same time, a more substantial revolt took place.[58] In Brittany, Maine and the Vendée, there was massive opposition to the conscription system. To the north of the Loire, the authorities were able to react quickly to the threat and avoid any general uprising. A kind of chronic rural agitation characterised by violence and isolated, episodic attacks occurred, especially after the mass conscriptions of the summer of 1793. This became known as *chouannerie*. To the south of the river, between the Loire and the Marais Poitevin, the refusal of conscription turned into a civil war. The Vendée war, as it was called, was so-named after only one of the four departments affected. The north-west of Deux-Sèvres, the south of Loire-Inférieure and the south-west of Maine-et-Loire formed the heartland of the Vendée zone of insurgency.

There were three distinct phases in the war of the Vendée. From March to June 1793, the movement conquered all. At the outset, the rebels were organised by villages with modest people at their head. Stofflet, an ex-soldier, was a gamekeeper; Cathelineau, a carter. But, once the fighting began, the squires of the region were sought to take up the leadership. The speed of events surprised the Convention and early replies were feeble; the federalist revolt which followed the fall of the Girondins was undoubtedly regarded as a more serious threat by government. All of a sudden, the Vendée revolt broke out of its isolated *bocage* landscape. The rebels took Saumur, then Angers, but were held at Nantes on 29 June. The war now entered its second phase of stalemate as many locals turned from fighting to work in the fields and the death of Cathelineau reduced the effectiveness of central command. A small republican army, defending the towns, watched events cautiously.

After the defeat of federalist forces elsewhere, the balance of military power shifted from rebels to government. Paris rapidly sent an experienced force to the area and a series of defeats for the rebels began. Republican forces moving from Niort and Nantes joined to crush the Vendée fighters at Cholet on 17 October 1793. Then the Count of La Rochejaquelein threw his forces into a desperate gamble. Hoping to receive foreign help he moved 100,000 people, women and children included, across the Loire and into Normandy. But the force was held at Granville. Despairing of receiving help from the English, they attempted to return to their districts but were crushed at le Mans and then Savenay on 23 September; few fighters returned to the safety of the *bocage*. In January 1794 the Convention ordered General Turreau to exterminate all semblances of rebellion in the region. Columns of the military wreaked a terrible vengeance in the area, massacring men, women and children in their wake. The Vendée was beaten. Only a residue of *chouannerie* survived, as it did in Brittany, which was finally pacified by Bonaparte in 1800. The region was drained of its life-blood. The war cost between 220,000 and 250,000 lives and destroyed some 20 per cent of all property.[59]

It is hardly surprising that an event of such magnitude has been interpreted differently by various historians. For the republicans in 1793, the rising was an aberration, an exception, the result of foreign interference fanned by the clergy and nobility. The opposing camp has insisted that the rising in the service of God and king was both spontaneous and popular. For the last thirty years, historical research has attempted to highlight the causes of the revolt through a detailed analysis of the economic and social structures of the region. In 1960, Paul Bois' *Paysans de l'Ouest* revealed the sharp conflicts of interest between town and country, peasantry and bourgeoisie in the *chouan* movement in the Sarthe.[60] The insurgent zones, he argues, were primarily in the *bocage*. There the peasant lived in a kind of individualist obscurity behind the thick hedges of his isolated farm. Social contacts were episodic and infrequent and religious events often provided the only semblance of collective life. By contrast, the open-field areas, with their nucleated, village settlement, remained patriotic. There the social horizons and contacts of the peasantry were much more extensive. As a result, the peasant was more aware of national events and more open to discussion and debate. For Paul Bois, as for Michelet, the Vendée war was primarily a revolution of the isolated.

This rather seductive thesis, however, needs to be qualified. Thus not all the isolated *bocage* joined the revolt; areas of *bocage* in Finistère, Côtes-du-Nord and Ille-et-Vilaine remained republican. Claude Petitfrère, taking up the debate, has examined the social and economic background of those who fought for either the Vendée army (the 'Whites') or the national volunteers (the 'Blues').[61] The contrasts are both striking and instructive. The Vendéan army had a powerful peasant backbone, with artisans and shopkeepers providing only small additional numbers. The republican army, on the other hand, was primarily artisanal and industrial in character. Further, it is clear that most insurgents came from the lightly populated, agricultural communes. The small towns, with administrative or economic functions, played relatively little part in the revolt.

The motivations for the insurrection were complex and intermingled. The Vendée revolt can be seen as one of a series of uprisings which sprang up after 1791, testimony perhaps to the sense of betrayal felt by many at the outcome of the Revolution. Undoubtedly, there were strong economic motives behind the revolt as well. Church properties had barely been touched. In the Cholet district the peasantry was able to acquire no more than 9.3 per cent of land sold, as against 56.3 per cent for the bourgeoisie and 23.5 per cent for the nobility. Deception in taxation was also much resented. Direct taxation remained at levels comparable with the last years of the ancien régime, largely because the Assembly felt it appropriate to impose extra taxes on those western zones distant from the theatre of war. The fact that the dismantling of feudalism remained so incomplete in the spring of 1793 further increased peasant unease. Such essentially economic motives were reinforced by religious conflict. Boundary reforms had led to the departure of a number of priests, whilst those who refused to pledge loyalty to the state were also removed. For many peasant communities, these departures removed the anchor that held a dispersed community together, the priest. In an essentially illiterate community he was the chief spokesman and, frequently of peasant origin, he reflected and supported peasant issues to the world outside. A sense of unhappiness with such interference in the organisation of religion was undoubtedly a key motive underlying the revolt and was a potent force in unifying many disparate groups.

Thus, the peasantry emerged from the revolutionary process profoundly transformed even if, in appearance at least, the old divisions seemed to remain. More than ever before, ownership of land was the pivot of differentiation. Seigneurial rights had been suppressed and the freedom to enclose upheld. The property market, too, had opened up; this perhaps was the key factor. Even if, as we have seen, the amounts of land released were not always large, they were sufficient for their sale to act as a catalyst for change. The Revolution brought about an increase in the number of owner-occupiers and, in an area such as the Paris Basin, actually acted as a brake on the relentless consolidation of land into ever-larger units. The clergy was the clear loser; members could no longer be regarded as significant landowners. For the nobility things were a little better and many nobles, rather than leave the country altogether, were content to remain in decent obscurity in the towns. Others, quickly getting themselves removed from the list of *émigrés*, were able to repurchase their lands in their own name or that of a surrogate. Thus, in the department of Nord, the 21 per cent or 22 per cent of the land held by the nobility in 1789 had fallen to a still respectable 13 per cent in 1802.[62] In the Chartres region, the nobility lost between one-quarter and one-third of its lands. Current opinion favours the view that voluntary sales were perhaps of equal, if not greater, importance than the national land disposals. At the very least it should be noted that, even if the hold of the nobility on property declined, it was far from eliminated, and nobles continued to hold around one-quarter of all land.[63] In many areas, bourgeois landowners simply replaced noble landowners. Thus in the Nord, between 1789 and 1802, their hold increased dramatically from 16 per cent to 28 per cent.

Even where the bourgeoisie bought massively, however, peasant land-ownership still increased; in the Nord, peasant ownership rose from 30 per cent to 42 per cent between 1789 and 1802. As a general rule, it can be suggested that the peasantry held around one-half of all land in many regions. Who then were the purchasers? Nor surprisingly, well-off farmers with savings bought in some quantity. Those poorer social groups at the onset of the Revolution found their position little improved afterwards. The property-owning peasantry was strengthened, both economically through purchases, but also ideologically, as ownership of land became the pinnacle of republican aspirations in the countryside. Republican festivals soon celebrated a mythical peasant, raised to a position of pride just behind the national guard in the processions of state. Not surprisingly, this ideal figure bore no resemblance to reality. But the exaltation of such a figure to prominence exemplifies the wish of the bourgeoisie who held power to rally peasant support to the republic. It was successful to the extent that it won over those better-off groups who profited from economic progress after 1794. For the majority of peasants, however, conditions remained much as before.

For the poorest groups, changes were very limited. Granted, the sale of national lands had increased the number of *minifundia*. But the tiny size of many plots hardly permitted an amelioration in economic and social status. Even where a division of communal land gave them a few parcels of often-mediocre land, this hardly compensated for the destruction of the community that resulted. Inevitably, their gains were limited because succeeding political regimes cared little for their status. The deputies of the Convention, including the Montagnards, hardly intervened in agricultural matters because they feared the awesome complexity of local problems. The Conspiracy of Equals, led by Babeuf in 1795–6, had no peasant interest-groups within it. Proposed reforms of farm leases and sharecropping never saw the light of day. For Albert Soboul, developing the thesis of the Russian historian A. Ado, the failure of the Revolution to attack the fundamental issues of the continuance of sharecropping as a system and the problem of land rents, meant that there could be no dramatic modernisation of agriculture in the nineteenth century. For him, the retardation of capitalist agriculture in France could be blamed squarely on the incomplete nature of the peasant revolution.[64] It was the peasantry, particularly those of it who had to rely on food purchases, which was the ultimate victim of the economic conjuncture at the end of the revolutionary period.

The winter of year III (1794–5) constituted the start of a spell of several years of continued misery for many country-dwellers. Bands of vagabonds, part-beggars, part-robbers, reappeared in Normandy, Picardy, the south of the Paris Basin and the Lyonnais. Agricultural labourers with neither employment nor land mingled with groups of rebels and failed adventurers from the towns. This shady and marginal world, previously hidden from view, was revealed by Michel Vovelle's study of the bloodthirsty Orgères band, who terrorised the country between the Seine and the Loire.[65] This band, well organised and devious, comprised several hundred people roaming the country, begging by day, in order to select and torture victims prior to robbing them of all they had. The upsurge in banditry in the Directory period is testimony both to the long tradition of such activity in rural areas and to the immediacy of the social crisis in the revolutionary period. This prevailing climate of insecurity, particularly amongst the better-off peasantry, inevitably introduced a yearning for order and security.

3. Imperial stability

When Napoleon seized power in 1799, the countryside appeared profoundly unstable. In many regions, insecurity was endemic, whilst the deflation consequent upon the withdrawal of paper money in 1797 provoked a severe fall in agricultural prices. This fall, furthermore, took place at precisely the time when the peasantry, faced with having to pay taxes in currency rather than devalued credit-notes, was flooding the cereal market. Whilst a divided peasantry was in no position to influence the course of events, the period was nonetheless a significant one for it. The new regime, aided by a favourable economic conjuncture, quickly sought to reestablish order in the countryside and to lay the foundations of the new ideology there. 'After the age of change came the age of institutions.'[66]

A new order

Pacification was the first priority of the Consulate, whose measures affected the countryside as much as, if not more than, the towns. In under five years internal peace was established and an administrative structure set in place that was to last more than a century.

For the new regime, the restoration of public order was a priority. Banditry was a chronic problem in many of the more-isolated areas, associated as it was with an opposition to conscription, an unfavourable economic climate and the activity of secretly returned *émigrés*. In the Haute-Loire, it remained unsafe to travel by road until 1804,[67] whilst in the Var, two years of armed repression were needed before a measure of peace was restored.[68] In the south-west secret royalist groups were able to organise a rural population which was increasingly hostile to the religious policies of the Directory and, especially, the Jourdan legislation of 1798, which aggravated the existing opposition to conscription. These groups were able to assemble an army of 5,000 people which threatened Toulouse before being crushed, albeit with some difficulty, at Montrejeau on 20 August 1799.[69]

Political changes accompanied force in this process of pacification. The Concordat signed with the Vatican in 1801 permitted the reestablishment of catholicism in the parish and was of fundamental importance in the pacification of western France. There, the reopening of churches and the rebirth of the old religious ceremonies symbolised a return to normality in many regions. At the same time, the regime sought to maintain the goodwill of the clergy, particularly the bishops, and to encourage a respect for civic obligations, especially conscription, on the part of their flock. Measures of appeasement with regard to *émigrés* permitted many to return to their districts and, in October 1800, some 52,000 were allowed to return. Their confiscated lands, if they had not yet been sold, were returned to them. In many villages, the nobility, taking advantage of the new political environment, was able to reassert its power over the peasantry.

A new, much more centralised administrative organisation of the countryside was also introduced.[70] The legislation of 17 February 1800 and 4 August 1802 introduced the commune as a unit of administration. Each commune with a minimum population of 2,500 had a mayor nominated by the prefect for a five-year renewable period. An assistant and ten municipal councillors were also nominated from amongst the more powerful and influential members of the canton. The power of the mayors could be extensive; at the very least they were the local eyes and ears of the administration, carrying out many tasks such as the collection of statistics and the implementation of legislation, tasks which proved beyond the capabilities of many. It was precisely because of this extensive power that many prefects found difficulties in recruitment, for many individuals feared the reprisals they might face for their actions. Others, more pragmatically, feared the workload for which no remuneration was forthcoming. Many of those who accepted the task turned out to be ignorant or incompetent or both, frequently failing to reply to administrative requests. In many departments of the west, royalist candidates had to be used because no one else would, or could, fulfil the tasks.

At the chief town in the canton, grouping several communes, a stronger administrative presence was required. There, nominated rather than elected bureaucrats would be placed to carry out basic administrative tasks. The justice of the peace, the tax-collector, the policeman would ensure that administrative and legal functions were properly carried out. The other levels of the hierarchy – the *arrondissement* with its sub-prefect, the departmental capital – remained distant from the daily lives of the peasant. This centralised administration served, above all, to remove a considerable degree of autonomy from the village community whilst, at the same time, its structure reflected the considerable importance that was attached to agriculture.

In terms of economic organisation, however, the government was rather more hesitant. Chaptal, Minister of the Interior under the Consulate and, therefore, charged with agricultural matters, was a supporter of physiocratic ideas. He strengthened the agricultural societies which were beginning to emerge. The commission charged by Bonaparte in 1801 to redraw the Rural Code was largely drawn from such society members. Its task was herculean – to assemble into a single document all the economic and social legislation relating to the countryside. Not surprisingly, it had barely advanced by the time the Empire fell in 1814. It was therefore an incomplete set of legislative texts, coupled with administrative reforms, that were the backbone of efforts at agricultural reform. Many prefects sought to institute change in a piecemeal, localised fashion. They encouraged, for example, the mutual assurance societies against agricultural calamities, such as hail damage or animal disease. In 1809, such groups were recognised as in the public interest. Frequently, however, the administration lacked the necessary statistics to be able to coordinate an efficient agricultural programme. To help provide the base for such programmes, a complete property census in each commune – the *cadastre* – was established in 1807. But the census, which dealt largely with land, took some twenty-five years (1810–35) to complete.

The Civil Code, promulgated in 1804, was the cornerstone of social policy. This massive synthesis of legislation and deliberations on civil matters had been advocated by the Constituent Assembly, and the other assemblies of the revolutionary period had worked on the documents. But it was Bonaparte who brought the project to fruition. The Civil Code confirmed the social advances of the Revolution: the abolition of feudalism, equality before the law, full individual, private property. Property, above all landed property, was central to the whole code which, amongst other things, established the rules of succession. Considerable importance was attached to marriage contracts and to the problems of inheritance. The main provisions are well known. The interests of legitimate children took priority over illegitimate ones.

A central question about the code concerns the extent to which it led to the continued subdivision of plots in equal parts between successors. But the question is not straightforward because the code allowed a parent to favour a particular child or to dispose of at least part of his property exactly as he wished (a proportion of between one-third and one-half could be freely disposed of). The important point to stress, then, is that families were able, if they so wished, to sort out a variety of arrangements to keep the property intact in the hands of one family member. The new code hardly marked a break with tradition at all in succession practices in the Midi. All that changed was the precise legal terminology used by solicitors. Only when no family agreement was forthcoming were there problems. Then, the Civil Code, in allowing all inheritors to receive their due portion of property, undoubtedly contributed to increasing division of the land.

Under the Empire, land remained the base of social organisation. Particularly after the inflation which was experienced with paper money, its possession meant security. In official documents, the use of the title of landowner was sufficient in itself. In this respect then, the regime confirmed the essential economic and ideological positions of the Revolution. The ownership of former national lands was not called into question and their sales continued, albeit at a reduced rate compared with earlier years.[71] Most of the remaining lots were of mediocre, low-revenue land which was hardly attractive to speculators. As a consequence, more modest buyers were able to enter the market. The Empire was thus marked by an increase in the number of individuals who owned at least 1 hectare of land. The overall reduction in land sales was also linked with the return of *émigrés* who reclaimed their unsold land. As well as these official land restitutions, private initiatives were also taken. Often, land returns were carried out by agreement and those who had bought land using devalued paper-notes were able to resell them at a later date to their original owners for hard currency. The move was, for the sellers at least, a clever one, especially as many had been able to draw a revenue on the land in the intervening period without any expenditure on improvements. Some *émigrés* sought to have their lands returned by legal means by arguing that the original sales were invalid. But the government quickly moved to quash such initiatives. Louis Bergeron has estimated that upwards of one-quarter of nobles' land lost during the Revolution was recovered under the Empire. In the enquiry launched under the Consulate to ascertain the twelve highest property-tax payers in different departments, the nobility frequently figures at the top. Many nobles, back on their land, embarked on agricultural experimentation, as in the case of La Fayette's experiments with merino sheep on his farm in the Champagne.

A favourable economic climate

Our knowledge of the agricultural economy for these years is far from adequate. The agricultural enquiries organised by departmental prefects have yet to be systematically studied, whilst monographs for this period are few and far between. As a result, important information on the reality of agricultural production remains hidden. What knowledge we do have relates to agricultural prices.

Both prices and salaries were on the increase between 1799 and 1817.[72] Between 1798–1802 and 1817–20 the price of wheat increased by 25 per cent, and rye by 14 per cent. The latter figure is interesting for, in the eighteenth century, rye prices had increased much faster than those of wheat. Can this be explained by changing patterns of consumption? Perhaps, for it is noticeable that the highest price rises were for those products demanded by either the army or the urban centres. Thus, during the same period, wine prices rose by 20 per cent, meat by 33 per cent. Wages also increased – by some 20 per cent in the case of agricultural workers. Conscription, which had borne most heavily on the peasantry, led to shortages of manpower, especially after 1809. In comparison with 1789, wage increases were considerable: rates for shepherds had doubled whilst those of day-labourers had risen by 67 per cent. Undoubtedly, such rises benefited the majority of peasants who, from time to time, did day work on other farms to complement their resources. These rises may well help to explain the ability of some modest day-labourers to purchase national land.[73]

Farmers and sharecroppers did not, however, benefit to the same extent. The level of farm rents, measured in currency terms, rose 40 per cent to 50 per cent between 1789–1802 and 1817–20, well over the price rises noted above. Was this rent rise perhaps a reflection of demographic pressure increasing demand for rented property? It is debatable. What is more likely is that landowners were acting to recover by other means those revenues lost by the suppression of seigneurial dues.

We know little of the impact of these higher prices on agricultural production. According to Montalivet, Minister of the Interior from 1809 to 1814, total production had increased by about 10 per cent since 1789.[74] Given the paucity of current research, one should treat such a figure as highly speculative. Demographic pressure, coupled with rising prices, at least created the climate for such increases. But one must ask how such increases were facilitated. Productivity does not appear to have risen and the increase in yields appears unspectacular. Nor can one detect any remarkable technical breakthroughs in farming in this period. What initiatives were taken by the administration (encouraging new crops, for example) appear to have met with little success. Production of potatoes did rise, especially after the shortages of 1811–12, but fell once supplies increased.[75] They remained an emergency foodstuff for most families; most were used for feeding pigs.

The administration in this period was preoccupied with industrial crops, which were in short supply because of the blockade. Since sugar cane was not arriving from abroad, it was decided in 1811 that some 32,000 hectares of sugar beet would be sown. The total figure was to be divided amongst those departments considered most suited to the crop, with the prefects deciding on the allocation by commune. Where no volunteer farmers were forthcoming, the municipality was required to rent land for the crop. The operation had only a limited success except in those areas – the Bas-Rhin, for example – where processing plants were located. There, the organisation of plantations had largely been in the hands of entrepreneurs, chemists or lawyers, rather than peasants. Elsewhere, the population remained apathetic; many mayors did not even trouble to reply to the circulars from the prefect. In the Haute-Garonne, only 7 hectares in all were planted. Attempts to encourage other crops – cotton or dye-plants, for example – met with the same response.[76] Only madder, used for dyeing, was partially successful in the Vaucluse.

No fundamental transformation, then, seems to have taken place, for too many obstacles stood in the way of dramatic agricultural progress. Traditional farming systems continued to dominate. Communal and collective farming rights encouraged the maintenance of tiny farming plots, reinforcing the place of the *minifundia*. Many peasants had exhausted their meagre financial resources in the purchase of a plot and could not afford to modernise their farming techniques. But, interestingly, this technical cul-de-sac was not confined to the peasant owner-occupier. It applied with equal force to the large landowners, many of whom sought only to maximise short-term rental income to the detriment of any long-term improvements in the conditions of estates. Given these stagnant conditions, then, how can one explain the general progress in living conditions amongst the peasantry in this period?

Improvements there undoubtedly were. The availability of food was greatly increased. The evidence of property declarations in wills reveals a wider range of furniture and possessions in even the most modest families. For the first time in many years, houses were repaired and improved. Demographic trends also bear out this steady improvement.[77] Despite the somewhat uncertain statistics, it would appear that the death rate fell from some 32/1,000 in 1792 to 26/1,000 between 1806 and 1810. This fall can be seen as part of a long-term demographic trend first begun in the mid eighteenth century. But does it also reveal a better standard of living? It is difficult to be sure. Birth rates also seemed to alter in this period and stabilised at levels somewhat lower than at the end of the ancien régime: 32/1,000 for the period 1806–10 compared with 36/1,000 between 1779 and 1789. The speed of this fall – 15 per cent in twenty years – is all the more significant when taken in conjunction with the increase in marriages after 1790. There is no doubt that methods of contraception began to be more widely used. What seems to have taken place is a transformation of attitudes and mentality which deserves further study through regional monographs. Could it be that reduced demographic pressure alone is sufficient to explain the improvements in peasant living conditions?

The abolition of seigneurial dues certainly played a large part in the improvement of living conditions. In many regions between 10 per cent and 30 per cent of revenue, once lost, may have been returning to the family budget. Within an economy based largely on subsistence, part of this revenue may have been used to improve daily life. This may also imply a reduction in the quantity of produce taken to market, since prior to 1789 seigneurial dues were largely paid out of the proceeds of marketed produce. It is by no means certain that the suppression of such dues would automatically have eased the passage from a subsistence to a market economy in the way in which Albert Soboul supposed.

Alterations in the fiscal regime also led to an improvement in conditions for the peasantry. The suppression of the tithe and the reorganisation of tax away from the country to the towns was a significant factor. In 1813, whilst property taxes represented three-quarters of all direct taxation, revenue from direct taxation provided only 29 per cent of state finances. Thus, the department of Calvados paid 15 million francs in property taxes in 1791, but only 4 million in 1813. Indirect taxation, in part through national customs dues established in 1804, was the preferred method of the Empire, and such taxes weighed more heavily on the urban population than on the still subsistence-oriented peasantry. For as long as the price rises facilitated an increase in indirect taxation, and whilst new conquests financed the war, the imperial regime was able to consolidate its popularity in the countryside.

Growing discontent?

These steady improvements during the Consulate and Empire were, however, fragile and they were brutally exposed by the economic crisis of 1810–12. Discontent, linked to military defeat, accumulated in the countryside to such an extent that most peasants seemed indifferent to the fall of the regime. The legend of Napoleon, later to become so powerful in the countryside, post-dated the end of his Empire by a number of years.

Industry was the first to be hit by crisis.[78] It was undergoing some form of recovery when the poor harvest of 1811 intervened. Storms here, drought there and, suddenly, the harvest was in doubt. The Paris Basin, western France and the south-east were especially hard-hit. The north, Lorraine and the Massif Central were largely untouched. Despite the action of prefects in attempting to direct flows of cereals between surplus and deficit regions, prices took off. In April 1812, at the start of the traditional period of shortage, a decree, similar to that of year II, established price ceilings. Farmers were obligated by decree to sell their produce at particular, specified markets and merchants had to declare their stocks to the authorities. But in the absence of any coercive measures, the decrees were largely ineffective. Banditry began to reappear, beggars returned to the roads and many markets experienced scenes of violence and robbery. Our knowledge of these troubles is scanty. Their eruption with such force and violence suggests that food shortages were a mere catalyst for more deep-seated discontent.

The general economic crisis served to reveal the full depth of such discontent amongst the population in general. From 1810 onwards, those factors which had helped maintain internal peace and equilibrium in the Consular period no longer operated. In the west, the conflict between government and the papacy was especially provoking and a considerable proportion of the clergy was hostile to the government as a result. The emergence of an atmosphere of social conservatism is also evident, as many nobles were named as mayors of communities they had once governed as feudal overlords in 1789. Some large landowners, after having remained prudently quiet for some fifteen years, began to snipe at village communities which, they argued, had overstepped the mark. Some tribunals lent the nobles support in their attacks.[79] In some instances, the prefect backed up the attacks on the communities.

Many villagers, not surprisingly, were disquieted by the attitude of the public authorities in attacking their hard-won rights. At the start of the Empire, public prudence had characterised the administration. The decree of 22 February 1804 confirmed the earlier law of *prairial* year IV. Only those divisions of communal land which had been properly sanctioned were maintained; many others were annulled. The prefects then began a policy of discreetly farming out blocks of communal land and using the revenues for paying the local clergy and maintaining local roads. However, as military defeat dictated higher state revenues, the process changed dramatically. The legislation of 20 March 1813 transferred the communal lands to a central bank and authorised their sale. Once the sales had been made, the communes would receive state rents in return. In theory the benefits should have been considerable. In practice the process was slow to get off the ground as a consequence of disagreements between the prefects and the central administration. Thus, at the collapse of the Empire, little land had been sold. But the glimpse that the peasants had had of the procedure was sufficient to disquiet them.

With military defeat, the burden of the war was felt more keenly. From 1812 onwards, fiscal pressure was intensified on a countryside already facing food shortages. At the same time, conscription was increased.

More and more and younger and younger seemed to be the pattern. In the class of 1812, two-thirds of those eligible were required to join up. In 1813, out of 963,000 men called to the colours, at least 250,000 refused and went into hiding. After the disaster of the Russian campaign, the heavy recruitment continued. As in 1793, a flood of deserters resulted, many forming themselves into bands of brigands and malcontents in isolated areas. There they joined the swelling ranks of beggars and criminals forced out of society by the crisis. Insecurity became endemic in the Massif Central, the Midi and the west. In the south-east a secret royalist group, the Chevaliers de la Foy, took many bands in hand in apparent readiness for the return of the Bourbons. With the invasion and general uncertainty of 1814–15 the old political differences amongst the peasantry appeared to return. In the north-east resistance groups fought the foreign invaders. In 1815, the Vendée rose again while Napoleon, returned from the island of Elba, was acclaimed by the mountain-dwellers of the Dauphiné. Two years of defeat had seemingly erased ten years of apparent indifference amongst the peasantry to the future of the regime.

How then can one explain the spread of the legend of Napoleon in the countryside?[80] To judge from the narrative of this chapter, it would seem incomprehensible. Indeed, in 1814 it was the black legend of 'Boney' which seemed strongest in the countryside, the tale of an ogre whispered from one village to the next. Yet, once the monarchy was restored, it needed only a few maladroit measures to make the difficulties of the last years of the Empire fade into insignificance. The unfavourable economic conjuncture after 1817, with falling agricultural prices, coupled with the demands of the returned *émigrés*, made many nostalgic for the high prices and salaries of past years. The Emperor became transformed into the epitome of material progress and personal freedom. Old soldiers invested the legend with the scent of battle and the aura of victory. Thus, the legend was born.

In the space of thirty years, then, the peasantry had experienced a series of dramatic changes which had thrown traditional agricultural systems into disarray. As far as the legal status of property was concerned, the changes were absolutely decisive. The destruction of feudalism and the affirmation of individualism reinforced the importance of private property. The relative fluidity of the property market also helped to at least rejig property distribution without fundamentally disturbing the social hierarchy of the countryside. The large, bourgeois property-owner was untouched, indeed, in many ways, was reinforced in some areas. Property rents increased, too, as landowners sought to recoup their lost feudal dues. At the same time, however, the proliferation of small properties increased. The Revolution paved the way for a period of some 150 years in which the small family farm, based on subsistence production and the intensive use of family labour, dominated the economic and social regime of the countryside.

2

A slow transformation: 1815–1870

The years between 1815 and 1870 represent half a century of relative calm in comparison with the upheavals of preceding decades. There was no dramatic agricultural revolution any more than there had been in earlier periods. Rather, there was a steady, unspectacular evolution of agriculture from which the peasantry nonetheless emerged profoundly changed. The economic climate also changed, permitting a steady and uninterrupted expansion of production, especially after 1850. Thanks to a combination of high prices and an easing of demographic pressure, there was a perceptible improvement in living conditions from the middle of the Second Empire onwards. These changes have led some observers to speak of these years as marking the apogee of peasant civilisation in France. But it should be noted that these improvements do not reflect radical changes within an essentially somnolent agricultural economy. Instead they came from other sectors, especially the growth of urban markets and the increasing role of the state. To be a peasant still implied a condition of subservience to the local squire and administration, a subservience reflected, above all, in the comments and observations of non-peasants on their rural brethren. Even universal male suffrage, granted to, rather than won by, them, did not lead to the political emancipation of the peasantry.

1. Agricultural progress
Agricultural production increased markedly between 1815 and 1870, but the credit for these increases can hardly be laid at the door of decisive transformations in farming systems. Rather, they have their roots in the increased demand for food and the opening out of urban markets. In many respects, traditional agricultural systems continued to represent a barrier to progress.

The evolution of production
The work of Maurice Lévy-Leboyer and Jean-Claude Toutain has clearly and unequivocally shown the dynamic nature of agricultural

48

production in this period.[1] It grew by around 1.2 per cent per annum between 1815–24 and 1865–74, a rate not far short of that of the economy as a whole. The evolution of prices divides the period into two. Between 1818 and 1845, prices tended to fall, thus wiping out some of the gains made through increased production. By contrast, the years of the Second Empire were marked by both high prices and abundant production.

Short-term fluctuations did not disappear altogether, however. In 1816–17, 1837, 1839–40, 1846–7, 1854–6 and 1867–8 many regions suffered severe shortages. As in the eighteenth century, the authorities, fearing the social unrest which might result from shortages, anxiously studied harvest returns. It is evident, however, that from about 1850 onwards, these chronic variations in supply and prices of cereals diminished markedly. The problem of famine and shortage appeared to have been overcome. Even if the fear of hunger remained ever-present, it no longer dictated the economic behaviour of the peasantry. From the Second Empire onwards, the cultivation of cereals at all costs, regardless of physical or economic conditions, was no longer regarded as essential. In any case, price movements meant that pastoral farming or viticulture were becoming much more attractive propositions to many peasants.

The area devoted to arable crops increased by some 20 per cent between 1815 and 1852, largely at the expense of wasteland. After that date, however, it remained static. These changes accompanied alterations in the crops grown. Thus, for example, mixed crops of rye and wheat, and rye itself, disappeared from all but the very poorest regions, whereas the area devoted to wheat increased. This decline in the traditional bread-making cereals coincided with dietary changes. White bread, already part of urban consumption patterns, spread to the better-off groups of the peasantry. The potato was more widely accepted as part of everyday meals and increased its hold in the Auvergne, Brittany and Provence, where the amount of bread consumed fell accordingly. Maize played a similar role, increasing in the south of the Paris Basin and the Rhône valley. These two high-yielding crops were especially attractive to small peasants because they permitted the marketing of cereals that were previously consumed, or the keeping of livestock. In the longer term they were an important factor in increasing the integration of the peasant into the money-based economy.

The vine also increased the commercial options of the farmer. During the Second Empire viticulture made spectacular gains with a 13 per cent increase in the area under vines between 1852 and 1874. This dynamism benefited above all the regions south of the Loire, especially Languedoc and Roussillon. There, the vine prospered within traditional polycultural systems.[2] Agricultural workers profited from good prices to purchase small plots of land and, between 1862 and 1872, in the Hérault, the number of *viticulteurs* grew from 14,000 to 25,000. The strong increases in urban demand meant that profits could be made even in years of poor harvest on land previously uncultivated.

Pastoral farming, encouraged by rising meat prices, also developed. The area under grass increased by 38 per cent between 1820 and 1880 and similar increases were noted for a range of other fodder crops. In some regions – the districts of Auge and Bessin, for example, in lower Normandy, pastoral farming played a dominant role.[3] There, a near-monoculture of grass, organised by large estates, dominated the landscape. Beef cattle, purchased from surrounding areas, were fattened on the rich grass and marketed in Paris. Cereals were no longer the 'necessary evil' they had once been.[4] Fallow lands also disappeared beneath grass as pastoral farming developed in the Mayenne, Maine-et-Loire and parts of the Massif Central. Here, root crops were grown to feed cattle. Elsewhere, pig farming was popular, primarily because it could easily fit into existing practices. Sheep farming declined somewhat, chased from the old fallow and communal lands, and further depressed by a fall in wool prices. But the development of other specialisations compensated for this decline. In this period, then, more than ever before, a herd of animals represented a good source of both revenue and capital which could swiftly be adapted to changing economic circumstances.

Progress was general if not uniform, and some regions developed more rapidly than others.[5] Undoubtedly, the proximity of large urban centres favoured the Paris Basin and the north. But, after 1850, the development of pastoral farming and viticulture tended to accentuate the differences between the north and the Midi. In the cereal zones of the north, previously well-favoured, farmers faced less-remunerative prices. As a consequence, many were faced with the need to improve their own production methods to maintain their revenues.

Weaknesses in the system

The increase in the quantities of agricultural produce cannot be explained in terms of spectacular changes in farm production methods. Up until the middle of the nineteenth century, it was an expansion of the farmed area and intensification of labour, rather than shifts in agricultural techniques, that explained these increases. With the onset of the Second Empire some regions began to adopt agricultural machinery but, geographically, such innovation was strictly limited.

The agronomists of the first half of the nineteenth century inherited the legacy of agronomic thought of the eighteenth century, coupled with some of the advances in recent scientific knowledge. But their empirical skills and experiments were strictly limited. The first agricultural schools were born out of private initiative, such as that of Mathieu de Dombasle at his estate of Roville in Lorraine, established in 1822. Use of the plough which was to bear his name spread but slowly after 1840. It was above all the landowning classes who influenced and controlled so many of the agricultural societies which developed rapidly after 1830.[6] Their publications bear witness to a frenzy of innovations, the majority of which was never followed up. Even if they could read, peasants rarely bothered to look at anything other than almanacs; to most, such specialised agricultural journals were literally a closed book. Many of the *comices agricoles* which were established after 1832 could organise all the exhibitions and competitions they wished for the local farming populace – these 'official' manifestations of agricultural innovation had little impact on peasant knowhow and traditions.

Progress in farming methods, as in mechanisation, was isolated and episodic, and it would be almost tedious to enumerate the examples of slow or strangled innovation.[7] Just two examples will suffice. In the Midi, the traditional method of threshing corn was to spread the grain on the ground to be trampled upon by a team of horses. In 1809, a corrugated wooden roller, drawn by a single animal, began to be used in the Orange region. This method was both more efficient and productive but it was not until the Second Empire that its use spread as far as the department of Bouches-du-Rhône. In the Beauce, the spread of technical innovations was scarcely much faster.[8] The scythe was forbidden under the ancien régime, because it both wasted grain and deprived the poor of much-needed straw. In 1791, the principle of individual freedom to cultivate having been established, such legal obstacles to innovation were lifted. The use of the scythe thus expanded between 1800 and 1850 because it more than doubled productivity. In one day a single harvester could cut 50 ares of wheat with a scythe as opposed to only 20 ares with a sickle. The threshing machine did not replace the flail until well into the Second Empire and then, largely for economic reasons, as wage rates rose. As for harvesting machines, they remained the exception before 1870. Yet such slow innovation was occurring in the Beauce, one of the more advanced farming regions of the nation!

A variety of reasons can be advanced to account for the survival of traditional tools and routines. Many, apparently psychological, reasons in fact reveal underlying economic and social rationales. Many agricultural societies castigated the peasantry for its traditionalist ethos, its

reliance on the 'tried and trusted' methods of past years, its distrust of
innovations introduced from elsewhere. But it is evident that many of the
objections to change were severely practical ones. Thus, the survival in
many regions of the sickle while the scythe appeared more practical and
efficient may seem illogical. But in practice, the peasants recognised that
the workload with the scythe could be much greater since an exclusively
male personnel was thought to be needed for such a heavy implement.
Furthermore, the scythe was regarded as cutting too low and destroying
quails' nests, thus depriving them of the hunting, so much prized by the
peasantry since the abolition of seigneurial rights. Thus, such innovations might threaten the careful social equilibrium of the countryside.
The threat of arson by harvesters was often sufficient to dissuade some
large farmers in the Beauce from using harvesting machines. As long as
labour was cheap and plentiful, innovations were regarded as both costly
and full of risk. From the Second Empire onwards, however, the situation
was reversed and mechanisation became the preferred option of many
large farmers in the Beauce when faced with rising salary demands. 'The
day the first harvesting machine appears in the countryside will herald
the independence of the farmer . . . it will mark the end of the despotic
stranglehold hitherto exercised by the labouring classes', stated the
Journal de Chartres of 28 July 1859.[9] Such problems were, however, largely
the concern of those large farms employing considerable numbers of
workers. For the small peasant farmer, such considerations were barely
significant.

For the large majority of peasants, the perfecting of particular innovations or the purchase of machinery was hardly a pressing priority. Many
preferred to sink their savings into purchasing more land rather than
farming their existing land better. A mowing or harvesting machine represented a large expenditure in money within an economy still based to
a large extent on barter. Such machines, furthermore, required horses
rather than cattle for their motive power. This level of investment, then,
was usually well beyond the means of most peasants, particularly as credit
was both expensive and poorly adapted to their needs. Any kind of
borrowing had unpleasant connotations to most peasants and implied,
furthermore, considerable risks, given the system of credit then in use.

Solicitors were usually the intermediaries for loans, assembling and
distributing capital in the countryside. In the Pas-de-Calais, 52 per cent
of borrowers were peasants; their creditors were usually landowners.[10]
With such a system, at least part of the rents paid on land was reinvested
back in farming. Even in borrowing from a solicitor rather than a money-
lender, the peasantry was not necessarily spared usurious rates of
interest, often through the expedient of recording false sums in the

actual deed of notice. Certain transactions were made simply through
an exchange of notes, which often gave rise to malpractice. In the
Bourgogne during the July Monarchy, rates of 8 per cent to 12 per cent
were common but, in exceptional cases, could reach 144 per cent.[11]
Loans at rates as low as 3 per cent or 4 per cent were usually only
practised between relatives. Usury then, was primarily a consequence of
a situation in which peasants rarely had access to urban circuits of capital. Bankers were, in any case, much more attracted by lucrative urban
lending portfolios than by loans to the agricultural sector. From the
middle of the nineteenth century, the societies of agriculture began to
focus on this problem and created, in 1861, the Agricultural Credit
Society, linked to the Crédit foncier. When this latter group failed in
1876, the damage was considerable. The directors had largely speculated
with the money and had devoted little time and attention to the problems of credit for the peasantry. On this question, France was evidently
well behind its German neighbours.[12]

Increases in production, then, had been achieved primarily through
an intensification of existing practices and systems, rather than through
their modernisation. The cultivated area thus increased, attaining its
maximum extent of 26 million hectares in 1862. A number of large, state-
financed projects after 1830 contributed to this total in spectacular
fashion. Parts of the Marais Poitevin and the lakes of the Dombes were
drained and there were major drainage programmes during the Second
Empire in the Landes and Camargue. Such operations were, however,
exceptional and were largely the action of large landowners with good
government connections. The Duke de Morny represented the arche-
typal improver in this respect. The large mass of the peasantry engaged
in a relentless nibbling away of remaining communal land. The authorities, anxious to maintain calm in the countryside, permitted municipalities to let parts of their communal land in a legislative act of 1818.
The July Monarchy maintained the process, seeing in the revenues thus
obtained a means of sustaining municipal expenditure. In some areas,
such as the upland parts of the Lyonnais, the habitual users of communal
land engaged in a kind of non-violent guerrilla war against the process
but were still unable to prevent the alienation of some 39 per cent of
communal land in their area.[13] The crucial step was taken in 1860.
Henceforth, municipalities could sell one-third of their communal land
in order to increase their financial resources. As a result, in 1877, communal land covered no more than 9 per cent of national territory.

The increase in the cultivated area indicated above was paralleled by
an increase in labour inputs. Demographic pressure and the proliferation of *minifundia* meant that working by hand was maintained, or even

increased, in some areas. Such was the case in the Limagne, for example, where potato cultivation was henceforth practised in open fields. The scratch plough, hardly an efficient tool for this form of cultivation, was replaced by the spade. It was not until the second half of the century that the metal plough took its place.[14] The agricultural census of 1852 revealed especially high labour inputs (measured in workdays per hectare) in the Nord, the uplands of Brittany, Alsace, Limagne and the departments of Rhône and Tarn.[15] This heavy workload was linked above all to agricultural specialisations which allowed peasants to draw a decent revenue from the smallest of plots. The vine is the example *par excellence* of such specialisation.

It is clear, then, that agricultural production continued to rely on huge inputs of human labour, often very poorly rewarded labour at that. Mechanisation proceeded at a snail's pace and was the concern of the large farms who thus secured a decisive advantage over the mass of the peasantry. As Ronald Hubscher has cogently argued: 'such changes were like a tiny film of progress spread over a traditional world'.[16] Additional efforts at mechanisation by peasants were tolerated primarily because they allowed larger families to be fed; increased demographic pressure remains at the root of the production increases in the countryside. A second motivation was economic: the increased prices for farm products consequent upon urbanisation. As transport improvements occurred, so the more dynamic farmers were able to take advantage of new markets, and better prices, for their products.

External stimuli to change

There were, however, a number of external stimuli which helped to shake up the rather stagnant agricultural sector. Transport improvements after 1840, whilst primarily intended to benefit industry and commerce, were of considerable, indirect benefit to agriculture in opening out the market economy. Was there perhaps a fundamental revolution in transport prior to 1870? The impact undoubtedly varied from one region to another.

At the start of the nineteenth century, the nation was criss-crossed by a network of national roads, but the regions they traversed remained largely unaffected by them. They barely constituted an integrated network, particularly in the centre and south.[17] This did not mean, however, that the countryside was totally isolated. On the contrary, the small tracks and roads often carried a dense traffic of men on horseback or on foot, whilst merchandise was transported on the backs of mules or on cattle-drawn carts. But such movement was primarily short-distance in nature. With the establishment of a system of classifying and financing routeways after the Thiers legislation of 1836, the situation improved considerably. The state undertook to maintain main roads, the communes the local network. The administration of bridges and roads embarked on the construction of some hundreds of bridges and laid out a network of routes south of the Loire, bringing a noticeable improvement in communications. But the communes barely had sufficient revenue to carry out their alloted tasks and the local squirearchies were vociferous in their complaints about the state of the roads. The complaint of a deputy from the department of Nord is indicative of the tone of such complaints: 'You have voted many millions to embellish our towns, you have voted for great monuments whilst we are still up to our knees in mud every time we venture out'.[18] A law passed on 11 July 1868 finally brought a solution to the problems of financing work, authorising communes to take out loans at low interest rates in order to undertake road construction. Only after this date can one detect an opening up of the countryside in most areas of central France and the Midi.

Railway construction did not dramatically alter this chronology. The task of the first lines was to transport industrial raw materials and finished goods, and, from the outset, agricultural products were viewed as relatively unimportant. Certainly the promoters of the lines largely ignored the potential agricultural traffic. In many rural areas the new lines met with indifference and even hostility from a population who feared their deleterious impact on crops. Possible land expropriation was a further source of disquiet. Once generous compensation was forthcoming and the lines were built, the advantages became more evident to the rural population, even if perennial complaints about the high tarrifs were made. Railway transport profited most those sections of the agricultural economy which were already commercialised, notably wine and cattle production. It was also useful in supplying goods such as fertiliser and agricultural machines. But the economic opening of the countryside by the railways remained limited to those areas which were close to the main lines and which, most importantly, had good road connections to local stations. By 1870, whilst an adequate north–south network was in place, transverse links had barely begun. It was not until after 1877 that Clermont-Ferrand was linked to Tulle and Lyon. The secondary network was little more than a sketch on a map. There is little doubt that where a good railway network existed, considerable economic transformation took place. But these changes acted to accentuate still further regional differences. By 1870, the revolution in transportation was still in its infancy.

The slow pace of change was also reflected in the very tentative process of national economic integration. At the start of the century, markets were heterogeneous, fragmented, diverse and barely integrated. Such fragmentation is displayed in the geography of wheat prices. In 1820, in the south-east, the price for a hectolitre of wheat was some 48 per cent higher than in the north-east. By 1869, the gap had narrowed to about 16 per cent.[19] The regional markets widened around the more dynamic towns and cities. Annual and biannual fairs multiplied during the Second Empire and reveal the growing significance of pastoral farming as well as increased peasant consumption. Every commune sought its own market but the overall pattern shows that the smallest declined with the shift of trade to larger centres.[20] Weekly markets were more stable, with a more loyal clientele of small peasants constrained to sell a few perishable products at their local village or town. Such small markets were largely the domain of women whilst the larger fairs were a masculine domain in which 'technical' rather than 'domestic' matters were dominant. Here the sale of animals was a crucial part of the proceedings and price levels were liable to make or break the farm budget.[21] Did such fairs and markets bring about the economic integration of the regions into a national economy? In so far as the railways reduced the problems of cereal supply at the end of the Second Empire, perhaps a national market had emerged. The same does not apply, however, to a range of other products and regions. Agriculture in the Beauce, for example, became increasingly commercial after 1850, orienting its production decisions to a national and international cereal market. But, interestingly, at the same time, the majority of peasants in other parts of France was constrained in its selling patterns by pressing monetary needs; production solely for the market remained some way off.

Agricultural structures and their effects

Between 1815 and 1870, agricultural structures slowly evolved into a pattern of increasingly small property and farming units. Ownership of land continued to be the decisive element in rural social hierarchies and landownership remained at the heart of productive systems and was, no less, the basis of society.

Our primary sources for the study of property are fiscal in nature. The *cadastre* provides a listing of all property units in every commune together with an indication of their taxable revenue.[22] This long and complex census, first proposed in 1807, was not completed until 1851; the majority of surveys was completed between 1820 and 1842. Unfortunately, it is impossible to use this source to draw up an account of national property structures because these cadastral account books have yet to be fully exploited by historians. This is why it is more usual to use the statistics relating to property units, which record the proportion of the property tax each owner had to pay. Using this source is far from satisfactory, since an owner could be counted several times if he held land in different communes. The administrative records of the period assumed that 100 property units would belong to about 60 owners. In 1815, 9 million units were recorded. By 1842, the number had reached 10 million. This was followed by a rapid increase to 14 million in 1865. Thus, in the space of some fifty years the number of owners had increased by 55 per cent. Once again, the years of the Second Empire saw the most dramatic changes.

The statistics of property units give an indication of value but not extent of the unit. In 1826, small units with a value of 30 francs or less accounted for 84 per cent of the total; in 1858, this had risen to 86 per cent. Large units, with a value over 300 francs were barely 1 per cent in 1826 and 0.8 per cent in 1858.[23] The inequalities of the earlier period thus continued with but a slight weakening in the position of large land units. Large property units fared relatively badly in some areas – especially in mountain zones and Brittany, but also in a swathe of territory from the Champagne to Alsace and in Provence. They remained of fundamental importance in the Paris Basin, Languedoc, and the area from the Haute-Garonne to Hérault and, to a lesser extent in Aquitaine, the Nord and the lower Rhine valley. It is difficult to explain these patterns. The factors leading to an increase in small units did not operate consistently across the national territory.

The Civil Code has been seen by some as a prime culprit in the multiplication of units. But, in many regions, all sorts of legal devices could be employed to ensure that the land was kept intact on succession. Birth control could also be used to prevent the division of the land. It is also evident that the increases in production from mid-century, coupled with a rise in prices, allowed many peasants to buy parcels of land as well as permitting agricultural labourers, favoured by salary increases, to get a step on the ladder of ownership. The increased trend towards land division was also fundamentally a reflection of the continued socio-economic importance of landownership. It represented the outcome, more accentuated than in previous years, of a continued struggle between those groups requiring land for production and those to whom land was an instrument of social prestige and financial security. The purchase of land provided a guarantee of good revenues and a careful use of capital. Because demand usually exceeded supply, the land market was highly speculative and prices continued to increase until 1881, increasing threefold from 1851 to 1881.[24]

In this struggle for land, the absentee landlord maintained his position, at least at the start of the period. Whilst rents remained at a good level (they almost doubled between 1821 and 1881), this form of speculation was attractive. But the real value of such returns is difficult to estimate because much depended on the size of the unit, the type of production, the economic conjuncture and the particular conditions of the lease. Returns, net of tax, varied from 2.5 per cent to 5 per cent of the value of the capital, depending on the region and period.[25] After 1860, with the rise of more remunerative investment opportunities in the towns, this form of speculation became less attractive. Nevertheless, such investment in land continued to confer a degree of social prestige, which was an important element in bourgeois and aristocratic life. Land was a social imperative, together with a small château at the centre of the territory. Up until 1848, too, possession of land was a requirement for those wishing to enter politics and only those paying a property tax at a certain level could participate in political life.

The landlord class represented an important group in mid-century with something approaching 1 million members. It was a highly stratified and diverse group. Despite the Revolution, large aristocratic landlords remained very powerful in some areas such as Mayenne, where they were easily able to recover their previous position.[26] The 1814 Charter permitted the return of those lands not yet sold to their old owners. To recover those lands which had been sold, certain aristocrats used a combination of force and menaces, prompting the monarchy to introduce a system of indemnities in 1825 – the *millard* – as compensation for lands which had been sold. The funds paid out by the state were not always used to repurchase lands previously lost. The 1830 revolution was more decisive for, by distancing legitimist aristocrats from the corridors of power, it led many of them to spend more of their time on their estates. Some sought to influence the farming practices of their sharecroppers, regarding themselves henceforth as farmers. In the Sarthe, such involvement brought spectacular results and previously poor land was planted or improved with lime. Pastoral farming also developed on many noble estates.[27] Many, however, preferred to leave the sharecropping system intact, as it had been under the ancien régime. The Second Empire was the golden age of the gentleman farmer, idealised in the novels of the Countess of Ségur. Such figures exercised a strong patronal control over their villagers, a control in which charity was the accustomed reward for servility and long service.

The urban bourgeoisie took as its model the landed aristocracy and, as in the eighteenth century, those who had made their fortunes in commerce or industry invested heavily in land which could bring them social standing. Thus, the bourgeoisie of Lyon invested in large estates in the Dombes and Beaujolais and the Parisian bourgeoisie made their influence felt as far away as the Pas-de-Calais.[28] Land was also the most important investment for many of the middle classes – doctors and pharmacists, solicitors, justices of the peace – in the small towns of the countryside. The few dozen hectares of land they owned brought with them an additional revenue. Such groups helped to constitute the 'village bourgeoisie' studied by Maurice Agulhon in Provence.[29] The term is not as contradictory as it would at first appear. Many of these people played an integral part in village life. They were resident rather than absentee landowners, frequently educated in urban ways and language, who exercised an important influence on the local peasantry with whom they were familiar.

If ownership of land represented a useful investment for the bourgeoisie, for the peasantry it represented security. It was a first necessity without which farming skills counted for nothing. To be the owner of one's farm conferred independence, or at least the illusion of independence. But for many, access to this precious security, this sought-after independence, was impossible because, at least up to the end of the Second Empire, parcels of land rarely became available, and, when they did, were usually too expensive. Where possible, peasants bought, no matter what the price, preferring to invest in more land rather than modernising their existing land. Did they thus achieve independence?

In 1862, only 25 per cent of all farms over 1 hectare were owner-occupied and one-third of farmers had to supplement what land they owned with rented plots. It can be argued that in mid-century only a farm of about 10 hectares could provide a degree of self-sufficiency for the whole family. For viticulture, the equivalent figure would have been about 4 hectares. Yet, in 1862, 85 per cent of all farms were below this figure of 10 hectares and *viticulteurs* farmed no more than 30 per cent of the cultivated area.[30] Undoubtedly, the threshold for survival could be put at a lower figure – perhaps 5 hectares, much less for the vine. But it is clear that a large majority of the peasantry was dependent on what work it could find elsewhere, particularly on larger farms. Even in the Beauce, an area of large units, small parcels of land continued to exist. Here were congregated those who were to win – or lose – the battle for land. Thus, the development of *minifundia* did not transform the economic structure of the countryside. What it did do, however, was make the struggle for land a central fact of countless lives in the course of the nineteenth century.

The place of the 400,000 farmers and 200,000 sharecroppers in 1862 is difficult to evaluate. Large farmers, powerful at the end of the eighteenth century, increased their importance in areas such as the Paris Basin and the Nord. Some, farming many hundreds of acres, were in an excellent position to take advantage of price rises. Because they employed a number of labourers and also loaned money to local villagers, their social position and influence was akin to that of the large landowner and the two groups dominated rural society.[31] They formed a veritable elite at the heart of the peasantry. The same did not apply, however, to the sharecroppers who found themselves closer to salaried workers. Sharecropping was widespread in the Vendée, the south-west and the Bourbonnais. In the department of Allier, the number of sharecroppers increased from 8,000 at the start of the century to 17,000 in 1870. They depended totally on their landlords and were frequently controlled by intermediaries who represented the landowner. These individuals were not averse to imposing one-year leases made all the harsher by clauses drawn from the practices of the ancien régime.

The world of the salaried worker was a heterogeneous one. In 1851, 44 per cent of males working in agriculture were labourers. In 1851, there were at least 900,000 day-labourers and 2 million domestic (live-in) workers. In mid-century wages continued to be paid according to local conditions, and there were considerable regional variations. Wages were especially low in Brittany: around one-third of the average wage in the Paris region. They were also low in the Nord, Aquitaine, the Pyrénées and the Auvergne.[32] But they tended to increase during the Second Empire. Salaries rose in this period by between 20 per cent and 50 per cent, depending on the region, between 1841 and 1875. This group should not be regarded in isolation from the rest of peasant society because its role was crucial to the functioning of medium and large farms. At least a part of this group, furthermore, owned some land or hoped to inherit a plot or two. Young people from large families were usually quick to engage as live-in workers, remaining in such employment whilst they saved money in preparation for marriage, or whilst waiting to inherit some land. A whole cycle of conditions existed, largely as a function of age. Only what Fernand Braudel called the 'ultra-poor' remained on the margins of society.[33] The beggars and outcasts often stayed in the village after a long, wandering career. Their numbers diminished under the Second Empire primarily because they were no longer able to exploit the dwindling communal rights and resources in the village or because the attractions of an urban life proved too strong.

2. The dynamics of the peasant population

Between 1815 and 1870, the peasantry continued to constitute the largest group in the population of France. But statistical information remains hazy until at least mid-century. It was only at the 1846 census that the rural population was defined as those communes with fewer than

2,000 people in the *chef lieu*. For the earlier period we have to rely on approximations. Using these it can be estimated that the rural population grew from 23.4 million in 1815 to 30.5 million in 1866.[34] In relative terms this represented about 79 per cent of the populace at the start of the Restoration and 70 per cent at the end of the Second Empire. As regards the precise size of the farming population, the figures are less certain still. The first census to include figures on professions was that of 1851, but this is unreliable. Nevertheless, we can estimate the active agricultural population then, including women, at about 14.3 million. Agriculture accounted for some 57 per cent of male employment at the same date. As for the total population dependent on farming, a figure of some 20 million is a fair estimate; some three-quarters of the rural population and 55 per cent of the total population.[35] Whilst these figures may exaggerate the importance of the rural and agricultural population in some areas, they do point to the tremendous demographic importance of the peasantry and emphasise that overpopulation was a potential problem in many rural areas. As a result, many peasant families were forced either to seek alternative forms of employment or to migrate, initially as a temporary measure, later as a more permanent solution.

Rural overpopulation

A high birth rate was at the heart of the demographic vitality of the rural population – not that such rates were universally high. In the Beauvais region, where Malthusian practices made an early appearance, they were only 25/1,000 in 1831. Similar figures appear in Normandy and the south-west.[36] But at Saint-Jean-de-Tromilon, in the Bigouden region of Brittany, they were as high as 40/1,000 throughout this period.[37] In most rural areas, birth rates were consistently higher than in urban areas; the average number of children per family was almost always higher in farming areas, where children were an important source of labour, than in urban areas. A large family obviated the need to employ salaried labour. Nonetheless, there was a tendency to adjust family size to the size of the farm. In the Pas-de-Calais, the 1851 census indicated that single-child families were much more common on tiny farms than on the larger plots.[38]

In the countryside, death rates fell more rapidly in this period than in urban areas, declining from about 24/1,000 in 1820 to 22/1,000 in 1880. This decline was not due to advances in medicine or sanitary conditions. Doctors, for example, were rarely, if ever, consulted by peasant families, for the cost of consultations, perhaps equivalent to two or three days' salary, was beyond the reach of most families.[39] Local healers, wise, usually elderly, women who spoke local dialect and offered traditional recipes and cures, were in any case much cheaper, could be paid in kind and prescribed simple, readily acceptable medicines. In the countryside they reigned supreme. Rather, the fall in mortality is probably accounted for by a better diet and the disappearance of food crises that reduced the susceptibility of the rural population to epidemics and disease.

The rate of natural increase in the countryside towards the middle of the Second Empire stood at about 0.4 per cent, an increase which was soon reflected in rural-population densities. But regional differences were important. In 1836, regions with densities above 90 people per square kilometre were mainly north of the Loire, from Brittany to the Belgian frontier as well as Alsace and Lorraine. By contrast, south of the Loire only two areas had such high densities – the departments of Rhône and Isère, and a swathe of territory in the south-west from Ariège to the Gironde. The east and south of the Paris Basin and the Massif Central were, by comparison, thinly settled with densities below 50 people per square kilometre. An average rural density of some 73 people per square kilometre was, by comparison with its European neighbours, low.

Despite this, numerous signs pointed to an overpopulated countryside. The most visible of these was the continuance of beggars in rural areas at least until the middle of the Second Empire. Another sign was the unease of many of the rural elite. A strong Malthusian philosophy took root from the 1830s which argued that both urban and rural populations were too large and were the cause of the poverty and poor living conditions in many areas. The solution advocated by these Malthusian advocates was to argue for birth limitation by the poorer sections of society. For the rural populations themselves, however, the solution lay not in limiting births, but rather in increasing the revenue of their family budgets.

The search for additional resources

Most peasant families engaged in a wide range of activities outside the traditional agricultural calendar and, in the first half of the nineteenth century, pluriactivity was widespread.[40] From one region to another, one particular situation to another, the peasant engaged in work as an artisan or worker, at home or in a workshop. The sheer diversity of situations is eloquent testimony to a basic fact of life – that agricultural activity alone was rarely sufficient to make ends meet; extra work elsewhere was needed. This multiple employment was a necessity, then, which flowed from overpopulation in the countryside and the imbalances in agricultural systems.

Artisanal activity was widespread. In the first half of the century, many peasants made their own tools and clothing. Such activity meant that peasants could provide for their own needs without recourse to the market. Some went beyond this autarkic activity and entered the market, selling such goods to others. The difference between a peasant engaging in artisanal activity and an artisan, also producing a little from his plot of land, is not easy to define for, in traditional rural society, artisans remained closely linked to the land. The peasantry constituted their chief clientele and, for many, revenue from land, was an important component of artisanal income. The more modest artisanal workers, furthermore, would not infrequently engage in work as day-labourers on the land, often accepting payment in kind rather than cash.[41] Such employment diversity changed somewhat with the impact of industrial-isation and the modernisation of farming. Thus, weavers largely disappeared after 1840 while the development of a more mechanised agriculture, powered by horses or cattle, increased the numbers of local metal-workers and smiths. Such artisans were independent workers, not to be confused with those home-workers whose numbers multiplied with the onset of industrialisation.

The towns provided good employment opportunities for a plentiful rural workforce which was out of work for at least part of the year.[42] Urban trader–manufacturers used local entrepreneurs to distribute work locally. They would usually provide the raw materials and undertake to market the finished product, often after final finishing in the towns. Pay-ment was usually at piecework rates since the entrepreneur could not supervise the work closely. Whilst rates of pay were usually poor, such work was a valuable supplement to an overstretched budget. Such forms of employment were highly diverse. Textile work was the most important branch. Thus, the cotton industry employed some 25,000 people in a 50-kilometre radius around Saint-Quentin in 1843. At the same time, many tens of thousands of peasants in the Vosges or in the Caux region span cotton during the slack agricultural season. In the Champagne, villagers processed wool. In the Haute-Loire some 40,000 women did lace-work. Forestry mobilised the peasants of the Alps and Vosges. Metal-working also held an important place in this economy. Knife-making employed around 15,000 people in the Thiers region of the Puy-de-Dôme. Locks were made in Picardy, clock manufacture was important in the Jura. The catalogue of jobs is hardly complete. It is likely that, around 1840, some 400,000 to 500,000 people in rural areas were engaged in work for urban merchants and entrepreneurs. In this same category can be placed less obvious forms of home-work such as the wetnurses of the Yonne and Nièvre, engaged in bringing up Parisian children. This assured a low but steady income. As with artisanal production, specialisation varied from time to time and from region to region. It was a changed pattern rather than an absolute decline which set in after about 1850.

Technical innovations prompted some industrialists to create new, more mechanised factories in rural areas. Such factories were able to recruit local manpower which retained its rural, agricultural roots. Such a workforce was both malleable and accustomed to low wages. Strikes by ribbon-makers in Saint-Etienne in 1834 and 1848 prompted the establishment of many factories in the surrounding countryside where factory workers remained essentially peasants. The forges at Savignac in the Périgord employed large numbers of sharecroppers and smallholders who retained their plots.[43] In the coal district of Brassac, on the borders of the Haute-Loire and Puy-de-Dôme, two-thirds of the miners owned land which they farmed on days off. At Carmaux, the workers did not hesitate to take time off from the mines when agricultural tasks were pressing, especially during harvest-time.

In some of the more isolated and mountainous districts, where the urban network was barely developed, such employment opportunities were few and far between. Here, an excess workforce had no option but to take to the roads and migrate. Seasonal and temporary migration were, of course, part of immemorial tradition, but rapid urban growth after 1840 quickened the rate of migration.[44] Agricultural migration, at least initially, remained more important.[45] In 1852, 880,000 people, that is, some 6 per cent of the active agricultural population engaged in such movement. Many shifted only within a limited geographic area and for a limited time: the grape-harvesters, for example, who, at a fixed date, descended from the uplands to the vineyards of the Beaujolais. At the end of the Second Empire, the department of Hérault alone attracted some 80,000 temporary vineyard workers. In the Beauce in 1852, 110,000 temporary workers from far afield were engaged in the harvest. Here, the onset of mechanisation was to greatly reduce their numbers. Other, more picturesque, regional specialisations disappeared in the course of time. The *piquers* of the Velay set off in groups with false certificates and wandered at will.

Normandy mole-catchers offered their services, as did the displayers of holy relics in Lorraine and the Bourgogne.[46] Other migrant artisans continued to ply their trade as in the eighteenth century. There were some half a million in the middle of the nineteenth century. Those specialisations linked to urban destinations tended to travel furthest. The stone masons of the Creuse – an estimated 40,000 out of a population of 220,000 in 1850 – profited from rising urban construction after 1840. By contrast, linen-workers suffered from industrial competition. The same was true of log-cutters, ousted by mechanical saws. These workers from the Corrèze were thus forced to turn to other forms of work, many becoming carriage-drivers in Paris. Most of these migrants remained essentially peasants whose prime objective was to return to their homes.

Whatever its particular form, pluriactivity was a permanent characteristic of the family farm in the nineteenth century. Patterns of work were organised within the family with a careful division of tasks between members. The father would engage as a worker or temporary migrant, at least until such time as his place could be taken by another family member. Such an organisation implied a considerable degree of cohesion in the management of the labour and revenue of the family. The primary aim of this multiple activity was to ensure a steady supply of cash into the family coffers, which would allow for some savings to be made with the ultimate aim of purchasing more land. Such activity, then, was essential to the survival of large families and gave that family economy considerable powers of resistance, a resistance often attributed, falsely, to the supposed autarky of the family. Such autarky, given the degree of outside activity a typical family was involved in, was little more than a myth.

Multiple activity meant as much to the towns as to the peasant families and the exchange of labour between town and country was always to the benefit of the former, for rural labour was both cheap and docile. Female salaries were especially low. When demand was high, the whole family might be involved in work at home. At times of economic difficulty, the industrialist would cut production by the simple expedient of restricting the supply of raw materials. The use of migrant labour was equally flexible. When the building industry in Paris struck a period of depression the migrant workers returned to their homes without threatening social peace in the city. Undoubtedly, such labour was hardly highly skilled and qualified. But, at a time when most industrial processes required simple repetition of tasks and when many of the simple tools and machinery were akin to those used in the countryside, this posed no problems. The peasant was far from being overwhelmed by the urban-industrial world of the nineteenth century. For the peasants who operated the forges of the Périgord, metal-working was neither disruptive nor alienating, for there was a kind of continuity between agriculture and the rest of the economy. The ease of adapting from one world to another, an ease greatly facilitated by pluriactivity, brought about the slow integration of the peasantry into the new economic climate. It also, undoubtedly, encouraged the process of migration.

Rural migration

The migration of country-dwellers to the towns was hardly a new phenomenon. In the eighteenth century, for example, some 70 per cent of Parisians had been born in the provinces. But migration greatly accelerated so that by the mid nineteenth century contemporaries began to express alarm at the depopulation of the countryside and the deleterious effects this might have on the nation. Some historians have thus spoken in terms of a 'rural exodus'.[47] Such a view seems unduly pessimistic. Between 1830 and 1850, 40,000 to 50,000 people were leaving the country regions each year. The crisis of 1846–51 does not seem to have accelerated this flow as has often been thought. Neither in the region of Apt nor the uplands of the Lyonnais did emigration increase markedly; undoubtedly the unfavourable economic climate dried up available jobs in the towns anyway. During the Second Empire the rate of migration did move upwards. From 1856, something of an upsurge occurred: between then and 1866 about 130,000 people a year migrated from country to town. But there was no sudden, massive exodus. As Henri Mendras has suggested, we would do better to speak of emigration rather than exodus.[48] The exaggerations of many local notables at the flow of people perhaps reflected less the pace of movement than the impact such departures were having on wage rates in the countryside.

Analysis of the geographical and social characteristics of population flows also suggests the lack of any massive structural changes. Those regions of emigration were the same ones that had contributed their people in the eighteenth century. The regions of departure were essentially on mountain fringes, especially the Massif Central, together with regions to the east of the Paris Basin, the *bocage* of Normandy and Maine, the valley of the Garonne, Lorraine and Alsace. They were precisely the regions where rural overpopulation was most acute. Only Brittany was an exception. Here it is probable that linguistic factors made the insertion of Breton migrants into urban life that much more difficult. Added to these long-distance patterns of migration were a series of migrations to second-rank towns. In the Lyonnais, a considerable flow of people moved from the mountain and plateau areas. The flow seemed to be downslope, but was geographically very restricted, and Lyon itself seems to have relied largely on migrants from a greater geographic distance.[49] Only a tiny proportion of migrants went overseas. Some Basques moved to the United States, whilst a number of inhabitants of the valley of Barcelonnette in the Alps chose Mexico. From 1840, there was also a small flow to Algeria. Such emigrants numbered around 20,000 people a year. But not all migrants were of rural origin and, in any case, their over-all numbers were tiny compared with the major population movements that occurred in other European countries.

Those who migrated were above all the young, especially young men, although a region such as the Lyonnais did send considerable numbers of young women to work as servants in Lyon itself.[50] Many migrants were unmarried. Research into the social origins of migrants is of funda-mental importance. In the Beauce, for example, it was above all the children of artisans and shopkeepers who left for the attractions of Paris; emigration was far from being the sole preserve of the farming popu-lation. Amongst the peasantry, it was those labourers without land who were the chief migrants, whilst those owning plots of land rarely left. Migration was predominantly the affair of individuals rather than families and the number of households in the Beauce did not diminish during the Second Empire. But the phenomenon is a complex one, with marked regional variations, which makes research into the seemingly obvious causes of migration very difficult.

Any attempt at classifying the reasons for the migration of the rural populace cannot be other than artificial because they were so complex and interlinked. Traditionally, so-called 'push' factors have emphasised the poverty of the rural environment as opposed to the 'pull' factors of the corresponding attractions of the urban environment.[51] Thus, rural overpopulation has often been put forward as a key factor in explaining both temporary migration and the rise in putting out industrial work. But why, then, were these two solutions not enough to stop permanent migration? Another factor often put forward is the pace of mechanis-ation, especially in the richer regions, which, it is argued, forced agricultural workers to migrate. Elsewhere, the development of pastoral farming with its reduced labour demands may have had similar effects. But the improvements in agricultural techniques were slow and there is evidence that in many areas agricultural workers were migrating despite plentiful offers of work at home.

Perhaps the answer is to be found in the attractiveness of urban wages. Thus an unskilled stone mason from the Creuse could earn twice as much in the towns as at home. Furthermore, a skilled mason, anxious to succeed, would be obliged to move permanently if he was to be able to bid for and undertake larger building projects. To what extent, further-more, was permanent migration simply the consequence of temporary migrants deciding to stay on? In France, one cannot argue that the indus-trial revolution served to attract crowds of peasants, chased from the land by the agricultural revolution. The temporal characteristics of industrialisation in France hardly fit in with such a picture. It has already been shown, in any case, that the so-called agricultural revolution was largely mythical in mid-century.

That there were limited movements of population from the country-side into the factories is evident in some regions, especially in textiles. One can also note the example of the Schneider factories at Creusot which attracted a predominantly peasant workforce. But the sheer number of migrants cannot be explained simply by a shift in the working population from the primary to the secondary sector. It would also seem that at least part of the workforce that serviced the new factories was already urban in character. Sociological explanations may also be of value, for urban centres exerted a pull which was not solely economic in nature. In the nineteenth century, the peasant did not see the town solely as a place where he could better his standard of living. For him, it was somewhere where he could escape the restraints and constrictions of family and village life. Such attitudes and perceptions of individuals were part and parcel of the migration process leading, ultimately to perma-nent migration. A whole nexus of feelings and beliefs – a balancing act between the security of the village and the dreams of the town – entered into the decision to move.

The consequences of rural emigration were still not widely felt prior to 1870. Naturally, the rural elite feared the increase in agricultural wages. Accustomed as they were to a docile and plentiful supply of labour, the diminution in this reservoir of cheap workers alarmed them. The com-plaints by large landowners were often accompanied by an urban paranoia about the 'barbarian forces camped at the gates of our towns'. But the real consequences of migration have to be studied in a longer-term context. The towns undoubtedly profited from migration, which provided an influx of youthful labour. The ways in which that migrant population integrated into urban life remain to be studied. In those regions which shed people, negative consequences were barely visible before 1860. Rural-population densities levelled off, relieving population pressure in some areas, but hardly creating swathes of empty territory. Migration did not, as yet, threaten the coherence of the peasantry: rather, in acting as a pressure valve to release excess people, it para-doxically permitted peasant society to flourish.

3. The nature of peasant life

The middle of the nineteenth century is often chosen as an appropriate moment to draw a composite picture of peasant life in France. Thanks to a steady increase in money, the standard of living was improving. The cultural opening out of the countryside helped to strengthen village life and institutions, maintaining its distinctive features and qualities. This impression of a mature, flourishing civilisation in the countryside is reinforced by abundant documentary evidence dealing with country life. Municipal enquiries, peasant memoirs, literary accounts all increased after 1870. But this growth in documentation carries with it its own problems. How are we to interpret those accounts of the 'good old days' which existed in minds alone? The huge diversity of the nation also militates against an overall picture. Each region, each district had its own way of life, often hidden behind local dialects and traditions. Such variety makes a composite picture difficult to draw. One can do little here, other than broadly sketch some of the main features.

The improvement of living conditions

Most of the descriptions of the countryside in the first half of the nineteenth century seem to tally on one feature: the extreme poverty and squalor of the population as a whole. Their landscapes seem exclusively peopled with miserable wretches in rags inhabiting equally miserable hovels which they share with their few animals. Such portrayals should be treated with some scepticism. In reality there were sharp differences beneath this apparent uniformity, which are readily gleaned from an examination of the material life of the peasantry at this period.

The domestic environment remains one of the slowest things to change in the rural world.[52] For the peasantry, fields rather than houses were what mattered, and it is this which explains the permanence of house styles over time, if not over space, given the great regional differences. The variety in peasant vernacular architecture was primarily a reflection of the locally available materials. At the start of the century, many houses were roofed with thatch, a material which was readily available and which provided good insulating shelter. But the risk of fire was ever-present with a chimney spark rapidly threatening a house and its neighbours. Municipal authorities, together with the insurance companies made strenuous efforts to reduce the use of thatch and, by 1856, it was used in only about 20 per cent of all houses, concentrated in a region from Brittany to Belgium, together with a few isolated mountain areas. Thatch was largely replaced by tiles, which became more widespread as their industrial production developed.

Despite a diversity of building materials, house forms fell into two, regionally differentiated types. The longhouse, in which both living quarters and working area were under the same roof, was the most widespread type in mid-century, especially in areas of polycultural farming. In the poorest regions (the Landes or Brittany, for example) people and animals cohabited. Elsewhere a partition separated the two, although the family continued to take advantage of the proximate warmth provided by its animals. In viticultural areas, the house was divided horizontally rather than vertically, with a storeroom forming the ground floor, over an underground wine-cellar. The living quarters were on the first floor with a grain-storage area above that. In the richest regions, the peasant house would comprise several buildings, forming a courtyard house where the working buildings were clearly separated from the living quarters. Depending on climatic conditions, the court-yard might be open or closed with a covered porch connecting the courtyard with the outside. This type of house, often a sign of increased affluence, became more widespread after 1850.

In most villages, even if one regional type of house dominated, there was a range of styles largely reflecting social differences. Thus at Saint-Germain-sur-l'Arbresle in the lower Beaujolais, those landowners who employed salaried workers built houses with several distinct buildings grouped around a courtyard, whilst more modest peasants had a simple longhouse with gallery, seen as the typical regional style.[53] As for bour-geois residences, these tended to be similar, regardless of region, with a residential rather than working function, with reception rooms and a pleasure garden, a sure sign of ease in regions where few could afford to leave land unproductive. In most senses then, house types were a good indicator of social status.

The internal character of houses further identified the social status of their occupants. Most houses had but a single living-room which was used for all purposes. Built against one wall, the fireplace served for both heat-ing and the preparation of meals. Close by, a chest would contain the cooking utensils. As required, it would also serve as a bench or footrest. A table, some benches and, except in the poorest house, a cupboard would, together with a bed, either separate or in a closed-off alcove, constitute the remainder of the furniture. Possession of several cupboards, a cabinet for crockery and a clock in its wooden case would indicate a well-off family. The peasant house could hardly be described as comfortable. The living-room was frequently dark, as light came mainly from the door and perhaps one window. The tax on windows and doors established under the Directory was not the sole cause for this.[54] The incorporation of several doors and windows in the course of build-ing a house was regarded as costly and unnecessary, creating currents of air which brought cold and discomfort. There was no running water in the house. This had to be brought from a well which, with luck, might be in front of the house, and deposited in the kitchen sink. In more nucleated villages, thanks to the initiative of the mayor or the squire, water fountains were installed in the centre of the village. But the drudgery of fetching water remained, hence economy in its use was essential.

Living conditions improved only slowly, primarily because notions of comfort and salubrity in housing were largely foreign to the peasant population at the end of the Second Empire. As far as improvements go, these were limited to cosmetic changes in the interiors of better-off houses near to towns, at least up to the 1860s. The opening out of the rural world, however, did slowly spread new, more comfortable living conditions from village to village. Thus, in the Paris region, petrol lamps slowly replaced the old candles and wooden faggots, particularly after the Exhibition of 1867. In the Massif Central and the Midi their triumph over the oil lamps common there was much slower. Furniture improved largely through inheritance or recycling to the better-off peasantry of the old bourgeois furniture of the eighteenth century which was no longer considered fashionable. Local cabinet-makers continued to use the old Louis XV styles with only minor adaptations through to the end of the nineteenth century.

Peasant diet did not change much between 1815 and 1870. Characterised, as always, by monotony and frugality, it reflected the constraints of a family farming system which had little recourse to the market.[55] Even if polycultural farming varied in character from region to region, diet appeared to show few changes from one place to the next. Except for part of the south-west where maize cake was eaten, bread was the basis of the diet. Around 700 grams to 1 kilogram was estimated as the average daily consumption in mid-century. In the poorer regions it was often made with crude, poorly sifted flours. White bread spread through the north and the central Paris Basin. Because its preparation was time-consuming and fuel was often short, bread was often prepared once a week or even monthly. In the Devoluy, one baking session a year had to suffice. The bread could be eaten hard because it was dipped, or cooked, in a soup usually made from vegetables, which was the basis of the peasant diet. Depending on the vagaries of place and season, the soup might be flavoured with pork fat or, in poorer areas, with onions alone. Use of the potato grew in the Auvergne, where it was cultivated widely as a field crop from the early nineteenth century. Cakes were made from its pulverised flesh. In the Pas-de-Calais, though, potatoes were regarded as a poor substitute for bread when the latter was in short supply. Meat was a rarity in everyday meals, despite the increase in pig farming. The same applied to those eggs, milk products and poultry which were sold at market to provide vital cash. For most peasant families, the Sunday chicken belonged to the realm of fairy-tales. The consumption of spirits was common in only a few regions. Overall, the diet was monotonous and the monotony was broken only on the occasional feast day. On such occasions the consumption of alcohol, of a variety of meats and other dishes, in short the heavy consumption of luxuries, served to reinforce the exceptional nature of such meals. Overall then, if there was no qualitative change in the diet, quantitative improvements were far from negligible.

In the realm of clothing, however, there were real changes between 1815 and 1870. At the start of the period, the family farm had to provide most of the raw material for clothes, such as flax, linen or wool according to region. The women of the household worked this, although often the weaving was left to specialists who would travel from household to household carrying out the work. Much of the clothing was crude, the peasant cloth, for example, was especially heavy and uncomfortable. Clothes then, for better or worse, were made at home. For children it was largely a matter of recycling old clothes.[56] Much of the clothing of the poorer peasantry came from charity, cast-offs from the local notables.

Under the Restoration the typical clothing for men included a short jacket, a large shirt, trousers and wooden clogs. Women wore a linen shift, a skirt, a blouse, an apron and a bonnet or traditional headdress. All the clothes were generally in poor condition. It was far from unusual to find children dressed in rags. Most clothes would be washed no more than two or three times a year, a tradition which at least ensured that they lasted a long time. Men possessed few clothes, but most families had an abundant supply of underclothes and household linen. In the Orthe region to the south of the Landes, marriage contracts drawn up at the start of the nineteenth century reveal impressive quantities of underclothes, sheets and handkerchiefs.[57] Such linen was an essential part of a young woman's bottom drawer and work on this would start not long after a girl took her first communion. The beauty of the embroidery was taken as a sign of the skills of the future wife. Such linen, transmitted from one generation to another, and an integral part of the marriage agreement was, paradoxically never actually used.

From 1830 onwards, change was perceptible, as industrial cottons and fabrics became more widespread. By 1850, they had conquered all areas, primarily because they were cheap, colourful and pleasant to wear, even if they provided little protection in a cold winter. They were bought in town along with sheets, which were now only rarely made at home. Henceforth, peasants were, for the first time, able to separate working clothes from holiday clothes. The former were always rustic and practical. During the Second Empire, the large blue blouse became the universal item of male clothing. Holiday clothes were more diverse.

Women's fashions increasingly followed those of the towns, adopting typically urban neckscarves and hats. The quality and quantity of embroidery and lace became a kind of social indicator in the village, especially in Brittany. Holiday clothes were greatly influenced, it seems, by urban fashions. As living conditions improved in the countryside, peasants were quick to adopt the prevailing urban fashions. But rarely did they follow subsequent fashion changes because clothes bought at the time of marriage were kept for the rest of their lives. Hence many of the descriptions of supposedly traditional 'folk' costumes worn by peasants at the end of the Second Empire were, in fact, descriptions of fossilised examples of urban fashions of the recent past.

By the end of the Second Empire, then, the living conditions of the peasantry had undoubtedly improved, although these improvements were neither geographically nor socially uniform. The underlying process would seem to have been one of a steady spread of urban values and mores into the country. But not everything was simply slavishly adopted and country-dwellers adopted and adapted at their will, both as regards material improvements and with regard to the organisation of community life.

The flowering of peasant sociability

Up until the end of the Second Empire, villages remained heavily populated, even in those areas that had experienced rural emigration. The dynamism of an essentially youthful population ensured the continued vitality of social relations. From the end of the eighteenth century, family and community ties held sway over rural society and manifestations of such solidarity were, if anything, further enforced by improved standards of living. Is there any evidence, then, of changes in these structures of social life?

Certainly the central force of family structures remained evident. In those regions where unequal inheritance was practised, the new Civil Code had little impact. Land remained at the heart of family relations, especially in regions south of the Loire. Family strategy remained to ensure the future of the farm, and marriages which threatened that future were largely forbidden. Under such conditions, then, the freedom of young people was restricted. If one took account of the restrictions of family and close relations and the need to avoid splitting the farm, the choice of a marriage partner would perhaps narrow down to just three or four people.[58] In such circumstances, recourse would often be made to marriage brokers able to find partners outside the traditional circles.

In Brittany, wandering tailors and dressmakers often fulfilled this role as they moved from farm to farm. But the lowering of the age of marriage and the increase in births outside marriage possibly points to the weakening of hitherto strong family controls.[59] Perhaps the strength of these controls has been exaggerated: in some societies (in the Vendée or around St-Jean-des-Monts, for example) young people were able to enjoy considerable sexual freedom before marriage. In the valleys of the Maurienne, young men and women mixed freely on Sunday evenings. At Tortefontaine in the Artois, among couples married between 1835 and 1848, some 40 per cent had a child before their ninth month of marriage.[60] Perhaps this toleration of freer sexual practices can be explained by local conditions. Thus, in the Maurienne communal lands covered some 90 per cent of the territory, putting most peasant families on an equal footing. What was more important than sexual freedom was the abandoning of a pregnant girl.

The structure of the family group was tied to economic functions. In the Stephanoise, most medium and large farms were run by extended families. Any farm above 5 hectares simply could not be managed by a single couple, and only small farmers could live in the setting of the nuclear family. In the Limousin, many sharecroppers had complex family structures, with several couples cooperating on the farm.[61] The peasant family was first and foremost a source of labour supply for the farm. If there were excessive numbers for a farm of a particular size, migration or celibacy were possible solutions. Undoubtedly, the demographic growth of the nineteenth century meant an increased recourse to such options. In the Hautes-Pyrénées, at Laborde, around one-fifth of the population was celibate. Economic transformations did provoke some changes. Thus, in the Beauce, economic modernisation seems to have reinforced the importance of the nuclear family. If the family farm was small, the work of the husband and wife would suffice and children would take jobs as *domestiques* on other farms. When they married, they would endeavour to lease some land and farm it themselves. By contrast, around Agen, it would appear that households became more complex in the second half of the century.[62]

The family remained the pivot on which agricultural work was organised. Age and sex largely determined the hierarchy of tasks and responsibilities. As population increase was primarily a consequence of a fall in the death rate, management of the farm remained for ever-longer periods in the hands of parents. In the Agen region, according to surveys in the second half of the century, it was only when they were aged between 68 and 70 that most men gave up the day-to-day management of the farm. More and more, the children of the family were obliged to spend much of their adult lives in positions of subservience. Younger sons in particular were condemned either to leave the farm or to accept a lowly position within the hierarchy for the rest of their lives. For the son who inherited the farm, the system of cohabitation severely restricted personal freedom. A cupboard containing linen and the conjugal bed were often the only personal space a young couple could lay claim to.[63] The basis of peasant life lay outside, in a pattern of work which tended to intensify for both the man and the woman. Each sex had its alloted place in the functional organisation of the farm. To the men fell the heavy tasks of preparing the land, while the women's domain was the courtyard, house and garden. But both would labour together at harvest-time or in the care of some of the animals. If men did the back-breaking work, women were never at peace.[64] Vibrant, but at the same time burdensome, the family contained and controlled each member, giving precious little scope for individualism.

The dynamism of village society remained, although, here and there, gradual changes were taking place. There was undoubtedly a weakening of the old economic bonds between members of the community, victim, it is clear, of the relentless rise of agrarian individualism. Thus communal institutions, such as the village cheese-factories of the Doubs, fell into decline.[65] Originally, these institutions served to pool the milk of small producers to manufacture 50-kilogram Gruyère cheeses which could be marketed outside the village. The development of a national market for cheese after 1840 prompted many large landowners to create and direct their own factories, thereby supplanting the role of the smaller village groups. In other areas, the Beauce, for example, systems of mutual aid between farmers quickly vanished.

At the same time, however, especially south of the Loire, social relations appeared to flourish in many festivals and manifestations, which seem to have been much more than the simple continuation of the social life of the ancien régime. Here, a decline in the traditional evening gatherings, or *veillées*, was accompanied by an increase in popular celebrations. The economic function of the evening gatherings had in any case declined as the putting-out system was eroded. As its economic function vanished, its festive aspect was reinforced, with dancing and card games at many gatherings. A sociability based on the separation of the sexes remained. Female gatherings usually had a strong utilitarian bias – occasions for women to carry out work tasks outside the home. The wash-house or river bank continued to be a favoured gossiping place. The so-called *couviges* of the Velay benefited from the increase in lace-work, with women gathering in summer on the village square to work at their lace and, in the process, attacking and defending reputations.[66]

Corresponding to such exclusively female gatherings were a range of male social activities which developed rapidly in the first half of the century. During the day the blacksmith's shop would be a gathering place for the old and idle – in some ways the counterpoint of the wash-house. Alongside these traditional meeting places other, less informal, gathering places developed after about 1840. The resurgence of old charitable and religious fraternities can be detected, such as the Normandy brotherhoods of charity or the Penitents of Provence, having as their aims the provision of free, and impressive, funerals for the dead of the village. In the Midi, the *chambrées* or *chambrettes* were an important social institution, where groups of men could meet for a glass of wine and to play cards or hold discussions.[67] There could be as many as three in villages in the Var with populations below 500. It was a form of social interaction which corresponded to the bourgeois circles of the town. Initially primarily for artisans, peasants joined in increased numbers after 1840. These *chambrées* served as centres for young, unmarried men who, in the years leading to 1848, often first experienced democratic ideas in such gatherings. But one should be cautious about imagining that the intense social life of the Midi existed in other regions of the country. In the Beauce, where there were none of these 'urbanised villages', but only small market towns or scattered hamlets, social inter-action remained severely limited.

It was the youth of the village who continued to be entrusted with celebrating communal festivals. The authorities did their best to limit the more exuberant of these activities. In the Midi, the carnivals and *charivaris* were regarded as veritable schools for inculcating popular subordination. They declined after 1840 and municipalities took the opportunity of encouraging more sedate forms of celebration, particu-larly village fêtes which would encourage trade. The general improve-ment in living standards ensured their success and their vitality rested to some extent on the popular religious revival of the Restoration years. The festival and religious ceremony went together, much as the revival of faith fed on the multiplication of ever-more spectacular public manifestations.

Religious festivals developed primarily from a combination of the efforts of the clergy to win over the rural population and peasants' insecurities and worries, which inclined them towards the super-natural.[68] At the start of the Restoration, the clergy tolerated the devel-opment of popular religious fervour, of a kind which placed much emphasis on healing saints and the cult of sacred shrines. The clergy allowed such cults to flourish in the hope of harnessing the upsurge of religious feeling to its own ends. The village community was deeply involved in this popular religious fervour and the support of the church for such cults seemed self-evident.

A new wave of recruitment to the priesthood around 1825–30 led many priests, often themselves of peasant or artisan stock, to play a more active role in channelling popular religious fervour in the direction they desired. Some sought to 're-christianise' the countryside by building. Many churches were restored or rebuilt. Countless *calvaires* – some 2,500, for example, in the diocese of Arras alone – were erected. They were often constructed during the celebration of solemn missions, whose aim was to direct the religious practices of the villagers along more orthodox paths. Among the enemies to be fought figured the 'superstitious', the old semi-religious cults which many priests now refused to sanction by their presence. Dancing was controlled or forbidden, leading to battles during festivals between the clergy and the parishioners. In the diocese of Arras, nuns created associations, such as the Children of Mary, whose young female members would forswear the pleasures of dancing and participation in 'profane' festivals. To replace the gaps in the calendar, the church organised pilgrimages and uniquely religious festivals. Their development and triumph mirrors nicely the expansion of the railway network. The proclamation of the Immaculate Conception in 1854, the apparitions of La Salette, Lourdes and Pontmain, helped to inculcate the cult of the virgin Mary and became occasions for huge gatherings. The priest of Ars, poor and of peasant origin, attracted huge crowds to his village in the Dombes between 1818 and 1859, although he never left the village himself during his lifetime.

The cultural opening up of the countryside

Between 1815 and 1870, the cultural influence of the towns steadily infiltrated the countryside, with the spread of urban values and cultural models being helped by the steady improvement in means of communication. As the power of these influences made themselves felt, so previously diverse rural cultures and civilisations became ever more uniform.

At the start of the nineteenth century, the influence of the towns was relatively slight. Undoubtedly the physical difficulties of communication explained much. Visiting a town more than a day's journey away on foot was outside the experience of many peasants. Go further than 30 or 40 kilometres and linguistic barriers alone could prove insurmountable. Language was a fundamental barrier, for over perhaps half of the country French was poorly understood. What Maurice Agulhon called the 'arrival of communications' in the countryside was achieved primarily when the improvement of the road network allowed more widespread travel by the peasantry. These improvements took place between about 1840 and 1870, depending on the region. In Provence, then, families bought a mule, an excellent all-purpose animal able both to pull a plough and, when necessary, a cart for the occasional journey into town. In other regions, horses filled this role. Transport improvements also helped the development of postal services and, under the July Monarchy, rural post offices multiplied. But the carrying of letters, paid for by the recipients, remained, at 12 *sous*, an expensive service. The introduction of a 4 *sous* stamp, paid by the sender, was an important innovation in 1848–9, adopted from the English model. Henceforth, the volume of mail increased markedly. From two letters per year per person in 1830, the average reached nine in 1869.[69] The developing importance of letters helped the peasantry to become aware of the benefits of education. Having to ask for help in reading or replying to a letter served to increase the humiliation felt by many at their poor level of instruction.

Greater ease of movement then, increased the contact between the countryside and the rest of the nation. Certain social groups filled a kind of mediating role between the peasant world and the towns. Thus, migrants played a key role, particularly as their numbers increased after 1840. Some artisans, the Breton mobile tailors, for example, played a similar role, acting as agents spreading political ideas among their clientele. The number of fairs increased, serving to encourage more frequent visits to the towns by men, whilst more local markets played a similar role for women. Such occasions encouraged greater commercialisation of the countryside – selling farm produce, buying urban merchandise – and, at the same time, increased contact with the French language.

The question of the extent of the use of dialects in the nineteenth century is a teasing one.[70] It would seem well nigh impossible, given the statistical lacunae, to draw a complete picture of the linguistic situation in France at this time. In 1794, the Abbé Grégoire had solemnly declared to the Convention that three-quarters of the French populace understood at least some French. A government survey carried out by the Minister of Public Instruction in 1863 revealed that in 22 per cent of all communes French was not the language in everyday use. At the same date, the number of pupils aged between seven and thirteen who were unable to speak any French stood at only 11 per cent. This seems to point to the success of the education policy, although Eugen Weber has argued that the figures may well underestimate the real total, especially for areas south of the Loire. The extent to which the various sources contradict one another shows the difficulties faced by those charged with collecting the relevant data.

How then are we to judge the real extent of French-speaking? Into which category should those who understood French but could not, or did not wish to, speak it be placed? What of those groups on the boundary between the *langue d'oc* and *langue d'oil* who spoke a language close to, but not identical with, French? The evolution of linguistic ability was both slow and episodic with important contrasts between different social groups, and, most especially, different generations. As a gross approximation, one can perhaps argue that in mid-century French was a foreign language to about one-half of the population. Patois remained the everyday language of thought and communication: however, it should be noted that only a small minority – perhaps 10 per cent, perhaps 20 per cent – neither ever used, nor understood the national language. The statement can perhaps be phrased differently. Under the Second Empire many peasants understood at least a modicum of French, even if it was not their natural first language. They were essentially bilingual. From 1860 onwards, only the older generation remained completely non-French-speaking.

The arguments about why French progressed steadily, too, are controversial. For Maurice Agulhon, French conquered much of the Midi well before the advent of national schooling.[71] In the traditional Noël, the angel spoke in French, the shepherd replied in Provençal. The conquest was largely spontaneous. The peasantry, far from being proud of its language, quickly realised that French was more useful for dealings with the administration and the towns, and from the Revolution onwards, was quick to adopt it. Patois was regarded as parochial and outmoded. Thus, from the moment that the cultural and geographic horizons of the peasantry began to open up, the advantages of French became evident. Migrants were especially active in propagating French-speaking. Thus French-speaking masons in the Creuse pushed the linguistic boundary between *langue d'oc* and *langue d'oil* from its position north of the department at the start of the nineteenth century, to the southern limits of the department some forty years later. Those who wished to improve their social position had to adopt French, all the more so as many dialects had neither formal structure nor grammar. It was only later, in 1854, that a group of poets and linguists founded the *Félibrige* to try to save the language and literature of Provence. For the peasantry, such literary language was both remote and incomprehensible.

By 1870, then, a common language existed for most rural-dwellers. This did not however, mean that regional languages vanished. Those regions with the greatest linguistic differences from French were especially resistant. One thinks, for example, of Flemish in the north and of Lorraine and Alsace. In Brittany, nevertheless, French penetrated along the lines of the railway and through the hinterlands of the major ports and came to be the language used for technical terms. Patois remained the language of everyday life, although it increasingly lost its place as the first language of younger people. In so many regions, the linguistic gap was increasingly to become a generation gap.

The triumph of French was inextricably linked to the greater penetration of writing skills into the countryside. This was a fundamental change, anticipated by the rapid spread of cheap, popular pictures from the July Monarchy onwards. The presses at Epinal produced millions of prints on such themes as Napoleon and the miraculous saints. They were bought avidly and displayed in places of honour in the house.[72] Travelling salesmen also offered almanacs, which were hugely popular. More than a simple calendar, these offered information, recipes, cures on a whole range of subjects from gardening to popular medicine. They were treated with respect and reverence, especially by those who were unable to read. Together with pamphlets and prayer books they were part of many households at the end of the Second Empire. Frequently read aloud in groups, they indicate how oral communication served to develop the written word, especially at a time when education was far from fully developed.

In 1815, the degree of instruction in the countryside showed dramatic regional variations.[73] North and north-eastern France had relatively high rates of literacy in contrast to other regions, especially a triangle of regions from Brittany to the Landes and the Massif Central, where rates were very low. The line linking Saint-Malo and Geneva often serves to distinguish these two zones. Even within regions with low rates of literacy, there were major contrasts between villages. Thus, in the Bourgogne, a contrast can be drawn between village societies with high levels of instruction and those, generally in the isolated *bocage*, where rates were low. François Furet and Jacques Ozouf have argued that the highest literacy rates were in the more advanced open-field areas of France: 'The ability to read and write was above all a product of the market economy which relied upon written communication'.[74] The more backward zones caught up slowly after 1820, primarily through the efforts of the clergy. In playing this role, the church saw a means of intellectual and social control which could help it put down ever-deeper roots in the countryside. But the quality of education was frequently poor with, in many classes, little beyond the rote learning of the catechism. It was also patchy. In 1832, 27 per cent of communes still had no school.

The crucial step came with the Guizot legislation of 1833 which required communes to create a primary school for local boys. In 1863, there were only 818 communes without such a school. From the Second Empire onwards, almost all peasant families at least had the opportunity to send their children to school. In 1872, 21.5 per cent of conscripts were unable to read. At the same date, 23 per cent of bridegrooms and 35 per cent of brides were unable to sign their names on the marriage register. The previously significant regional gaps, had been largely closed by then, particularly to the east of a line linking Dijon and Bayonne. Only a zone from Brittany to the Morvan remained behind. One cannot, however, evaluate instruction solely on a quantitative level, for qualitative factors were important. Thus, school attendance was often very poor at the busy spring and autumn periods, and female school attendance also remained low. Progress, however, whilst incomplete, was nevertheless significant. But, for poorer families who could not perceive the value of education, school continued to be regarded as an interference and an inconvenience. It seemed, furthermore, to have little to offer in terms of improving agricultural practices and methods. However, demand for schooling did develop, especially amongst the non-farming rural population and the better-off peasantry.

The shift, then, from an essentially oral, collective culture to one based on the written word and the individual was slow, but, ultimately, decisive. It was an 'interminable rending apart'.[75]

4. Peasants and politics

Up until 1848, the peasantry remained largely marginal to the national political debate of the times. With the institution of universal male suffrage in that year, it became the majority of the electorate. Even so, the right to vote did not mean that the peasantry henceforth participated actively in political life – the peasantry remained politically passive.

The monarchy: 1815–1848

During the Restoration, peasants played no part in the electoral process. In order to vote at legislative elections, a minimum tax charge of 300 francs had to be paid as a qualification. Not surprisingly, such a high figure was paid only by the large landowners. In total, there were fewer than 100,000 electors in this period. The peasantry was distanced from political life for, even at local level, positions such as municipal or district councillors were nominated by the administration and not subject to election.

The 1830 revolution brought with it a slight easing of the position and a somewhat more open system of voting was instituted. The tax minimum was lowered from 300 francs to 200 francs, increasing the number of voters to 200,000. This shift at least allowed a number of large farmers onto the lists, but the peasantry was hardly affected by the move. The legislation of 24 March 1831, however, instituted elected municipal councillors. Those tax-payers in the top 10 per cent to 14 per cent of their commune (the figures varied depending on commune size) were placed

on the voting lists. The mayor and his assistants continued to be nominated by the prefect from the body of elected councillors. In some areas
– the thinly populated communes of the Var, for example, the lower
ranks of the peasantry found themselves with the right to vote.[76] From
this date, about one million electors were able to vote. In most regions,
however, the move hardly stirred the political apathy of the country
areas, which remained largely under the heel of the local elite, who
continued to act as the representatives of authority.

During the Restoration, the functions of the mayor remained
modest.[77] In any case, his continued office was subject to the will of the
prefect. In country areas his role was both difficult and sometimes
unclear and the powerful elite preferred, in any case, a direct approach
which ignored the local mayor. Contrary to popular belief, few aristocrats
and squires were attracted by the post: 11 per cent of mayors were aristocrats in 1824; the figure fell to only 4 per cent after the revolution of
1830, which, in this respect at least, was an important event. In the conservative parts of France – the west, Velay, the south of the Morvan, such
aristocratic mayors were common. But many preferred posts in the small
or medium-sized towns close to their country estates where their role was
often purely nominal, leaving the running of affairs to assistants of more
modest origin. The post of mayor was most frequently filled by more
modest *notables*, chosen from amongst that small group of individuals
with sufficient education to deal with official business. In 1824, 73 per
cent of them had a direct link with the land – hardly a surprising statistic,
given that land remained the key to social standing and prestige in the
countryside. But only 31 per cent were landlords, as opposed to the
41 per cent who farmed their land. Such statistics contradict the tradition
popularised by Balzac that the large landowner had, necessarily, to be the
local mayor.[78]

The monarchy had in the clergy another efficient system of inculcating loyalty in the countryside, relying on priests and curates to maintain
its power there. For its part, the church looked on the Restoration as a
means of restoring itself to the power and influence it had exercised
under the ancien régime. Undoubtedly, in some cases the church went
too far, as in the Pas-de-Calais, after 1815.[79] There, over-zealous church
officials breathed fire and damnation on those who had bought ecclesiastical property and refused to restore it to the church. Under pressure
from the bishop, the worst excesses of this trend were curbed but, even
under the Second Empire, some confessants were only able to obtain for-
giveness if they also restored church property. But the reconquering
efforts of the church were undoubtedly spiritual as well as material, leading, as we have noted, to an often excessive interference in traditional

village festivities by the more intransigent clerics. On such occasions, conflicts would often ensue with the mayor, even where both individuals shared similar ideological standpoints. The civil power of the mayor, in any case, was often perceived as in direct competition to the ecclesiastical power of the incumbent priest. Another frequent source of conflict was money, and more than one mayor clashed with the local priest over the financing of church restoration. The efforts made by the clergy to literally rebuild the faith were, in any case, often resented by the peasantry as a return to a past that it had long left behind.

There was a marked decline in religious observance from 1840 in a number of areas – the centre-west, the south-east, part of the Paris Basin. In some regions, a kind of apathy prevailed, especially amongst the men. The quality of priests was sometimes advanced as a reason for this indifference. In the Var, at the beginning of the Restoration, recourse was made to migrant Italian priests who treated a spell in France as a means not of saving souls but of saving money. Such temporary incumbents were regarded as unsatisfactory, if for no other reason than that, since the signing of the Concordat, their salary was paid by the state. The old arguments about working on Sundays quickly resurfaced, especially amongst those small peasants who worked as paid labourers in the week and cultivated their fields on a Sunday. Prohibitions on dancing were also much resented and the accumulation of such bones of contention was one reason why, to the horror of the authorities, some villages in the Limousin and Périgord demanded that protestant churches be set up. To many, protestantism appeared an essentially laicised religion, cheap, easy to live with and preferable to a catholicism which seemed to represent a return to the days of the ancien régime.[80] The old conflicts born of the Revolution were far from being worked out.

A further glimpse at how such conflicts reappeared can be gained from some of the sporadic disputes which sprang up in the countryside. One finds the tell-tale signs of an essentially loyal, yet resentful countryside: traditional *charivaris* turning unpleasant, defence of traditional rights, protests against the taxing of drinks and so forth. Their development depended on local circumstances but some, undoubtedly, were linked to political events, as in the uprisings which broke out in 1817 in some regions. In the market-places, the populace demanded that the price of bread be fixed officially and also tried to prevent the departure of grain convoys. Alarm was all the more serious for the monarchy because of the widespread rumour that Napoleon was on the point of returning. In the Lyonnais, repression was brutal, with guillotines installed in several villages and around thirty villagers executed as an example to the rest.[81]

Equally serious were the reactions to the Forest Code introduced in 1827. Designed to protect forest land from unplanned destruction and logging, it gave extensive power to the forest guards who represented the authorities. Numerous woods, previously open to communal use, were closed off by the legislation and the new code was neither understood nor accepted by many peasants. In the Gers, an angry peasantry destroyed thousands of trees. In the Ariège there were very serious troubles between 1829 and 1832. This was the so-called *guerre des Demoiselles*, instigated by peasants dressed as women to disguise their identity. They circulated in bands of twenty or thirty or, on one occasion, as many as eight hundred. Their targets were the forest guards and forge masters who bought wood from the administration. The revolt, suppressed with difficulty in 1832, continued to simmer through to 1872.

Such reactions were essentially those of an ill-educated peasantry for whom violence was the sole means of expression. Clearly, then, to properly understand such events, we need to undertake a study of popular mentalities rather than popular political opinion for, at this time, the politicisation of the countryside had barely begun. Maurice Agulhon has shown how, in the Var from 1830 on, political ideas 'descended' towards the peasantry from the petty bourgeoisie who animated the *chambrées* of the region.[82] The press also played a part in regions of relatively high literacy. This steady awakening of political opinion has also been underlined in Phillipe Vigier's study of the Alps. It had not yet occurred throughout the country, it is true, but it laid the foundations for what was to come.

Entry into political life: 1848–1851

The 1848 revolution was of fundamental importance to the peasantry. With the introduction of universal suffrage for all men aged over twenty-one, the peasantry found itself the arbiter of the nation's political life. But the possibility of the vote did not necessarily mean that there was more active involvement in political life and in great national debates.

The news of the February days and the proclamation of the republic were initially regarded with surprise and, rather later, by an almost unanimous rallying to the republic. With varying alacrity from one commune to the next, trees of liberty were planted or, perhaps, a celebratory bonfire lit. Undoubtedly, the change of regime excited new hopes. The dawn of the republic was seen by some as a return to the ideals of the original Revolution and held the hope that the conflicts between the peasant community and large landowners and the administration over communal lands or forests would be decided in favour of the community. The power vacuum that resulted at departmental level led to an upsurge of peasant unrest, long simmering in places since the onset of economic crisis. In Alsace, the Pyrénées and the southern Alps, bands of peasants invaded forested areas. More rarely, some directed their attack at representatives of the old order. Some châteaux were ransacked and more hard-line clerics roughly treated in the south-east. The new republican commissioners, however, acted speedily to restore order in most departments. Set the task of rallying the peasantry to the new republic, many made promises which could not be kept.[83] By the beginning of March peace had largely been restored.

In the meantime, attention was focused on a series of elections to the new government. On 23 April, a new National Assembly was elected. The election campaign, a very short one, was chaotic. Numerous candidates, often with confused and confusing electoral programmes, sought the support of the somewhat naive peasantry. Overall, some 8 million people were eligible to vote for the first time. The influence of the rural elite was assured, in part because the method of voting was open to influence. The fact that voting fell on Easter Sunday further meant that there were large crowds in church where the peasants could be persuaded of the right vote to cast. The vote took place in the main district towns and villagers travelled in groups to the urns, often with the local squire and priest at their head. Alexis de Tocqueville in Normandy thus led 'his peasants' two by two and in alphabetical order to the town of Saint-Pierre where they obligingly elected him to office. Almost everywhere, turnout was high – 84 per cent nationally, though it was as high as 90 per cent in some rural communes.

In most of the country, support went to moderate republicans – lawyers and solicitors, doctors, the local squire, the rural bourgeoisie. Republican undoubtedly, but also resolutely anti-socialist. Elections to municipal bodies and to cantonal offices in July and August produced more conservative bodies, probably because electors chose those locals they knew. Many of the elite who were in place during the July Monarchy kept their posts in the elections: more than half of those mayors appointed before 1848 remained after the elections. Only in a few rural cantons of the Midi and central France were more radical republicans elected.

The importance of the electoral influence of the peasantry was confirmed most strikingly with the election for the post of president on 10 December 1848. Louis-Napoleon-Bonaparte, despite having no clear programme, won an overwhelming victory in most rural areas. In the Limousin, for example, he took over 85 per cent of the rural vote.[84] Undoubtedly, the name itself carried an aura of the past glories of the

Napoleonic era. But the size of his victory attested above all to the errors of his rivals. Cavaignac, for example, was tainted by the rather maladroit administration which in the spring had ordered a 45 per cent increase in direct (primarily property) taxation. This move alone alienated many owner-occupiers and gave powerful ammunition to his opponents. Can one argue then, that the vote was primarily a protest vote against the fiscal policy of the government? Or did it rather represent the expression of an essentially conservative peasantry for the candidate – Louis-Napoleon-Bonaparte – of the rural elite? Perhaps in voting as it did, the peasantry was indicating its opposition to a republic which it perceived as emanating from the towns.

Whatever the reasons for the triumph, most politicians were stunned by Napoleon's success. It was clear to many that the peasant vote had to be won. Whilst conservatives believed that the countryside was firmly committed to order and stability, their opponents sought to seduce the peasant electorate. The Constituent Assembly, moderately republican in tone, learnt the fiscal lessons of its predecessor and voted for a substantial reduction in indirect taxation. The democratic-socialists, who called themselves the Montagnards were especially active under Ledru-Rollin. In their campaigns, they laid great stress on spoken propaganda, marching from village to village and spreading the word at fairs and markets. Free pamphlets were distributed in even the most isolated hamlets. They sought to focus on themes relevant to the small peasantry: the excessive weight of indirect taxation, the need to defend communal lands and traditions, the necessity for loans at low rates of interest. These efforts paid off, for, on 13 May 1848, the 'party of order' gained only 53 per cent of the vote with 35 per cent going to the democratic-socialists. In sixteen departments they enjoyed an absolute majority. Three regions voted massively for them: the centre-east from Cher to the Jura, the valleys of the Saône and Rhône and a part of the Alps.[85]

This clear indication of a supposedly 'red peasantry' which could be persuaded to vote with the popular masses in the towns, had a major influence on the attitudes and behaviour of conservative parties in subsequent years. Henceforth, the countryside was the stage for an intensive ideological campaign against the so-called *partageurs* who, it was said, would not hesitate to abolish private property if they ever took power. It is also important not to underestimate the popularity of the president-prince who was perceived as someone who would protect the poor and the country-dweller. This provincial bonapartism perhaps explains why those areas which resisted the December 1851 *coup d'état* were not necessarily the same as those that voted for democratic-socialist candidates in 1849. In most regions, the peasantry was indifferent to the news coming from Paris. Zones of insurrection were isolated, revolt was episodic. Only in parts of the Var, Basses-Alpes, Drôme, Gers and Lot-et-Garonne was real resistance evident. In the Allier and Nièvre, discontent was slight. Within a week, and after some energetic army intervention, calm returned to the countryside.

The peasantry, bulwark of the Empire: 1852–1870

Up to the beginning of the Second Empire, literary and artistic portrayals of the peasantry tended to be hesitant and uncertain.[86] The peasant was, above all, a figure of suspicion and fear. Balzac, for example, described peasants variously as brutal beings, cunning, greedy, and obsessed with a lust for property which drove them to the worst excesses. This pessimistic and brutal portrayal can perhaps be explained by the fear people felt for such a miserably poor section of society, but also by the inability of urbanites to penetrate the closed shutters of the peasant world that could only be glimpsed from outside. Alongside this brute realism was the pastoral vision of peasant society as developed by George Sand in, for example, *La Mare au Diable* (1846). Her fictional peasant world was one of simple, honest sentiment, cheerful goodwill and a world distant from the corrupting influence of the towns. Her descriptions were drawn from imagination rather than the somewhat harsher reality. This same uncertainty about the peasant – a beast to be feared or a noble being worthy of emulation pervaded painting circles, too, at this time.[87] Millet's *Le Semeur* (1850) and *Les Glaneuses* (1857) show peasants at their labours. Their struggles, the harshness of their features, are translated through a kind of exaggerated primitivism of form and colour. But such a vision of the peasant world was not accepted. It was strongly criticised and rejected. Jules Breton's *Les Glaneuses* (1855), with its poetic and noble vision of the peasantry, was a much more popular picture with contemporaries. In his representations, peasants are young and vigorous individuals, happy in their work, at one with their world. Millet himself bowed to such artistic fashions in his *Angélus* (1859) which was an extraordinary success with contemporaries. This painting became, henceforth, the symbol of patient resignation and the courage of hard work. The peasant as symbol of order and harmony was born.

The countryside was firmly controlled by an administration which carefully nurtured the rural vote. A widely recognised system of clientilism and official candidates was the favoured means. Prefects used both methods to orient the results of their departments in the desired direction. Official support for a candidate was openly admitted. This was said to be used to 'help' novice voters who could not be expected to know how to cast their votes without guidance. Those in power were allowed to use white posters (the colour of official government announcements) for electoral purposes. The posters were pasted on official boards free of charge. Other candidates had to provide their own coloured posters and distribute them at their own expense. The official candidate benefited from the support of all government agents, large and small. Gendarmes, rural constables, teachers and other officials were mobilised. The support of postal workers should also not be underestimated. To ensure electors made no mistakes, voting cards were delivered together with the electoral literature of the favoured candidate. The nominated mayor would be charged with ensuring the rural vote came in. Gerrymandering was widespread to ensure that 'loyal' rural cantons would counter-balance urban areas judged hostile to the official candidate. Such practices led many opposition candidates to despair of ever being able to gain the peasant vote.

Was the peasantry, then, simply manipulated for political ends? Probably not, for there were solid enough reasons why it supported the Empire. A favourable economic climate had led to a rise in both agricultural prices and salaries. A lessening of demographic pressure in the countryside, which reduced social and economic conflict, also indirectly benefited the regime. Infrastructural changes set in train in these years brought some further tangible benefits. The opening of a new railway line figures prominently in many an election promise. Even international commercial treaties were regarded with favour by many peasants and few negative effects were felt until after 1870. The attention that the state devoted to farming matters was a key plank in the arguments of many prefects: Napoleon III: the Peasants' Emperor!

Undoubtedly, then, bonapartism was a powerful force in the country-side. Was it simply the expression of rural conservatism? It is difficult to reply one way or another, for the regime itself consciously sought to be neither 'white' nor 'red'. A vote for an official candidate might be a vote against a traditional *notable*, as much as an expression of submission to authority. Perhaps it is in this sense that the Empire marked the start of the '*fin des notables*'.[88] Certainly this was the case in the Limousin where the electorate, freed from the clutches of both the rural landowning elite and the towns, rallied temporarily to a government which brought clear economic benefits. The Empire also allowed the thorough establishment of the principle of universal male suffrage. The rural populace became much more familiar with voting procedures, which now took place at communal level. The game of politics was not completely smothered, even if the dice were partly loaded in favour of the establishment party. Opposition parties thus managed to survive, if not always prosper, throughout this period.

The monarchist opposition was the first to regroup. Its resurgence was due primarily to the conflict between government and the catholic church. Certain bishops sought to encourage voting for opposition candidates following French intervention in Italian affairs. In regions won over to anti-clericalism, the voice of the church carried little weight. There, republican parties prospered, particularly when the weight of administrative control diminished with the later, liberal Empire. In 1869, in the Morvan, the republicans, led by a former dismissed teacher who spoke the local patois, spent huge sums on a massive campaign. They increased the distribution of newspapers, created local support committees in many villages and found a ready audience in the many drinking-clubs in the countryside.[89] They consciously sought to exploit the old hatred of the countryside for governments which pandered to urban interests, ignored the rural electorate and imposed crushing taxes in order to wage foreign wars. These republicans made some impression on the elections of 1869, even if official candidates were in the majority. Although few of the candidates were elected, their votes at least indicated a renaissance of rural, democratic sentiments in the Midi, the centre, Charente-Inférieure and Côtes-du-Nord. The republicans did not recover all their old strongholds of 1849, but they at least had a wide spread of votes. However, they were far from gaining the support of the mass of the peasantry. Politically, the years of the Empire cannot be regarded as a kind of apolitical interlude. They were years which marked the beginnings of change which was to prepare the peasantry for a more active part in national political life.

Within the space of half a century, then, the peasantry had made tangible, if slow, gains. Increased agricultural prices and incomes had been accompanied by an increased external influence on the material fabric and way of life of the peasantry. The spectre of famine was gone; that was an achievement not to be underestimated. But the fear of shortages and hardship was not wholly banished from the collective consciousness. The majority of families had merely progressed from misery to mediocrity in their daily lives. The economic horizons and technical skill of the great majority of farmers remained very limited. Progress, considerable though it was in relation to the recent past, remained fragile because it continued to be linked not to the implantation of new economic structures in the countryside, but to an ever-fluctuating economic climate. This link was to be clearly exposed in the economic crises after 1870.

3

The difficult years: 1870–1914

With the close of the Second Empire, problems began to develop in the agricultural sector although, at the time, they appeared to be isolated events. Ultimately, they conjoined to create a serious and lasting crisis, one which was both earlier and more severe than that which was to affect industry. For at least a quarter of a century, farm incomes either stagnated or fell. The crisis was particularly hard felt, coming as it did at the end of a long period of rising prices which had contributed to a kind of euphoria in farming circles. These price rises, as we have seen, had served, not as a stimulus to modernise farms, but rather to multiply the number of farm units. The end of this favourable economic climate was to force farmers to adapt to new conditions. Their reactions, it is clear, differed depending on farming systems and farm sizes, and hence changes varied regionally. The state, under pressure from an increasingly vociferous and organised peasantry, was forced to intervene by adopting a range of protectionist measures. Whilst these may have stabilised prices, they did not bring back the relative ease of earlier decades. The long depression also brought in its train a number of social and political changes, the seeds of which had been present before. For Eugen Weber, these years marked a crucial turning-point in the history of the French peasantry.

1. A complex crisis

What contemporaries termed simply the 'agricultural crisis' was in fact a complex phenomenon. Its initial character was a series of problems affecting specific agricultural products which were aggravated towards the end of the 1870s by a more general fall in prices and the collapse of many viticultural economies.

The fall of prices and incomes

The departments of the Midi were the first to be affected by the disappearance of traditional employment opportunities essential for the survival of populous areas. Thus in the Gard, Drôme, Ardèche and

Vaucluse, the raising of silkworms had long provided an important additional revenue, especially as the work could be done by women, children and the elderly during otherwise slack periods of the year. From mid-century, a series of mysterious diseases struck for which, despite the efforts of Pasteur, no cure could be found.[1] The only solution, a much more rigorous selection of silkworm eggs, increased costs for what was anyway, only a barely profitable pursuit. From 1875, the arrival of cheap silks from the Far East depressed prices for the raw material, and production had collapsed in most villages by 1914. In the lowland areas of the same departments, madder, a bright red vegetable dye was an easy and profitable crop for many farmers.[2] But, in 1868, the chemical industry developed a much cheaper dye, glizarine, produced from petrol. Prices fell rapidly from 1871 and by 1876 the cultivation of madder was little more than a memory. Another serious crisis was that in oilseed crops. Competition from other parts of the Mediterranean and, later, the African colonies, affected the production of rapeseed oil, poppyseed oil and, above all, olive oil from the end of the Second Empire.

These price falls, at first limited to a few products, were extended to most agricultural products after 1875.[3] Medium-term falls were spectacular. Thus, wheat prices fell by 34 per cent between 1875 and 1896, after which the crisis eased. Potato prices, too, experienced similar falls. Animal products were less affected but still fell by around 20 per cent. Only sugar beet was excepted, helped by a rise in demand. Overall, the wholesale price of foodstuffs fell by about 39 per cent. The size and duration of these falls, spread as they were over a quarter of a century, is nonetheless striking.

It was not until the start of the 1880s that contemporaries first became conscious of the gravity of the crisis.[4] The fall in wheat prices was regarded as especially symbolic and was greatly resented. The blame for the crisis was laid largely at the door of forces outside France, and imports, favoured by a range of commercial treaties, were the main target of attack. But internal factors were also blamed. The railway companies, whose tariffs were regarded as too high, or the fiscal policy of the state, were popular targets. Contemporary economists preferred to explain the durability of the crisis in terms of money supply. It coincided, they argued, with a slowing down in the global production of gold and the demonetarisation of the currency in many countries. No relief could come, they argued, until the supply of money increased once more.

In this deflationary context, demand fell. But the crisis can also be explained more simply by pointing to excess supplies, both in France and on the world market. Since mid-century, the new territories of the

United States, Argentina, Australia and Canada had developed their productive capacity in agriculture. The development of cheap and efficient maritime transport meant that the European markets were open to them. The poorly protected French market was an obvious target. Net imports of wheat in France, which stood at 0.3 per cent of total production in 1851–60, rose to 10 per cent in 1871–80 and to as much as 19 per cent in 1888–92. At the same time, demand was stagnant because population growth had slowed. Above all, dietary habits had changed and, as pastoral products became more widely available, consumption of cereals fell. From the crisis of shortage, which had previously marked the agricultural sector, a lasting crisis of oversupply soon developed.

It is hardly surprising that such circumstances led to a reduction in peasant incomes. It is difficult to be precise about the extent of the fall. Those farms that sold little of their produce were only marginally affected but, since mid-century, ever-fewer farms fell into this category. To a greater or lesser extent then, almost all farms were affected, particularly since the option of compensating for low prices by selling more was not open to most. Neither the farmed area nor the amount of produce sold increased in this period. Jean-Claude Toutain has estimated that total agricultural production in fact fell by some 10 per cent between 1865–74 and 1895–1904.[5] To ascertain the effect on net revenues some estimate of production costs is required. This is no easy task for these undoubtedly varied greatly from farm to farm. Salaries of live-in workers increased whilst those of day-labourers stagnated. These changes almost certainly more than compensated for the slight fall in the cost of industrial products used in farming. Undoubtedly, then, net incomes of most farmers fell. In the Loir-et-Cher one estimate suggests a fall of between 20 per cent and 30 per cent.[6] As most farmers hardly kept serviceable accounts, they often tended to exaggerate the size of the fall primarily because they focused on that key, symbolic item, wheat. But there can be little doubt that the crisis restricted the possibilities of purchasing those goods on the market which had played their part in improving living conditions in an earlier age.

The decline in rental incomes was yet more spectacular. On land rented to sharecroppers, owners immediately suffered the consequences of a fall in price of those products given over as rent. In principle, the fact that many farm leases were for nine years should have lessened the severity of the crisis for landlords. But by no means all farmers were able to honour their leases. In the Pas-de-Calais, for example, arrears accumulated rapidly, and when leases were renewed, many farmers demanded a reduction in their rental payments. Between 1875 and the end of the century it is estimated that land-rental income fell by between 30 per cent and 50 per cent, depending on the region. Return on capital was, at less than 3 per cent, much lower than the dividends and interest to be found in other, less risky investments. Thus, in 1880, overseas investments yielded around 5.5 per cent on capital with no management costs involved. As a result, the resale value of land fell by as much as 25 per cent in some areas. Non-farming landlords were, then, the principal victims of the crisis.

The phylloxera crisis

Viticulture played a vital socio-economic role during the nineteenth century[7] and had spread over a wide area since the 1800s. Rooted in a polycultural economy, the vine consumed little capital and, with large inputs of labour, could flourish on land otherwise unsuitable for cereal cultivation. For a family with plenty of surplus unpaid labour, the vine yielded a high revenue for a small area of land. In lower Languedoc and Roussillon the vine spread onto the plains after 1840, once the fear of food shortages had disappeared. The development of the railway network further removed one of the major brakes on the search for new markets. Henceforth, the development of large, exclusively viticultural farms, was evident, especially in the Midi, to take advantage of the market for poor-quality, cheap wines. The vine was an important source of income for many peasant families. It was, furthermore, important throughout France: a tax survey of 1874 revealed that 72 out of the 84 departments of France cultivated at least 500 hectares of vines. Exports of wine ranked second behind textiles, whilst government was able to draw one-sixth of the revenue from viticulture in taxes. Wine, then, was of prime importance, as politically sensitive a product as wheat. The seriousness of two successive crises in its production had wide ramifications.

In 1863 a previously unknown disease was identified in vineyards in Gard, which appeared to rot and ultimately destroy the vine roots.[8] The cause, a microscopic bug and its larvae, was identified in 1868 by Planchon who gave it the name *Phylloxera vastatrix*. It had been brought into France by contaminated American vines in 1862. Through the 1860s, the disease spread through vineyards in lower Languedoc and Provence – no solution to its spread could be found. It was not, furthermore, the only disease to strike the vine. Throughout the Second Empire, vineyard owners had struggled against oidiom (a vine mildew), which could at least be prevented by the application of sulphates. Phylloxera, however, carried a mortal blow, With a gap of between two and six years between the first attack and the death of the vines, it was an invisible enemy, cleverly manifesting itself only when the damage was irreversible. Hence the indifference, even jubilation of those in uncontaminated regions, when they witnessed the difficulties of their neighbours in the Midi. No doubt, they thought, such punishments were a just reward for all their unnatural attempts to increase production. Of course, their vines were so worn out, they were bound to succumb! General apathy reigned because the fall in production meant that wine prices remained high and government pronouncements sought to calm fears. Not until 1871, did the government finally 'discover' the true nature of the impending crisis. Given such apathy, the spread of phylloxera seemed ineluctable and inevitable. Thus in the 1870s, the Bordelais, Charentes and Beaujolais were hit. In the 1880s, it had spread as far as the Sarthe and Haute-Saône. After 1890, those previously untouched areas, such as the Champagne, Vosges, Ardennes and Auvergne, were hit in their turn. The catastrophe, then, was a drawn-out affair taking some thirty years before almost all the areas of viticulture were affected. All attempts at preventing the spread, let alone coming up with a cure, failed.

Apathy and ineffective administrative action by the authorities, as much as tradition and fatalism on the part of the peasant, can all be held to account for the disaster. In 1874, a phylloxera commission was created and, from that date, posters and pamphlets on what was to be done proliferated. Prefects created special commissions of enquiry on which the local elite from viticultural areas sat and deliberated. After numerous so-called miracle cures had been proposed by a whole army of tricksters and charlatans, just two remedies were officially sanctioned. Where local conditions allowed, one method was to drown the roots of the vines long enough to destroy the deadly insect and its eggs. Clearly, such a remedy was feasible only in low-lying areas. A second method was to use carbon sulphates. Grants were made after 1878 to viticulturalists willing to inject their vines with the necessary solution. But such treatments were onerous, difficult and soon showed themselves to be only partially successful. Yet again delays in finding a solution were fatal.

Only slowly did the ultimate solution, the replanting of vines, come to be adopted. In 1874, Planchon had brought a series of phylloxera-resistant vines from the United States. In 1877, experiments in planting these vines were begun. The early results were not encouraging. The wine tasted foxy, rough and could hardly be sold commercially. The intergrafting of French with American vines produced a much better final product. But the task of convincing the partisans of sulphur treatment remained. Major interests were involved – the chemical companies which made the product, the PLM railway which was the transporter, the

Vermorel factories, which developed the special injecting tools – and these succeeded in ensuring government support and subsidies until 1889. Furthermore, replanting seemed such a brutal, definitive act that many small viticulturalists hesitated before taking such a step, and sought to carry on, as best they could, with existing sulphur treatments. Only when their vines were well and truly dead did they turn to replanting. Legislation passed on 1 December 1887 exempted newly planted vineyards from taxes for their first four years. Even so, the costs of replanting were high, at around 3,000 francs per hectare. Only with the creation of a number of departmental and communal nurseries could the new vines be purchased cheaply. A number of agricultural societies opened training schools to teach viticulturalists how to graft and replant more cheaply.

A wave of replanting took place between 1888 and 1900. By then, the area under vines exceeded the 1876 total. The phylloxera crisis was over. French vineyards emerged from the crisis greatly altered. Their geographical distribution was different. Now, the vine was much more than one element of a polycultural system. Where that had been the case, in many areas the dead vines were never replaced. In specialised areas, Languedoc, Roussillon and Provence, for example, viticulture gravitated to the plains. The chalky hillsides were often abandoned because the new American varieties did badly there. The length of the crisis ultimately favoured those areas first affected since, once their vines had been reconstituted, they were able to benefit from rising prices. Such was the case in the south-east. On the other hand, a region such as the Auvergne, one of the last to be hit, never fully recovered its vineyard area. The redevelopment of the vineyards was led by those large landowners who had sufficient capital for the work required. In Roussillon, new groups appeared such as the Compagnie des salins du Midi[9] which oriented its product to the national market with all that implied in terms of organising the enterprise. The smallest viticulturalists could only replant if they had the capital and would, in any case, have to wait four years for the first harvest and income. For many the choice was stark: to sink back to a subsistence polyculture or to sell the land and abandon the region.[10]

The crisis brought in its train a much more scientific approach to the treatment of vines and the manufacture of wine – in short, it brought about modernisation. But is it really justifiable to speak in terms of long-term benefits when the phylloxera epidemic inflicted such economic and social damage on a whole generation of viticulturalists? Particularly so, when a veritable crisis of overproduction followed hard on the heels of the period of shortage.

The viticultural revolt in the Midi

From 1895, the phylloxera crisis appeared spent in Languedoc and Roussillon. The vineyards had been replanted and were now oriented towards production for the mass market. The Aude, Gard, Hérault and Pyrénées-Orientales had between them, almost one-third of the vineyard area in France, compared with about 14 per cent in 1880–5. This apparently prosperous recovery was ended abruptly in 1900 when prices began to fall.[11] A hectolitre of wine, worth 19 francs in 1899 fell to 11 francs the following year. Despite a slight recovery in 1902 and 1903, the general trend was downwards with a low point of 6 francs reached in 1905. The fall was primarily linked to an excess of cheaper, everyday wines on the market. Alternative wines, brought in during the period of shortages, had, in particular, served to modify patterns of demand. Imports of foreign wines, especially Spanish wine, had increased to a point where they represented 38 per cent of French consumption during the crisis years of 1886–91. At the start of the century, however, their role was unimportant at only 1.4 per cent of consumption. They went hand in hand with wines from Algeria, which avoided customs duties. The extent of vineyards in Algeria had increased tenfold between 1870 and 1890 and production there represented about 10 per cent of the French total. These wines made considerable inroads into the market, particularly amongst those wanting a stronger, sweeter wine. The crisis had also seen the establishment on the market of 'manufactured' wines created from imported grapes. These wines, however, heavily taxed from 1897, were eventually eliminated from the market.

Such was not the case however for so-called *vins de sucre*, made by a second fermentation of the grape pulp with the addition of sugar. As long as the price of sugar was low, such practices were profitable. This apparent 'fraud' was the subject of many an attack from the viticulturalists of the Midi. But it can hardly be held to account for the crisis as a whole.

Viticulture in Languedoc was in some ways the victim of its own growth. Undoubtedly, this speculative monoculture paid handsomely at the end of the century. For the period 1893–9, an average growth rate of some 13.5 per cent was recorded for the estates of the Compagnie des salins du Midi and 11 per cent for the small farms. Such results almost certainly led to massive over-investment. The whole regional economy depended dangerously on this one speculative production, and the fall in prices threatened all social groups. Once production costs had been deducted, most viticulturalists were working at a loss from 1904 to 1907. Their initial reaction was to lower agricultural wages by 25 per cent to 30 per cent as the crisis unfolded. At the same time, periods of unemployment increased.

The social crisis hit the waged workers first. They constituted a numerous and varied group. Those in regular employment lived in the region and often owned a small plot of land. At harvest-time, numbers were swollen by an influx of seasonal workers from the south of the Massif Central or Spain. Work was usually done in teams, and workers would congregate after work in the cafés of the large viticultural villages, a prime place for organising labour. In August 1903 the first meeting of the Fédération des travailleurs agricoles du Midi, a revolutionary-syndicalist group was held. A series of hard-fought strikes in 1904 brought some temporary improvement in salaries and a reduction in the working day. To compete with this body, the owners created their own, mixed syndicates, grouping viticulturalists and workers together. Faced with the continuing fall in prices, a massive *Congrès de défense du Midi viticole* was held at Béziers in January 1905, mobilising some 350 local syndicates and representatives from 250 municipalities, and demanding that measures be taken to prevent fraud in wine manufacture.

The discontent simmered through to the start of 1907. Wine prices remained chronically low. A number of deputies from the Midi persuaded the Chamber of Deputies to create a special commission to investigate the causes of the crisis. It began its deliberations in March 1907, triggering off widespread excitement throughout the region. Marcellin Albert, a café-owner and viticulturalist from Argelliers in Aude, skilled in oratory and the tricks of the theatre, quickly assumed the leadership of a *comité de défense viticole*.[12] His journal clearly spelt out who the guilty party was: fraud. Against it the whole of the Midi was united. A second accusation was laid at the door of a parliament which, it was argued, was far too solicitous of the interests of sugar-beet producers in the north. The government, it was argued, seemed impotent. The regional allegiances of the movement were clear – the Midi had to be defended against the north.

The local demonstrations organised by the committee quickly became unpredictably well attended. On 5 May, 80,000 people gathered at Narbonne, on 12 May, 120,000 at Béziers. Then it was the turn of Perpignan, Carcassone and Nîmes to welcome the huge crowds that flocked in on specially chartered trains. The demonstrations reached their high point at Montpellier on 9 June with half a million people taking part in what was undoubtedly the largest public gathering of the Third Republic. The meeting marked the culmination of the first phase of a movement which was pacifist and law-abiding, and, as Marcellin Albert ceaselessly affirmed, avowedly non-political.

Many opposition groups were quick to seize the opportunity to attack the government. Thus the royalist right had keenly supported the demonstration. The Bishop of Montpellier, a noted legitimist, went so far as to open the churches of the city to welcome the crowds on the evening of 9 July. The most spectacular case of jumping on the bandwagon was that of Doctor Ferroul, the socialist mayor of Narbonne. In front of the assembled crowds, he delivered an ultimatum to the government. If no action had been taken within the next day, there would be, he declared, a tax-strike and mass resignation of municipal councils. The following day, in a gesture of defiance, he closed the mayor's office after having ceremonially raised the black flag. Some newspapers began to speak of federalism, even of separatism. The government, which up till then had been largely tolerant, reacted with brutality to the sudden politicisation of this movement. Clemenceau, anxious to demonstrate the authority of the state, sent in powerful military forces. Between 18 and 22 June there was large-scale, brutal intervention. Doctor Ferroul was arrested, Marcellin Albert went into hiding. On 20 June, in poor light, troops fired at a crowd, leaving six dead. The news provoked a wave of violence. The prefecture at Perpignan was burned down, attacks took place at Montpellier. The 17th Infantry Regiment, based at Béziers and composed largely of local recruits, was sent on manoeuvres to Agde, as its loyalty was felt to be compromised. The regiment rebelled, refusing to be sent to maintain order. The situation seemed to be spiralling out of control.

After 22 June the situation eased and peace quickly returned to the region. This change occurred for two reasons: the large landowners who had supported the movement began to fear the influence of the socialists, and Clemenceau himself sought subtly to find a political solution. The government proposed legislation to 'prevent the mixing of wines and the excessive use of sugar in wine making'. This was to be enforced by requiring owners to declare the exact size of their harvest and merchants to declare all sugar purchases of over 25 kilograms. The law was passed on 29 June.

In the meantime Clemenceau, profiting from the naivety of Marcellin Albert, succeeded in discrediting him. The latter, alarmed by the turn of events, went to Paris on 23 June. There he met Clemenceau and received for his pains, a 100 franc note to pay for his return ticket. The 'Saviour' appeared to have sold out for the sake of a train ticket and his popularity collapsed overnight. The government smoothed troubled waters by freeing many prisoners and giving large tax rebates. The situation was stabilised when, on 22 September, under the presidency of Doctor Ferroul, the Confédération générale des vignerons was created. Its task was to control fraudulent treatment of wine. Abuses slowly disappeared.

The price of wine slowly rose. The 1907 revolt, then, although largely a failure in economic terms, nonetheless left a profound ideological legacy. Increasingly, the events of that year took on a mythical dimension, becoming *a posteriori* symbolic of the revolt of the Midi against a domineering north.

2. Reactions to the crisis

Faced with the evident difficulties of the period, the peasantry did not remain inactive. Many farmers sought, by a variety of means, to adapt to the fall in revenue. Others simply packed up and left. Others still sought the more active intervention and help of the state.

Adaptation and change

The depression dealt a body-blow to growth. Production stagnated and the urge to clear and cultivate, so important in earlier years, disappeared. In the poorer farming regions, wasteland increased. Farming systems also changed in line with the evolution of prices. Thus, cultivated land fell by about 9 per cent between 1882 and 1912, especially in mountain areas. The area under rye fell by one-third. Those products least affected by price falls progressed. In the south-east, market-gardening, fruit and floristry profited from an enlarged market. Railway-wagons loaded with flowers moved regularly to Switzerland, Germany or Austria from the Nice region. In western France, the production of cider brought appreciable additional revenue to many farms, helping to soften the effect of the crisis.[13] But such shifts in production were not possible everywhere.

The most widely adopted solution was to shift into animal production, particularly the more extensive and cheaper forms of this specialisation. In the Limousin and Auvergne, land previously devoted to the poorer cereals was converted to meadow. In those areas of Poitou and Charentes where vines were not replaced, a major specialisation in milk developed, aided by the development of a number of cooperatives which marketed butter in Paris. In Normandy, too, where dairying was already well established, it was reinforced in the crisis years. The development of pastoral farming to replace the traditional polycultural systems had fundamental social and economic implications. Henceforth, many farms reduced their labour requirements.

A desire to reduce salary payments was an important underlying reason for the pursuit of more modern farming methods in many medium-sized and large farms, both because, and in spite, of the crisis. For those farms which were integrated into the market and had no plentiful supply of family labour to draw on, productivity improvements and higher returns would reduce the relative weight of labour payments in the farm accounts. The increase in mechanisation, interrupted at the start of the crisis, began again after 1885. This trend was also linked to a fall in the cost of imported goods. Thus, the price of reaper-binders fell by one-half between 1878 and 1912. Their use, even after deducting costs of maintenance and depreciation, allowed a reduction of some 25 per cent in labour costs.

Improvements in yields depended largely on advances in agricultural genetics.[14] In animal husbandry spectacular progress was made. At the start of the nineteenth century, each region had its own particular cattle breeds. From the Second Empire onwards a series of improvements can be noted. Two particular schools advanced their theories: those that sought to cross with English breeds and those preferring to renew local breeds by more rigorous selection methods. Cereal varieties were also improved through better selection, and local varieties declined. Fertilisers and other additives were used ever more widely as a consequence of the railway network. The addition of lime permitted much higher cereal yields on many of the poorer lands of the Massif Central. Chemical fertilisers became much more widely used. The net result of all these efforts was an overall increase in yields. Wheat yields, for example, rose 30 per cent between 1890 and 1900.

But such technical progress was the affair of only a minority of farmers. Most simply had too few resources with which to experiment. For such groups adaptation rather than modernisation was a more appropriate term. At this level, perhaps the greatest change was the triumph of the heavy plough. In 1892, there were some 3.7 million recorded for the 3.47 million farms over 1 hectare. Many, however, were simple, not to say crude. In Alsace, Poitou and the Limagne, the soil was still worked partly with a spade. Use of the scythe spread slowly, replacing the traditional sickle in all but the most isolated areas. Still, there were only some 23,000 scythes recorded in 1892. As in earlier periods, technical innovation was slow and faced numerous barriers. Before adoption, an innovation had to undergo a long proving period.

Finance was a major problem during the crisis, and such problems served to underline the archaic nature of credit organisation.[15] Up till 1880, farmers really had recourse only to one source for short-term credit – the local solicitor. But the security of the creditor's assets weakened as the price of land fell and, very quickly, many lenders hesitated in the face of these risks and turned instead to urban investments. The capital of the landed elite began to be invested elsewhere, whilst farmers themselves were only rarely able to take out loans from the various mutual banks which existed in some areas. In the department of

Rhône, rural borrowers and depositors were solicited by many of the Lyon banks which opened rural branches. But much of the money placed with them was not reinvested in the rural sector. The Caisse nationale d'épargne, founded in 1881, used local post offices as its banking network and also helped to siphon money from beneath the mattresses of the peasantry to more profitable urban investments.

These various efforts at adapting to the changed social and economic environment differed from one farming system and farm structure to another.[16] This fact helps to explain why the longevity and seriousness of the crisis varied regionally. The Paris Basin felt the most serious repercussions. By contrast, the intensive farming regions of the east and south-east, dominated by small, under-equipped farms often strongly market-oriented, recovered quickly. Their experience in having had to readjust and reorient to commercial crops at several stages in the past undoubtedly speeded their recovery. Similarly, recovery was quick in the Vaucluse from 1881 and lower Languedoc from 1885. In the Champagne, Aisne and Normandy, however, pre-crisis production levels were not achieved before 1914. Michel Hau sees in this fact the operation of the notion of 'creativity and adversity' suggested by Alfred Sauvy. The most rapid adjustment to the new growth came from those relatively under-equipped farmers who were able, without drastic modification of farm structures, to simply intensify the input of an abundant family labour-force. Other regions sought greater extensification with markedly different demographic consequences.

The demographic reversal

The agricultural depression coincided with a marked decline in the demographic dynamism of the countryside. The relative numerical importance of the rural population fell from 69 per cent of the total in 1872 to only 56 per cent in 1911. At the end of the century, migration to the towns was becoming ever more significant: 85,000 to 100,000 each year from 1881 to 1891, then 100,000 to 130,000 from 1891 to 1913, according to most sources. Examination of the occupational structure of the population confirms a shift away from the primary sector: 43 per cent of the total in 1906 compared with 49 per cent in 1876. Nevertheless, in absolute terms more people than ever were employed in agriculture, with the total increasing from 8 million in 1876 to 8.9 million in 1906. Statistics on women and children in farming occupations are much less certain because they were not always properly counted. But simply examining the active male population in farming confirms the view that to argue for a massive agricultural exodus is inaccurate.

As in earlier years, those who left were primarily in non-agricultural occupations except in a few villages badly hit by phylloxera. However, many of the migrants were not landowning peasants but were often the sons of peasant families – young people attracted to the towns by the possibility of work as servants or in administrative posts. Many contemporaries argued that the development of primary education was responsible for this flow of migrants, increasing young people's consciousness of the precarious nature of the peasant economy at a time of crisis. What is clear is that purely economic arguments, in terms of hardship and the lack of alternative jobs in the countryside, are insufficient to explain the migration process. Psychological factors such as the fear of a life with no future in farming and the mirage of a better life in the towns undoubtedly played their part. These also played a part in the decline of temporary migration. Rather than dreaming of an eventual return to their native hearths, migrants moved permanently to the towns with their wives and families. This was the case, for example with the stone masons of the Creuse. The demographic decline of the department was so marked that the supply of such workers eventually dried up.

The process transformed many peasant families at the same time. The number of people in farming families began to fall as those on the margins of the family, especially the youngest members, left to chance their arm elsewhere. Young women, in particular, left in droves to take up tailoring work and, especially, domestic work for bourgeois families. The phenomenon was well known in Brittany. At the end of the nineteenth century, religious establishments served as a kind of employment bureau for poorer girls, a function caricatured in a children's comic strip, *Becassine*.

The effects of this migration to the towns – and here we can note a fundamental difference from earlier periods – were not compensated for by the demographic dynamism of the countryside. Birth rates in peasant families fell dramatically. Regions which had previously been highly prolific recorded falling fertility rates. In the Lyonnais, the fall in birth rates was marked from the onset of the Second Empire. With the phylloxera crisis, a particularly strong fall was recorded in the Beaujolais. The communes of upland Lyonnais resisted rather longer, through to the end of the century. In 1911, in the rural areas of Rhône department, the average number of children per household fell to only two.[17] Some have argued for a link between demographic behaviour and religious practice. But the question is complex. Should one argue that birth rates fell because of the progress of de-christianisation, or rather did de-christianisation take place because birth-control practices were combatted by the clergy? Nor is the religious factor the only one to take into account. Claude Mesliand has argued for a link between Malthusian attitudes and economic modernisation of farm units. Too many mouths to feed meant, he argues, a limitation on what could be sold on the market and a requirement to purchase more goods for consumption. Common sense, furthermore, persuaded peasant families to take action to prevent their hard-won land from being split on succession. Limiting family size was an effective way of ensuring this.

Equally important were a range of psychological rather than economic factors. As rural society opened up to the outside world, other models of behaviour became apparent. Many newcomers to villages – teachers or policemen, for example – had fewer children in order to be able to offer them a better chance of social advancement. Military service also taught many peasants the rudiments of birth control.[18] The effects of this fall in birth rates was accentuated because mortality rates remained relatively high in the countryside. Infant mortality, in particular, was still high at the turn of the century. Pregnancy and birth were frequently experienced without any medical supervision. The number of typhoid cases also points to the poor sanitary conditions still prevailing in many rural areas.

The combination of these trends – the exodus of the young and a fall in birth rates – produced an increasingly ageing population, already visible on departmental age pyramids at the beginning of the century. Many contemporaries spoke worryingly of depopulation but, in reality, this was far from the case. What was happening was that peasant society was losing a little of its demographic vitality, it was retreating, closing back in on itself, uncertain of its future. More than ever before, the peasant world was on the defensive.

The development of agricultural syndicalism

The crisis prompted the development of agricultural syndicalism.[19] At a time of falling prices, the heavy dependence on market fluctuations was greatly resented. Competition from abroad coupled with the role of intermediaries were the favourite targets of attack. For the attack to succeed, organisation was required. But most of the initiatives taken to organise the peasantry came from outside. Agrarian interests – that is to say, all those individuals who sought to defend the farming population – were dominated by non-farmers.

Economic difficulties had reinforced the importance of mutual-aid groups, especially mutual-insurance associations which offered some security against fire, loss of harvest or animal sickness. Between 1860 and 1880, the movement spread through most of France, primarily through a diverse range of local initiatives and without any formal, legislative structure. A law passed on 4 July 1904 gave a clear mutualist structure and statute. By 1910, there were some 8,000 groups and 60 regional unions. This spirit of mutual cooperation was further reflected in the creation of many associations for the bulk purchase of fertiliser – so-called syndicates – which were able to bypass fertiliser merchants, whose often unscrupulous practices had damaged peasant confidence in the products. The phylloxera crisis also encouraged the development of these shop-syndicates for the purchase of carbon sulphates and, later, of American vines. With the overproduction crisis, viticultural cooperatives developed rapidly, stockpiling wine and keeping it in good condition. The dairy sector was the only other area of farming where a cooperative sector was able to compete with commercial interests. The Charente, Jura and Alps had strong dairy cooperatives. In all there were some 5,400 cooperatives in 1903. It was hardly an impressive total and many lacked the financial base from which to expand. But these essentially utilitarian groups nevertheless soon attracted the interest of those groups with more political axes to grind.

The first organisation which sought to federate these various local groups sprang from the Société des agriculteurs de France (SAF), which was founded in 1867 by Lecouteux. Its headquarters was at 8 rue d'Athènes in Paris, and its membership mainly comprised large aristocratic and bourgeois landowners. After the law of 21 March 1884 legalising syndicates, the Society founded, in 1886, the Union centrale des syndicats agricoles de France. It was primarily a federation of regional unions whose membership was drawn from numerous local syndicates. The Union du Sud-Est was the most powerful regional body.[20] The leaders of the Union centrale were conservatives, hiding their anti-republicanism behind constant proclamations of the apolitical nature of their organisation. Paternalistic in nature, many directors were strongly influenced by social catholicism. They saw their mission as creating a wide network of local organisations in rural France, whose strength would serve to counterbalance the power of the state and the threat of urban socialism. In order to extend and cement its influence, the rue d'Athènes created a series of allied groups around the pivotal local syndicate. Cooperatives and mutual-insurance groups were especially popular creations. A powerful syndical press and efforts to develop agricultural education were also part of their task. In many regional and communal syndicates, well-off peasants, large landowners and interested priests found themselves side by side.

The hold that the rural elite exercised on so many of these syndicates – it was, many argued, 'a syndicalism of dukes and squires' – soon led to disquiet in republican circles. For that reason, Gambetta created a rival Société nationale d'encouragement à l'agriculture (SNEA) based on the

Bd Saint-Germain. It could count on the firm support of both government and the prefects and received financial subsidies in return for its
support of government candidates. Like its rival, it saw the creation of a
range of cooperatives, mutualist groups and credit banks as essential to
its development. Its leaders, too, were essentially the rural elite, if of
more modest origin – landowners, doctors, solicitors. The administration, especially the departmental professors of agriculture, also lent
their support but, despite such help, growth was slow. Only after 1900,
with the triumph of a united left, did the SNEA take on a national dimension. In 1912, all these essentially republican groups were regrouped into
the Fédération nationale de la mutualité et de la coopération agricole.

Beyond their fundamentally opposite political standpoints, the two
federations in fact had much in common. Both wished to develop a form
of professional, non-sectional unionism in the countryside which would
see its task as the defence of all agricultural interests at government level.
Both professed to speak in the name of all peasants. It was a syndicalism
with a common cause which functioned as a pressure group. National
action was strongly influenced by electoral considerations on the part of
rural deputies and senators who dispensed largesse on a grand scale to
ensure their reelection. Demonstrations of strength were organised in
Paris to reinforce the arguments of the federation representatives in the
Chambers. One can detect in this the beginnings of a new form of agricultural protest which was to become a powerful model and example for
the rural world. The impact of such activities at local level was perhaps
small. In the Var, whilst small owner-occupiers constituted the largest
occupational group in the syndicates, fully one-fifth of members were not
engaged in agriculture.[21] This varied recruitment base meant that uni-
fied aims had largely to be imposed, a fact reflected in somewhat similar
aims from rival groups. But communal rivalry flourished nonetheless. In
the south-east it was not uncommon for two syndicates to exist in each
commune, divided along political lines. Many, as a consequence, were
weak and enfeebled. In the Var, many syndicates sprang up, on paper at
least, only to vegetate and quickly disappear.

Much the same applied to those syndicates that catered for specific
groups within the rural world – particularly the sharecroppers and
salaried workers – who were most affected by the vagaries of the economic situation.[22] These syndicates did not develop spontaneously but
were rather the product of anarcho-syndicalist workers in other sectors
of the economy. The leaders of the Bourse du travail sought to take
advantage of discontent in the countryside to put their militants in
positions of power and influence. Thus, for example, a cut in the wages
of woodcutters in the winter of 1891–2 led to the creation of a Fédération

des bûcherons du Cher, which extended its influence in a number of neighbouring departments. Similar action developed amongst the timber workers of the Limousin between 1899 and 1901 and the resin-collectors of the Landes from 1905–8. In the viticultural zones of the Midi, the Bourse du travail at Montpellier helped in the creation in 1903 of the Fédération des travailleurs agricoles de la région du Midi. After a series of hard-fought strikes in 1903 and 1904, it was eventually absorbed within the great demonstrations of 1907. In the Paris region, syndicates grouping market-garden workers also had an episodic existence. It is perhaps in the department of Allier that the best-known example of such syndicalism developed. If such syndicates were rare, it was even rarer that they were led by such a personality as Emile Guillaumin, both a peasant and a writer. The success of his autobiography *La Vie d'un simple* (1904) brought him to the attention of Daniel Halévy who popularised his work in his *Visites au paysans du Centre.*[23] The Fédération des travailleurs de la terre, co-founded by Guillaumin at Bourbon-l'Archambault, sought to group small peasants, sharecroppers and small landowners in their struggle against the large absentee landlords of the region. But, after the collapse of a projected general strike, the syndicate developed into a cooperative. The example was, nonetheless, important in developing socialist ideas in Allier.

The influence of these particular syndicates was spectacular but episodic and restricted in geographic extent. Their demands and aspirations were largely submerged under the dominant agrarian demands of the large unions, who were able to attract government attention. Only the two large national federations had any real influence on government policy. Even so, their roots were hardly deep amongst the peasantry: in 1914, some three-quarters of all peasants played no part in this cooperative and syndicalist movement. But the important thing was that at least a professional organisation existed. To outside eyes, at least, the peasantry appeared to constitute a structured and organised body with which the state and society at large had, *a fortiori* to deal.

State intervention

Up until the onset of the agricultural crisis in 1870, state intervention in agriculture was slight. Public action was largely confined to hoping for a good harvest and ensuring the even distribution of what produce there was across the country. The agricultural depression at the end of the century changed this. The fact that it lasted so long meant that the state was ultimately obliged to intervene. But interests were so complex that, coupled with the liberal attitude of government, only limited measures were adopted. Various governments confined themselves to a slow return to protectionism, coupled with the provision of a framework for developing the technical and financial modernisation of farming.

The mobilisation of the farming population against free trade was a slow affair. Thus, the farmers and viticulturalists of the Champagne and Bordelais remained sceptical about the disappearance of a free-trade system which had assured a market for their produce. But, after 1880, opposition to free trade developed more widely, stimulated both by the fall in prices and rental income, and by the growth of protectionism elsewhere in Europe and the United States, where the markets for French products were contracting. The Société des agriculteurs de France was the first to demand the establishment of customs duties, which would reestablish equilibrium between French and foreign products. The Société nationale d'encouragement à l'agriculture also made similar demands. The rivals of the rue d'Athènes and Bd Saint-Germain were in accord on the need for protectionist measures.

The first measures taken were of limited application. Between 1881 and 1884, a series of light taxes were imposed on pastoral products; by contrast, industrialists quickly gained most of the measures they had sought. Many, indeed, were hardly disturbed by a fall in agricultural prices which, they perceived, might relieve pressures for industrial wage rises. A decisive step was taken by Jules Méline (1838–1925), recently arrived at the Ministry of Agriculture.[24] He succeeded in obtaining a duty of 3 francs per quintal on imported wheat in 1884; the duty was raised to 5 francs in 1887. In general, industrial interests swung in favour of an increase in protectionism. After long debates in the Chamber, Méline, coordinator of the customs-tariffs legislation, intervened with some force to demand parity of treatment for agriculture and the law of January 1892 established a new set of customs duties. Duties of 5 per cent to 20 per cent (the size varied with the product and country of origin) henceforth protected domestic agriculture. It was a considerable advantage for French agriculture. These measures were completed by the sliding-scale tariffs introduced in 1898 which produced a more subtle, flexible and efficient system of protectionism, allowing customs duties on cereals, wine and meat to be altered as circumstances dictated. In 1910, following a range of complementary measures, the average tax on imported agricultural products was about 11 per cent. Certainly, the level of protection was moderate in comparison with, say, the United States. Conceived initially as a short-term measure, they remained in force for a long period primarily because they were perceived as having beneficial effects on agriculture.

In the short term they achieved the desired effect of slowing down imports. Agricultural prices slowly began to recover after 1896, except for wine. Exports, however, also slowed down, as neighbouring countries retaliated with their own protectionist measures. Wine was a prime victim of protectionism. In the longer term, the effects are more difficult to evaluate. The least that can be said is that many farmers believed that this type of political intervention represented the best solution to their problems. It was to the state that they looked to safeguard their interests. For government, protectionism seemed to avoid the necessity of a complete restructuring of a rural world which they preferred to leave as it was.

Other government measures can be viewed in the same light. The state confined itself to encouragement and advice, proffered largely through the major professional organisations which served to relay government opinion to the farming population. Government in any case lacked the administrative means to create and manage a coherent agricultural strategy. The creation of an agricultural ministry by Gambetta in 1882 had marked only a first tentative step towards an efficient administrative structure. Some specialist ministerial services were created to deal with technical aspects of agricultural development, such as encouraging irrigation, drainage or the updating of the *cadastre*. But severe financial and ideological limitations on action existed and, on questions such as the availability of credit to farmers, little was done.

The availability of long-term low-interest loans to farmers was held to be a priority amongst the rural elite of all political colourings.[25] A first initiative had been taken by the syndicate at Poligny, Jura, which, in 1885, created a mutual-credit association with the support of such local notables as the Bishop of Saint-Claude and the Prince of Arenberg. It offered loans at 4 per cent for the purchase of animals, seed and fertilisers. The model credit system established in Westerland in Germany by Raiffeisen, a civil servant, was regarded with some envy by many rural elite in France. The scheme was popularised in France by a Lyon lawyer, Louis Durand, and had a limited success in the south-east from 1893 onwards. The Durand–Raiffeisen movement drew inspiration from the tenets of social catholicism and was ideologically close to the rue d'Athènes. Such initiatives from the right forced Méline and the republicans to propose their own groupings. On 5 November 1894, credit groups which could be based on existing professional syndicates were given special legal status, and accorded certain tax exemptions. Méline, in organising these groups on a 'one-man, one-vote' basis hoped to give them a firm base in the countryside.

But these republican groups, unable to draw on the support and resources of the business community as were its rivals, were slow to develop. In 1897, only 75 had been created compared with the 500 of its social catholic rivals. As a pump-priming measure, Méline, in legislation passed in 1897, authorised the advance of some 40 million francs from the Banque de France, together with annual subsidies. The role of the state was limited to overseeing the proper functioning of the groups, and no changes to the mutualist basis were made. In 1899, another law created a series of regional unions whose role was to regroup local associations and act as intermediaries with the government. They rapidly developed in all departments except the Ardennes. On the eve of the First World War, the implantation of these groups had advanced somewhat, with a total of 4,533 local groups and 240,000 members. But the total still represented barely 10 per cent of all farmers. Most groups were led largely by a radical rural elite who felt that cooperation and mutual aid were the best ways of ensuring the smooth insertion of the peasant into the market economy. In 1914, the official Crédit agricole was still in its infancy.

3. The transformation of the peasant world
Towards a more simplified society?

On the surface at least, the crisis marked a shift in the rules of social interaction in the countryside. An easing of demographic pressure coupled with a fall in the price of land should have allowed for the full development of peasant landownership. Migration to the towns further reduced the number of peasants competing in the land market, whilst the collapse in rents encouraged many landlords to abandon the land for more profitable investments elsewhere. This shift was reflected in a steady reduction in the number of property units: a fall of about 2 per cent per year during 1882–92. Not that it was always easy to find ready buyers for land. In the Lyonnais, for example, many sellers experienced long delays because of the lack of buyers. Was there, then, a massive upsurge in peasants buying land as has popularly been supposed? Whilst the regional studies that we have paint a varied picture, none reveal any sudden, brutal change. It would appear, indeed, that the decline of the large landlord has been somewhat exaggerated. In the Mayenne, it was only slightly affected. In Calvados, aristocratic property was barely touched, whilst in the department of Rhône, large property units represented an island of stability. Instead of selling, many well-off urbanites increased their holdings in order to construct ever-more impressive second homes.

On the other hand, in the Beauce and Pas-de-Calais, large properties did decline, particularly in those cantons distant from the larger towns, allowing the number of typically peasant units to increase. The same applied in the Vaucluse, where property units over 30 hectares suffered a decline. Much of this reinforcement of the middle-peasant holdings

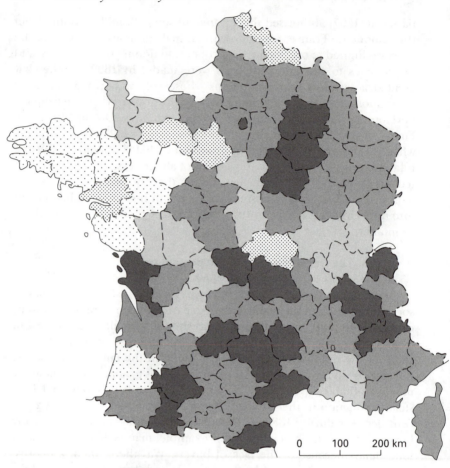

Proportion of owner–occupiers as a percentage of all farmers

☐ Less than 50%	▦ 60-69%	▨ 80-89%
⊡ 50-59%	▦ 70-79%	■ Over 90%

Figure 2 Direct and indirect exploitation of the land in 1882. (*Source: Atlas historique de la France contemporaine, 1800–1965*, Paris, Colin, 1966, p. 50; from the map drawn by G. Dupeux, after the agricultural enquiry of 1882.)

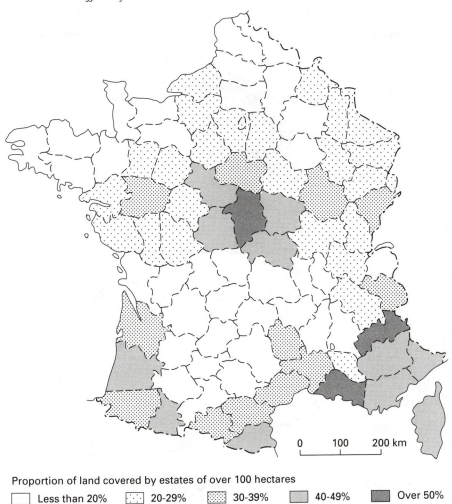

Proportion of land covered by estates of over 100 hectares

☐ Less than 20% ▫ 20-29% ▪ 30-39% ▨ 40-49% ■ Over 50%

Figure 3 The great estates in 1884. (*Source: Atlas historique de la France contemporaine, 1880–1965*, Paris, Colin, 1966, p. 48; from the map drawn by G. Dupeux, from *Documents statistiques sur les cotes foncières*, Paris, Imprimerie nationale, 1889.)

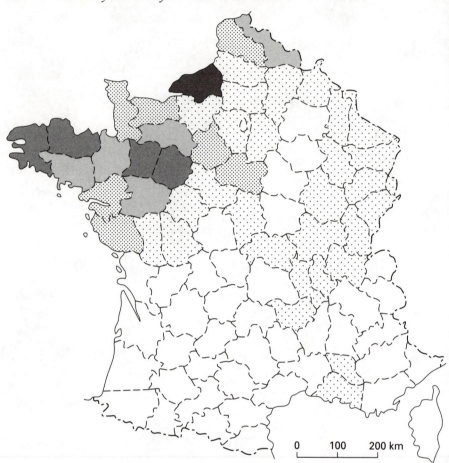

Proportion of tenant–farmers as a percentage of all farmers

☐ Less than 10%   ▨ 20-29%   ▨ 40-49%

▨ 10-19%   ▨ 30-39%   ■ Over 50%

Figure 4 Tenant-farming in 1882. (*Source: Atlas historique de la France contemporaine, 1800–1965*, Paris, Colin, 1966, p. 49; from the map drawn by G. Dupeux, after the agricultural enquiry of 1882.)

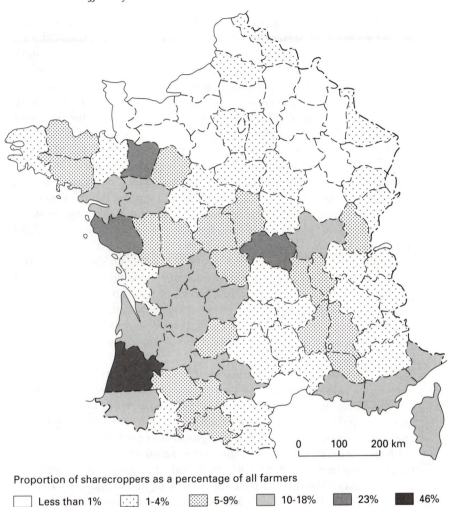

Proportion of sharecroppers as a percentage of all farmers

☐ Less than 1%   ▦ 1-4%   ▦ 5-9%   ▦ 10-18%   ▦ 23%   ■ 46%

Figure 5 Sharecropping in 1882. (*Source: Atlas historique de la France contemporaine, 1800–1965*, Paris, Colin, 1966, p. 48; from the map drawn by G. Dupeux, after the agricultural enquiry of 1882.)

was at the expense of the poorest rural inhabitants whose children had left the holding. In Mayenne, for example, one can detect the birth of a kind of 'bourgeois-peasant' steadily accumulating land on the strength of a powerful and efficient pastoral economy.

Changes in the average size of holdings do not appear to have been especially dramatic. According to the agricultural census of 1882, there were 142,000 farms of 40 hectares and above. By 1892, this total had fallen to 138,700, a reduction of 2.4 per cent. Over the same period, the number of farms between 5 and 10 hectares increased by 20,000 or 2.5 per cent.[26] In the long term, what is perhaps most remarkable is that, despite the crisis, the number of typical small farms between 1 and 10 hectares (a rather arbitrary but nonetheless pragmatic figure) remained very stable.[27] The strongest trend one can detect is a slight fall in those below 5 hectares. It is not easy to judge just how efficient the small farm really was. Was its 'resistance' to the effects of the agricultural crisis a consequence of a feeble involvement in the market? Or should we rather emphasise a remarkable capacity to adapt to changing conditions of production and demand? Ronald Hubscher has shown in a series of examples from the Pas-de-Calais, how many such farms performed very well by objective economic criteria. At the beginning of the twentieth century, when prices became more remunerative, the small farm did remarkably well.

Nevertheless, the reality of rural society was a long way from the 'rural democracy' whose seeming virtues were eulogised by agrarians of all colours. Certainly, in 1882, 75 per cent of all farms were owner-occupied. Sharecropping covered no more than 6 per cent and rented farms the remaining 19 per cent. But this last group occupied almost half of the cultivated area! Despite these figures, the republicans in power argued that the structural trend, a trend which had its origins in the Revolution and was fostered by the Third Republic, was for just such a 'rural democracy'. In 1909, Joseph Ruau, Minister of Agriculture in the Bloc des Gauches government, instituted a survey which purported to show the dominance of the small owner-occupier, the foundation of social harmony and economic prosperity. Jean Jaurès himself was quick to contest this too-idyllic picture. Using the same statistics, he showed what little change there had been in the dominance of large property units in the west, south-west and centre.

Rural society was, however, steadily purged of its poorest members. Those on the margins of the agricultural economy disappeared completely from Gascony and the Paris Basin. Salaried workers benefited from the general shortage of labour in the countryside. In the Pas-de-

Calais, for example, seasonal unemployment virtually disappeared.[28] An agricultural worker who worked on average only 263 days in 1852, would have worked around 304 days in 1913, which would translate into a considerable improvement in pay. Greater security of employment undoubtedly led many workers to absent themselves freely from their place of employment in order to work their own plots, or at the very least, to indulge in go-slows when at work. The pace and nature of the work were undoubtedly less strenuous than in the factories and the food served to farm workers was also much improved. In areas such as the Beauce more and more labourers were able, in the twilight of their lives, to buy a plot of land, and with the help of a few rented plots achieve a measure of independence.[29] But such steps on the ladder to ownership were always tentative and uncertain. Only rarely would succeeding generations reap the benefits – more frequently they would have to follow the same social path, beginning working life as a domestic or day-labourer. The path from poverty to mediocrity would be a lifetime's slog. For those who had small plots of land, this period did allow some consolidation. By dint of personal sacrifices and careful bargains, many were able to survive the crisis with the prospect of better times ahead at the turn of the century.

Overall, then, rural society became more homogeneous in social and economic terms. Thus, many landlords, hit by the decline in rents, were obliged to swell the ranks of the petty bourgeoisie in the towns to increase their income. Becoming a government official or lawyer usually required an urban residence, a first step to a complete disengagement from the countryside. The decline of many small artisanal productions in the countryside also led to an impoverished social structure, as villages became increasingly dominated by the agricultural community.[30] The number of ironmongers, coopers, rope-makers, basket-makers, clog-makers, saddlers and wheelwrights all declined.

At the start of the twentieth century, those that remained were often solitary, with no helpers or apprentices ready to take over when they retired. Sons no longer worked with their fathers in workshops which had once held three or four people half a century earlier. Only blacksmiths resisted urban competition, as the repair of agricultural machinery became an increasingly important part of their business. A few artisans were able to drift into the retail sector.Small grocery shops entered many villages with a vengeance, particularly as the tradition of making bread at home very quickly died out. In the Pas-de-Calais, the aping of urban customs and values was revealed in the appearance of bakers and butchers in many villages.

The spread of urban influences

The transformation of the daily lives of the peasantry, slow and steady after 1870, increased more quickly after 1900. The nature of urban influence was not much different from earlier periods, what had changed was its pace. Thus, dramatic changes were wrought in the way of life and traditional social organisation of the rural world. Did such changes, then, amount to that loss of identity so feared by the rural elite and the folklorists?

The steady widening of peasant perceptions, the opening out of their mental world, proceeded apace, even in the most isolated regions. Improved and widely available means of communication played a fundamental part in this process. Communal roads increased dramatically from 331,000 kilometres in 1871 to 539,000 in 1911. Improvements in roads stimulated the spread of the bicycle after 1890. The Freycinet plan, operative after 1878, permitted the expansion of the railway network from some 24,300 kilometres of track in 1881 to 40,770 kilometres in 1913. Taking the train was no longer a major event for many peasants. The train also allowed those who had migrated from the countryside to visit and maintain links with their native hearths. The receipt of mail became a normal occurrence, encouraged by a fashion for sending short postcards that grew up at the start of the century. In 1880, an average of fourteen letters a year per person were received. By 1913, this had risen to forty. What is more, the art of writing was no longer alien to the majority of the peasantry.

Schooling played a great part in the declining rates of illiteracy amongst the younger generations after 1880. The spread of education, as has been noted, largely predated the Ferry legislation of 1881 and 1882, although rural areas continued to lag behind. As late as 1887, 15 per cent of peasant conscripts were illiterate.[31] The education legislation reduced the disparities between the sexes. Even if absenteeism continued to be a problem between April and October (and this in spite of compulsory attendance), progress was clear and unequivocal. By 1914, fewer than 4 per cent of conscripts were illiterate. The school, however, did not simply teach the skills of reading and writing, but also served to transmit an essentially urban culture.[32] It stressed the importance of washing and grooming, of promptness and politeness. One particular consequence was to breed a sense of inferiority amongst country-dwellers, who were henceforth hesitant about speaking their patois. Education brought bilingualism in its train – many young people began to see that only French seemed to have real value. For some peasant families, the school came to be regarded as the means by which their children could get on in the world, find employment elsewhere and, it was hoped, avoid splitting up the farm. In the Pas-de-Calais, many small owner-occupiers encouraged their sons to take up jobs in the towns; the daughters stayed at home with their husbands.[33] The Midi, well advanced in its educational attainments at the end of the nineteenth century, furnished the republic with countless bureaucrats, thereby removing many of the most dynamic village members from the countryside. It was this process which explains the legendary generational social accession so common in the area. The peasant's son, trained by his teacher, became a teacher in turn. His son, in turn, would climb further up the educational ladder, becoming perhaps a professor, doctor or engineer. But this positive, optimistic vision of the role of education breaks down when confronted with the reality of educational achievement. Few peasant sons gained even their certificate of primary study. Rarer still were those who progressed any further. As for the teachers, by far the majority was of modest, urban extraction.[34]

The development of education, albeit of a limited sort, at least ensured the growing importance of the press in the countryside, which further served to spread urban values. Local newspapers proliferated after 1880. Their readership was a vast public which had learned to read during the development of schooling from the middle of the Second Empire onwards. The peasants were avid readers above all of the weekly journals published at arrondissement or canton level.[35] Popular Parisian newspapers also sold well. Circulation of *le Petit Journal* and, after 1890, *le Petit Parisien* spread into the countryside. They contained comic strips and simple political commentaries. Whether provincial or Parisian, the newspapers portrayed and identified with essentially urban fashions and trends. Advertisements enticed with their range of essentially urban offerings – photographers' shops, bicycle shops, dentists or fashion emporiums. As with the schools, the press was a powerful force for uniformity.

Military service was another well-recognised factor in spreading urban influences. Up until mid-century, only about 10 per cent of each age-class was actually called up. Of that number, one-quarter would be composed of replacement candidates. Between 1872 and 1889, the system was profoundly reshaped. Military service became obligatory through the law of July 1872. In 1873, the purchasing of replacements (bought by parents who did not wish their sons to be called up) was abolished. It still remained possible, however, to shorten service to one year by paying a fine of 1,500 francs. Otherwise, five-year service was the norm. But there were numerous dispensations that could be applied, and it was not until 1889 that a roughly equal treatment was applied to the whole age-class. Those with dispensations, clerics for example, were still required to serve for one year. All others served three years. As a rule, most young countrymen could expect to spend at least one year away from their homes and families. Even if the maintenance of regional recruitment to regiments continued, ensuring that the break for conscripts was not total, military service still brought many face to face with comrades from totally different levels of society in town and city barracks. This was undoubtedly a factor for change. The army was very much an urban institution. What is more, the standard of living for most conscripts was considerably better than that of most country-dwellers. Milk coffee for breakfast, white bread, fresh meat every day, wine, tobacco were all part of daily life. Outside the barracks lurked all the temptations of urban life. It is hardly surprising, then, that the end of military service was for many a moment of truth when the decision was made to break with their former, peasant world. In the Doubs, between 1887 and 1898, one in two conscripts chose not to return to their villages.[36] Those who did go back took with them new customs, habits and thoughts.

Changing ways of life

Changes in daily life came slowly at first and then, after 1900 as incomes rose, much more quickly. Diet, based on an essentially sub-sistence economy, remained frugal, but, even in the poorest regions, it was improved by the purchase locally of products which had previously been restricted to the towns.[37] In the north and east, sweetened coffee with bread and butter increasingly replaced the old morning soup, help-ing to lighten the domestic chores. In the Paris Basin, meat was bought from the butcher several times a week, but, in an area such as the Var, it was still only eaten on Sundays and festive occasions. Hard bread was eaten less and less frequently. The family oven was increasingly aban-doned when bakers began to install themselves in the village. The change represented both a lightening of domestic tasks and a shift towards more urban habits. Desserts made with eggs and sugar began to make their appearance on Sundays, served in particular to the children of the family. It marked the start of experimentation with recipes printed in journals and almanacs. Traditional peasant cuisine, far less ancient than is often supposed, began to be 'invented' in this period. Wine was more widely consumed in non-producing regions as military service created a population accustomed to regular consumption. In the west, where water was the usual daily drink and alcohol was consumed heavily on feast days and pilgrimages, habitual consumption of alcohol developed after 1870.[38] The penetration of urban habits tended to break down regional differences in diet. Thus in the Limousin, Périgord and

Ardèche, consumption of chestnuts declined in a spectacular manner between 1880 and 1900, being increasingly regarded with a kind of moral distaste.[39] But, despite general improvement, differences between social groups remained considerable. In the Var, white bread was the privilege of landowners, whilst agricultural workers had to content themselves with cruder wholemeal bread.[40]

Housing conditions changed more slowly and, here, regional differences remained strong. The more frequent use of lime and cement improved the general quality of construction. The most decisive change, available to the better-off, was the creation of a first floor which allowed private bedrooms, one for each generation of the family, to be built. In the west, the shift was marked by the abandonment of the *lit clos* or 'box bed', generally too bulky to be transferred to the upper floor. In the Limagne, struck by phylloxera fairly late, the high prices of wine sustained feverish building activity. In many villages, forged-iron balconies and heavy oak doors point to a newly acquired wealth. In the Paris Basin, furniture became much more varied. Much of it was of industrial manufacture, bought in the towns. But in the Var, more meagre provision of peasant furniture remained the rule. Improvements in village infrastructure were the most widely felt feature of this period, with the provision of running water often becoming a decisive factor in local electoral debates.

Perhaps the key area in which urban values were adopted was in the realm of clothing. Wardrobes were both larger and more diverse. The young led the way. The use of underwear increased after 1890. Working clothes were increasingly bought at fairs or from mail-order catalogues. But women nevertheless continued to make some of their clothes at home, helped, in part, by the spread of sewing machines which became the norm in peasant households around the turn of the century. Newspapers contributed to the standardisation of much of this domestic production with their portrayals of the latest fashions and styles, sometimes accompanied by dressmaking patterns. The evolution of wedding dresses is especially revealing of the spread of urban influences.[41] In 1870, in most regions, peasant brides wore brightly coloured garments, depending on local traditions, whilst in the towns, white dresses were the norm. In Languedoc or Bresse, green clothing, the symbol of hope, was used. In the poorer regions, the bride would often content herself with a multicoloured shawl worn over a black dress, which could be put to good use after the ceremony. White veils began to be used in the Ariège only around 1890. The wearing of white dresses, both more costly and difficult to re-use, spread rather more slowly. But by 1914, urban fashions had certainly triumphed in the better-off families. The standardisation of dress was by no means the least significant of urban triumphs in this period.

It is much more difficult to detect changes in the notion of time in the countryside.[42] The old peasant tradition of measuring time by the height of the sun was gradually replaced by a more structured day drawn from the urban model. Such organisation of time was introduced by, for example, railway timetables which imposed on country-dwellers a previously unheard-of degree of punctuality and precision. Arrivals and departures were organised to the minute, rather than the half-hour which had characterised the old coaches. Children had to learn punctuality at school. All these trends encouraged the spread of watches and clocks into the peasant family. Pocket-watches began to appear in the countryside at the end of the Second Empire. Their ownership was a sign of some social standing and a male privilege. After 1880, they spread more widely, becoming the favoured gift at first communion or when passing the primary certificate of education. In 1886, in a village in the Morvan, there were some 20 watches and 70 clocks amongst the 120 households of the village. After 1870, more and more public clocks were installed on the facades of the mayor's office, schools and clock-towers. Time was ever present, profoundly modifying the rhythms of peasant life.

Collective life was also subject to urban influences. After 1890, many traditional forms of collective behaviour began to be modified throughout France. In those areas where it still existed, the *veillée* remained little more than a gathering of women and the elderly to exchange gossip. Youngsters preferred to gather in the cafés to play cards or billiards. There they could also read the newspapers which linked them to urban values. The café, then, symbol of the opening out of rural society, replaced the *veillée*, that old gathering in which the peasant world turned in on itself. Other forms of recreation for young people increasingly followed urban models. Excursions by bicycle became increasingly popular, initially at least because they liberated the young from family constraints. Village festivities were also changed. Republican ceremonies displaced many more local gatherings. After 1880, the 14 July festivities competed with other more religious celebrations. Sometimes, the torch-lit procession became a substitute for processions previously forbidden by municipal authorities. The dance for new conscripts came to replace older dances. In the Limousin, Parisian-style dances were widespread: quadrilles, polkas and mazurkas triumphed over the traditional *bourrées*. Only a few continued to be performed by the elders of the village, to the amused curiosity of the rest. In the Auvergne, from the end of the century, accordions replaced the hurdy-gurdy, which was poorly suited to the new tunes of the age. In many respects, the rural fêtes became rather impersonal affairs, whilst private celebrations became more widespread. Marriages and communions were, more than ever before, occasions for family reunions. A photograph served to solemnise the occasion for posterity.

The social life of the village came increasingly to be modelled on urban patterns.[43] Associations frequently grafted a modern structure onto existing social networks. They multiplied in rural areas after 1880. In Saône-et-Loire, for example, a nucleated habitat favoured their growth: all communes of five hundred inhabitants and more had at least one. They were a varied lot: political circles, sporting and musical societies, professional groups. Their birth seems to have reflected both local needs and the wish of some individuals to control local political life. Many were founded by merchants and shopkeepers or the petty bourgeoisie, who sought to channel and control local community spirit, even though the membership was predominantly peasant. In communes riven by political opposition, parallel, rival societies were often created. The role of many associations was not without significance. Because their members had to attend meetings at particular times, they taught punctuality. They served to introduce the idea of leisure time into peasant life. Such an introduction was novel for many women, who were able, for the first time, to escape from their daily tasks and the confines of their homes. Since many groups were integrated into departmental, even national, networks, they served to open out the perceptions of many of their members. Social life had shifted a long way from the old networks based exclusively on family and village groups.

A changing cultural identity?

For many contemporaries these various changes seemed to amount to a veritable loss of identity. The growing interest in folklore was one expression of this disquiet.[44] The folklorist movement, in its infancy during the Second Empire, developed rapidly after 1870. The founding of many of the great regional journals, such as the *Revue des langues romanes* and the *Revue celtique* in 1870, *Romania* in 1872 and *Mélusine* in 1877, pointed to the success of the folklorist movement. After 1880, folklore societies were created in most regions. They saw their role as compiling an inventory of local traditions, everyday objects and tools; a range of books and papers on such subjects resulted. For the general public, photographers provided postcards in which peasant actors in regional costume illustrated local songs and proverbs and acted out popular scenes: marriage customs, harvest or grape-picking festivals, country cottages and angelic shepherdesses. Sometimes, folklore enthusiasts, usually urban-dwellers, dressed as peasants for a day under the bemused gaze of local peasants dressed in urban clothes. The most highly developed of these movements was in Provence, where folklore interests were reflected in the personality of Mistral – a rural *notable*, nevertheless, not a peasant. In assembling a range of practices, some of them undated, others abandoned long since, yet others, of recent introduction, many enthusiasts sought the re-creation of an idealised society which, in fact, had never existed.

The development of interest in folklore was not always as unpremeditated as it seemed. Many of the elite who developed and ran such societies were more conscious of the need to preserve their influence than of the wish to respect the peasant identity. In Brittany, at the end of the century, the clergy freely conversed in dialect. Many priests assiduously drew up parish monographs in the hope of reinforcing traditional, and threatened, ways of life. Frequently, they entered into competition with the local schoolteachers who sought to inculcate republican values which, they argued, had created a landowning peasantry. Folklorists participated in a rediscovery of the provinces, helped by many first- and second-generation emigrants eager to cultivate a nostalgia for their rustic roots.[45] These images of the provinces were mostly constructed from outside by groups who had not lived there for many years.

The development of folklore helped to shape a new image of the peasant in literature and art.[46] The peasant world became increasingly one of contentment and harmony. Up until 1890, the novels of Zola or Maupassant describe that world as shut off, even repellant. A reinvigorated literature focused rather on rustic and nostalgic portrayals of the peasantry. The works of René Bazin, whose titles – *la Terre qui meurt* (1899), *le Blé qui lève* (1907) are significant – focus on the fragility of the rural world. Eugène le Roy, whose ideological position was very different, does much the same thing in his *Jacquou le Croquant* (1899). The peasant represents a moral, virtuous world, set well apart from the vice and corruption of the town. Even Emile Guillaumin, one of the rare breed of genuine peasant writers, could not escape such stereotypes. Painters also participated in the creation of a peasant myth; a peasant race which was universally virtuous, courageous and prolific, so different from the towns which were the 'tombs of the race'.[47] Amongst the paintings submitted to the *salons*, those of harvesters and shepherds multiplied. Regional characteristics are an essential component of such paintings, which often have a quasi-photographic aspect. But they are expressive of naturalism rather than realism. Peasant labour was portrayed as anything but hard. It was a perpetual celebration, a festival. The work of Jules-Bastien Lepage, particularly successful after 1870, illustrates such trends well. His reassuring peasant figures, serene or joyful are refracted through a distorting lens. They reflect less the reality of peasant life than the image of that life that the bourgeoisie wished to see.

This rural idealisation was also seen in the pronouncements of the agrarian elite, whether republican or conservative. The peasant was represented as the cornerstone of the nation, the fountainhead of basic values. Were such sentiments merely a defensive reaction to the economic crisis and to an industrialising world which seemed to threaten the countryside? Perhaps the creation of this image of a 'model peasantry' served a convenient political purpose. Agrarian leaders of the right, inspired by the social catholicism of Le Play and La Tour du Pin, defended a hierarchical, yet united, rural world as conforming to the 'natural order of things'. Republican sentiments took a less religious tone but were otherwise in a similar vein. The peasant could if won over, be the best support for a republic which had given him land, liberty and the vote. For both right and left, the peasant occupied a central place in the electoral contest.

4. The peasants and the republic

The years between 1870 and 1914 are generally regarded as marking the awakening of political consciousness amongst the peasantry. It rallied to the republic, helping to consolidate the regime. After a period of uncertainty lasting about ten years, political activity developed at village level. But was the political mobilisation of the peasantry as deep-seated as is often believed?

The republic woos the peasant vote

In the countryside, the success of Napoleon III in the plebiscite of 8 May 1870 was overwhelming. But after only a few weeks, the fragility of the victory was clear. The Empire found few defenders after the defeat of Sedan. But that fact did not mean that the peasantry automatically rallied to the republic, declared on 4 September 1870 in Paris.[48] In the Var, it was undoubtedly welcomed by the peasantry. But in the Limousin, hostility to the government of national defence and its policies carried the day. The war was largely responsible for such attitudes. The advances of the German army set off widespread panic which, combined with local problems, produced many dramas. At Hautefaye in the Dordogne, a noble was massacred by villagers who accused him of being a Prussian. In areas distant from the front, the intensification of the war effort, led by prefects often employing authoritarian methods, was unpopular among peasants who could see little point in a fight to the last. In the Limousin, conscription lists drawn up at the end of November provoked serious trouble. Much of the army of the Loire was eventually supplied with docile Breton conscripts. In occupied areas, sniper activities provoked brutal repression by the authorities and brought no real benefit to the local populace. Throughout the countryside the war was highly unpopular, a fact which was reflected in the voting of 8 February 1871.

These elections were exceptional in more ways than one.[49] More than forty departments were under occupation; 400,000 men were imprisoned. The electoral lists were compiled in great haste and campaigning was non-existent. Does that mean, then, that the results had no significance? Conservative forces had drawn up large unitary lists of candidates. They proposed to recognise the military defeat and accept the armistice. The republicans, on the other hand, at least appeared to favour continuing the war. Their policies were incarnated in the figure of Gambetta, recognisably Parisian, who was not popular in rural areas. Only the departments of the east, the Rhône valley and the south-east lent their support. Most of the 250 republican deputies came from urban constituencies, whilst rural areas elected some 400 monarchists. The traditional rural elite had won a notable victory. This majority, at its first meeting in Bordeaux on 13 February 1871, loudly heckled Garibaldi, elected in Paris. From the public benches, Gaston Cremieux, a young republican lawyer, threw out his famous phrase to the assembled deputies: 'Rural majority, shame of France!'[50] In reality, however, the peasants were not as securely behind the banners of the old rural elite as the figures might suggest.

The Paris Commune did not provoke any brutal reactions in the countryside. In the Limousin, those peasants in non-migrant regions were little concerned by events, rumours of which barely penetrated their villages. On the contrary, in areas which had long supplied stone masons to the capital, the suppression of the Commune excited great indignation, although public order was not greatly disturbed. The stone masons of the Creuse and Haute-Vienne were amongst those imprisoned and executed in the troubles.[51] Many Breton peasants, on the other hand, took part in the crushing of the Commune, although holding no particular political opinion on the events. In most of the country, rural opinion did not appear markedly more conservative as a consequence of the events in Paris. 'All is saved, provincial France was not afraid', Clemenceau would have said. The republicans could start the political reconquest of positions which at one time had appeared lost.

Gambetta was acutely conscious of the importance of the peasant vote. He appointed himself as a kind of 'travelling salesman for the Republic', encouraging local organisations and coordinating national groups. He advocated prudent policies to ensure that the rural vote would not be lost.[52] With Jules Ferry, he never missed an occasion to underline that the republic meant order. The reassuring and moderate image he created of republicanism – which would guarantee social peace – contrasted with the maladroit politicking of royalist interests. The insistence by certain legitimists that the white flag replace the tricolore was exploited by the republicans, who were quick to associate the white flag with a return to the tithe and feudal dues. The political activism of some of the clergy, who encouraged pilgrimages and advanced their support for the royalist cause, further served to increase fears about the alternatives to the republic.

An electoral system which permitted multiple candidatures meant there were numerous partial elections. The progress of the republicans can be traced through the ballot box. Year in, year out, they steadily increased their importance in the Assembly. In 1875, they had 353 members to the 352 monarchists. The Wallon amendment permitted the use of the word Republic in the constitution. In the 1876 legislative elections, the republicans reconquered many of their old 1849 bastions: the north-west Massif Central, the south-east and the Rhône valley. They also made spectacular gains in the north and east. But large swathes of country appeared unconquerable – the west, from the Pyrénées to Calvados, the south of the Massif Central. After the dissolution of the Chamber, the 1877 elections confirmed this basic geographical pattern. Municipal elections in 1879 verified the solid local roots of the republican movement, and gave them a majority in the Senate. After the resignation of Mac-Mahon and the election of Jules Grévy to the presidency of the republic, the republicans were masters of their own destiny.

The deep-rootedness of the republican vote in the countryside was assured by legislation in 1881–2: freedom of expression, election of mayors by the municipal council, legislation on schooling. With the Freycinet plan, large sums of money were spent in many of the poorest regions where the newly established railways brought new jobs. All these measures were aimed primarily at rural communes. The regime took a calculated risk of closely associating the peasantry with democracy in the hope that this would ensure democracy's survival. But republicans were equally adept at using a range of less noble means, already well tried by their predecessors, to remain in power.[53] The intervention of the administration in districts judged to be lukewarm to the republican cause did not disappear. Bureaucrats were charged with ensuring the republican zeal of the electorate if they wished to advance their careers. Henceforth, political battles were more often won in the village than in the town.

'Village politics'

After 1890, there was a marked increase in political activity in many communes.[54] Depending on prior conditions, this can be regarded as either a new awakening of political consciousness or a resurgence of existing forces. The development of schooling and the growth of the press also meant that public opinion became an important element in politics. But political opinions continued to be shaped by discussions in many places – in the *cercles* of the south-east, elsewhere in cafés and bars.[55] These functioned as centres for discussion and debate and were often places where a passion for political matters was conceived. But undoubtedly the most efficient agent of politicisation was the electoral process itself. The stability of the regime meant that elections took place at regular intervals, often with long periods of preparation. Voting itself took place at communal level and in most areas, turnout was impressively high. In the Vaucluse, 90 per cent of those on the list took part in elections.[56] But abstentions remained high in the Pyrénées, the Massif Central, the west and the Vosges, particularly for national elections. In general, municipal elections were more animated affairs.

The mayor played a key role as arbiter within the commune and as the representative of the village in administrative affairs. He was to become a vital cog in the machinery of the republic. Legislation passed between 1882 and 1884 reinforced his power. He was elected by his municipal councillors, themselves elected by popular vote. Citizens could control the action of their councillors thanks to the opening of their sessions to the public. The requirement that every commune must possess a municipal office of some sort gave a material and symbolic structure to local power.[57] Even in the smallest communes, new buildings were erected to this end. Where finances permitted, a symmetrical building was often constructed with the mayor's office at the centre and a school and post office forming the wings.[58] Some councillors were quick to choose ostentatious quasi-urban designs which would architecturally rival the local church. This symbolic 'monumentalisation' of the village did not stop there. *Mariannes* multiplied after 1876, especially in public squares and on the facades of the mayor's office.[59] On moral grounds, these often represented a direct affront to monarchist sentiments. Perched above the drinking fountain, they became the symbol of a wise and benevolent republic that brought water, hence progress, to its peoples. Such costly innovations were not without electoral risks to over-enthusiastic municipal councils.

Did, then, the growth of democratic practices signify the increased participation of peasants in power? For the municipal councils, the response is positive. A growing number of mayors were listed as being employed in farming.[60] More and more peasants were able to assume such offices even though the rural population had begun to fall. In the Limousin, from 1878, farmers constituted the great majority of councillors. In the Var, in 1912, one-half of the mayors and three-quarters of their assistants were classed as being engaged in agriculture.[61] The same did not apply, however, to the Conseil général and legislative elections. In the Var, farmers furnished only one-fifth of *conseilleurs généraux* in 1913. Few became senators. In the National Assembly, the under-representation of the peasantry was more flagrant still. In 1889, out of 576 deputies, only 10 could be classed as real farmers. There were still only 36 in 1910.[62] The peasantry was still content to allow itself to be represented by others.

Rural voters continued to look to the rural elite. The most traditional of these did lose some support, except in the west and on the southern borders of the Massif Central. In the southern Morvan, too, the squire-archy continued to exert considerable pressure on its sharecroppers. Prior to elections, the squires' collectors were sent to deliver voting slips on the estates.[63] In 1912, in two rural cantons in the Nièvre dominated by large landowners, more than one-half of all mayors were squires. Elsewhere, the petty bourgeoisie was able to accumulate the peasant vote. Members of the liberal professions, solicitors or doctors, kept their power at legislative elections. For regional and local office, more modest members of the bourgeoisie came into their own. In the Limousin, shop-keepers and artisans were often elected. At Compreignac, butchers, grocers, café owners and wine-sellers solicited the votes of the electorate. In the Vaucluse, by contrast, such people absented themselves from the more disputatious elections, commercial discretion proving the better part of valour. Only the café owners did not hesitate to enter the fray.[64] Formal organisations played little part; personal standing continued to be important in local elections. Voters sought first and foremost men they knew to be trustworthy and influential. Such figures were able to control, at least in part, the voting process. Voting was done without envelopes or booths until 1914; the elector simply presented his voting-slip to the president of the office. It was not difficult to discreetly mark such slips in order to identify political attitudes afterwards.[65] Political life in the village was, to all intents and purposes, transparently open, which explains much of the passion which accompanied some political issues.

The central issues in political life were those which had a direct bearing on country-dwellers. The Dreyfus Affair, of great interest in Limoges, left much of the countryside apparently indifferent.[66] Two themes dominated – the church and the school – where local and national issues

were often intermingled. Conflicts over material issues clearly predated
the republican legislation. Witness, for example, the debates at the end
of the Second Empire between traditionalists and advocates of modern
hygiene over the repositioning of cemeteries.[67] Demographic growth in
the first half of the nineteenth century had meant that many cemeteries
around the village were full, requiring the creation of new sites on the
village outskirts. Many traditional catholics resented such transfers of
burial grounds as symbolic of the decline of the faith. Another source of
conflict was over the financial requests of church incumbents who
sought to undertake restoration and rebuilding work on their churches.
The Ferry laws served to introduce yet one more bone of financial contention between the clergy and municipal authorities anxious to balance
their budgets.

The schooling question was first and foremost a financial one, because
most communities could hardly afford to run two establishments at the
same time. Church schools survived only in those areas strongly loyal to
catholicism, such as the west and part of the Massif Central. The conflict
worsened around the turn of the century. In 1902, members of religious
orders were no longer authorised to teach and some of their number
were expelled, leading to serious incidents, especially in Brittany. In
1906, the application of the law of Separation of Church and State
unleashed an avalanche of protest. It required the municipality to take
over the control and maintenance of church buildings, to draw up an
inventory of the contents of the church and to distribute those goods to
cultural organisations. Violent incidents broke out in the west, the
Basque country, the south-east Massif Central. In Flanders, one protester
was killed. In the diocese of Arras, the doors of at least half the rural
churches had to be forcibly broken open.[68]

The war between church and state did not only take the form of
violent protests. Frequently, quarrels were of the most banal kind. Such
quarrels have often been personified by the fervent opposition of the
teacher and the priest. In few communes was the struggle an equal one.
More often than not, one party held most of the cards, creating both
victims and persecutors. In anti-clerical regions, the clergy, isolated, was
on the defensive. In the Limousin, priests were discouraged as they saw
their flock become increasingly distant from their influence. Some
priests compensated for their diminished church attendances by erect-
ing more and more inexpensive, factory-made statues in their churches.
Others contented themselves with violent diatribes against the teachers,
fulminating against the 'poison' they were spreading in the countryside.
Teachers themselves were usually held in some regard and many felt
themselves to be the representatives of education and, by extension, of

the future.[69] In strongly religious areas, where catholic schools were all-powerful, the lay teacher survived in a meagre, uncomfortable school with few pupils.[70] In some cases, local shopkeepers and peasants refused to sell food to them. At best, they faced the hostility of a population who considered them as town-dwellers, not rural teachers. Indeed, contrary to popular opinion, at the beginning of this century, only 10 per cent of teachers were sons of peasants, whilst 40 per cent came from the urban middle classes. Women teachers were especially resented. Such a variety of situations serves to highlight the fundamental political divisions that existed in the countryside.

The geography of political behaviour

At the end of the nineteenth century, the political geography of the country was much as it would be for at least the next fifty years. As early as 1913, André Siegfried noted the stability of political attitudes in rural France which clearly marked off republican from conservative areas. Pierre Barral has attempted to describe this diversity. The typology he proposed some twenty years ago has not been fundamentally questioned.[71] His basic distinction marked off 'democratic' regions from 'hierarchical' ones.

The 'democratic' regions were rural societies where small peasant owners predominated within a rural habitat characterised by nucleated villages with a distinctive and rich social life. A high degree of political consciousness introduced some regional variants. Thus in the north-east, the centre and the northern Paris Basin, as well as in Dauphiné and Savoie and viticultural areas north of the Loire, a 'democratic republicanism' quickly developed. Religious affiliation still existed but the population could not be regarded as subservient to the clergy. Other regions, republican bastions in 1849, moved more markedly to the left. These 'anti-clerical democracies' were won over by successive, often extreme, positions. Radical when the rest of the country was opportunist, they became radical-socialists, then socialists when France was governed by radicals. The penetration of the countryside by socialism came at the end of the nineteenth century. The agricultural programme elaborated by the socialist party in 1892 concentrated on the position of agricultural labourers. But, from 1893, certain leaders became conscious that progress depended on the peasant vote. Jean Jaurès played a formative role in the evolution of the party, developing the idea that small peasant ownership was worthy of defence. The 'red' rural zones were to be found in the Limousin, in the south and west of the Paris Basin and, above all, in Languedoc and lower Provence. One can also add to these the 'protestant democracies' comprising the protestant populations of areas such as the southern Massif Central and the borders of the Charentes, Vienne and Deux-Sèvres. Hostile to the catholic church, the protestants joined free-thinkers in supporting the left.

Other regions are more difficult to classify. In south-west Aquitaine, radicals took up where the bonapartists left off. In Normandy, the party in power, whatever its colour, was supported as long as it defended peasant interests. These were the 'neutral democrats' of Barral's typology. But democratic social structures did not necessarily imply a commitment to republicanism. In Flanders, in north-west Brittany, in the Basque country, the small independent peasantry remained close to the church, forming a kind of 'clerical democracy'.

In the 'hierarchical' areas, large landowners were instrumental in controlling the votes of 'their' peasants. Their influence and opinion, usually transmitted via the clergy, guaranteed the triumph of the conservatives. The isolation of the *bocage* slowed down the spread of urban influences. Another cementing influence, the memory of the Chouan revolt, was ever-present in the countryside of the west. These were the 'undisputed hierarchies'. But, where religious affiliation was waning, the power of the large landowners also fell. Among these regions of 'disputed hierarchies', the example of the Bourbonnais is perhaps most typical. In this sharecropping region, most large landowners visited their estates only in the hunting season. Their interests were looked after by managers who were anxious to feather their own nests. Hence, many peasants in such areas voted on the left for radical, then socialist, candidates. Finally, there were the 'capitalist hierarchies', where the large bourgeois landowners were opportunist rather than ideological and often ended by supporting moderate republicanism. The Loire valley and parts of the Paris Basin typified such groups.

This detailed typology drawn up by Pierre Barral rests on a detailed analysis of two variables – landownership and attitudes to the church. However, the latter is particularly complex and difficult to isolate. Between anti-clericalism and agnosticism, apathy towards the church and de-christianisation, there exists a range of sympathies that the sources hardly allow us to discern.[72] Louis Perouas has shown that in the Limousin, a comparison of the geography of voting and the geography of religious practice reveals few meaningful correlations. In certain cantons of the Haute Vienne and Corrèze, voting was massively radical after 1885, although the average gap between births and baptisms remained very short. In the Limousin, developments in political attitudes seemed to precede changes in religious behaviour. Note must also be taken of the fact that voting was exclusively male, whilst religious practice was very much in the female domain. Only more local studies of mentalities and attitudes will permit us to take account of the diversity of peasant society.

In the space of half a century, real, perceptible changes had taken place. The crisis had accelerated a little the slow evolution of economic structures. Peasant ownership of land was reinforced, as land lost some of its powers of attraction for other social groups. The small family farm was largely dominant in a rural society which was becoming less and less diverse. Ways of life were becoming more and more uniform under the pressures of urban models. Because the peasantry was no longer such a distinct and distinctive group, it no longer appeared a threat. The peasantry, having become a powerful and influential political force, was solicited by politicians and government, and came eventually to represent the social ideal of the III Republic. But the loss of demographic dynamism and the slow pace of modernisation of the unproductive family farm meant that the peasantry came increasingly to depend on the state, a state which tended increasingly to marginalise peasant interests.

4

Towards a separate world: 1914–1950

In 1911, the peasantry still represented more than one-third of the total population; by 1954, the proportion had fallen to one-quarter. The loss of more than 5 million people in under fifty years points to profound changes. Such changes, moreover, were not always clearly recognised by contemporaries. The two wars and the crisis that separated them, had, apparently, rather contradictory effects. Even if events seem to have been chaotic, they have to be carefully considered because of their unprecedented impact on the future of the peasantry. The First World War facilitated the strengthening of the small family farm. The rural exodus was accentuated during the prosperity of the immediate post-war period. The collapse of agricultural prices during the crisis of the 1930s transformed farmers into protesters. The long period of shortages between 1940 and 1948 gave them, however, some respite, whilst the Vichy regime relied on the farming population, regarding it as the very cornerstone of the state. But, with the Liberation, the Corporation paysanne was suppressed. Henceforth, the view that the peasantry must quickly modernise itself became an accepted dogma of government.

1. The peasantry during the First World War

Peasants during the First World War appeared as rather a silent majority. Most work on the period gives us only fleeting glimpses of their role,[1] whilst many rural-history monographs end at 1914.[2] How far, then, can we accept the brutal judgement of one police inspector from Noirétable in the Loire who commented in August 1918 that 'the war seems to occupy little place in the thoughts of our cultivators, an appetite for profit seems to have conquered all'?[3]

Peasants and the war

General mobilisation was declared in the countryside on 2 August 1914.[4] Peasants were called up and assembled beneath the insistent peals of the village church bells. In northern France, it was the middle of harvest time; south of the Loire, the harvest had been brought in but much farm work remained to be done. The notes drawn up by local teachers, on the orders of the Ministry of Public Instruction, about how the mobilisation was effected are a useful source of information on rural attitudes. News of the declaration of war was not received as enthusiastically as is often supposed. A sense of worry, consternation and sadness seemed to be the initial reaction. A few days later, after the conscripts had been assembled in the main urban centres, the sight of the first convoys of troops excited a patriotic fervour and noisy demonstrations of support, at least on the part of the urban population. But allusions to a revenging of the defeats of 1870 and to the return of Alsace-Lorraine were rare. Rather, received opinion seemed to be that, since France had been attacked, aggression demanded a firm response. This sense was reinforced by the view that the war would be a short one, six months at most.

For those left behind, the most pressing problem was to continue agricultural work. From the outset of war, more than one-third of all agricultural workers had been conscripted. The limited spread of mechanisation meant that farmers relied heavily on intense manual labour. Yet the peasantry constituted the largest contingent of conscripts and, amongst them, exemptions were few and far between. Unlike factory workers or public servants engaged in sectors such as transport, they were rarely withdrawn from the front to their former occupations. All in all, about half of the active agricultural male population, that is, some 3.7 million men, participated in the conflict. To deal with the consequences of such a loss in the workforce, a series of rather derisory measures were put into effect once it became clear that the war was going to last some time. From 1915, leave was granted for periods of sowing and harvesting. But these were still few and far between, because the major military offensives were timed in the main for the summer months. Farmers aged from forty-seven to fifty were exempted only in January 1917. The Office national de la main d'oeuvre agricole, created in 1915, had the task of introducing immigrant workers to fill the gaps left by the departing troops. About 150,000 were recruited – mainly Spanish and Portuguese – and the office also sent some 60,000 prisoners of war to help in agricultural work. The vast majority found its way onto those large farms whose owners had access to the corridors of power.

The measures taken to cope with the manpower shortages were limited primarily because the authorities relied on the ability of family farmers to adapt to the changed situation. Women, children and elderly men all had to redouble their efforts on the farm. Intense work by women was hardly a novelty in the countryside, but many women found themselves carrying out a range of tasks once exclusively in the male domain, such as ploughing and selling at market.[5] Because of the war, more than one-third of all farms had women at their head. But it is important not to exaggerate their emancipation. They remained under the close scrutiny of other members of the family, even of their husbands who, at times, demanded precise accounts of what was happening on the farm and did not hesitate to give written instructions in their daily missives.[6] Nevertheless, informal cooperation and the intensification of labour could only go so far to fill the gaps.

In addition to manpower shortages, there was also the requisition of about one-third of all horses, still the principal form of motive power in agriculture. In the Beauce, for example, the army tended to prefer the geldings used on the smaller farms rather than the less docile stallions used in the larger farms.[7] Such preferences forced small farmers to reduce the amount of land they could work and, consequently, their cereal production. In 1916, Etienne Clémentel sought to develop farm mechanisation. Some experiments were carried out using American tractors. Still, by 1918 there were barely one hundred tractors in the whole department of Eure-et-Loir.[8] They could not provide a solution to pressing manpower shortages. The reduction in labour inputs was also difficult to compensate for in other ways. A shortage of rail wagons slowed down the supply of industrial goods. Fertilisers were no longer manufactured in great quantity, for chemical factories had switched to supplying the needs of the army. The employment of fertilisers had been widespread, especially in the better farming areas. Viticulturalists, already hit by the shortage of manpower, now had difficulty in securing supplies of sulphur and copper treatments for their vines.

These shortages hit the more intensive farming systems especially hard. They implied a falling back into a more subsistence-oriented economy and a fall in yields. Thus wheat yields fell from 13.3 quintals per hectare in 1913 to 8.7 in 1917. The general fall in production was further aggravated by the partial or full occupation from the start of the war of ten departments. The front eventually stabilised for four years over the rich lands of northern and eastern France. The enemy controlled some 6 per cent of the national agricultural area. Cereal production fell – for wheat, for example, the 1918 harvest represented only 69 per cent of the average for 1904–13.[9] More and more farms gave priority to potato production, which could feed a family adequately and which was less liable to official requisition. The area under pasture, less labour intensive, also increased. These shifts reveal the inability of farmers to adjust to the new demands of the war years. As a consequence, the way was prepared for greater state intervention.

The politics of food supply

At the outbreak of the conflict, there were no ready-made plans
to deal with agricultural production. Because it was widely believed that
the war would be a short one, no general economic mobilisation to
support the war effort was planned. The prevailing economic liberalism
was hardly able to envisage any intervention in the running of farms or
threats on the inviolability of private property. To ensure the provision-
ing of the army and the towns, the government relied on the market
economy.

The needs of the army were considerable, particularly because the
rations to be supplied to some 8 million mobilised men were not
ungenerous. In operational periods, the authorities supplied 500 grams
of meat and 1 litre of wine per soldier per day. The wastage was
enormous. There was also the question of food supply to the civilian
population. The army supply organisation practised widespread and ill-
thought-out requisitioning. In the Loire, one-quarter of all meat
production was thus taken. At the national level, about 5 per cent of all
beef was requisitioned in only five months.[10] At this pace of consumption, the national herd risked massive diminutions. To cope with the
problem, a new administrative cohort was created and became an independent ministry in December 1916. Prefects were given the right to
requisition cereals and flour and to control their circulation, whilst
farmers were subjected to meticulous declarations of their produce. But
as official prices rapidly fell below accepted commercial ones, the market
halls quickly emptied. In the Forez, the wholesalers of Saint-Etienne
circulated the countryside in cars, stealthily buying up local butter which
their middlemen had sought out for them.[11]

The administration had no real means of controlling the production
of subsistence farms. The difficulties of elaborating any coherent policy
of food supply were immense. Successive ministers of agriculture sought
to gain the help of national professional organisations but gained only
meagre results. They remained committed to economic liberalism and
had no stomach for the task of controlling and directing the productive
apparatus of the country. In 1916, Jules Méline enacted legislative
measures creating a Comité d'action agricole in each commune,
charged with the task of requisitioning uncultivated land and placing it
under plough or grass. Still the basic problem of labour shortages
remained paramount. This requisitioning, the only measure which
might have threatened the sanctity of private property, had a negligible
impact. Only some 1,401 hectares in 56 communes were actually
redistributed.

The supply of food to the towns and army was ultimately maintained through imports. With effect from the autumn of 1914, protectionism was suspended and export bans were imposed on most food products. Massive recourse to overseas suppliers was made, especially for cereals which arrived in great quantity from those newer countries which had been prohibited access to the French market since the end of the nineteenth century. Technical problems, especially over the import of meat, also had to be tackled. The problem was solved thanks to the supply of ships and refrigerating material from Great Britain. By the end of 1915, some 60 per cent of the army demand for meat was being met by imports of frozen meat, especially from Argentina and the United States. Only wine and alcohol continued to be supplied from domestic producers, who had, in any case, considerable stocks in 1914. Imports, then, allowed satisfactory supplies to be maintained of most products except sugar, at least until the intensification of submarine warfare began to threaten supplies once more. Then, butchers and cake shops would often close on certain days. Sweets and soap were rarities. But the bread ration card was not introduced until June 1918: inconvenience to consumers was largely minimal, especially compared with the problems that faced German consumers.

This recourse to imports could in some ways be regarded as a defeat for French agriculture, from which the public authorities were unable to gain the necessary increases in production to sustain the war effort. But, on the other hand, the authorities did little to help the peasant population. Farms were, by and large, left to cope as best they could with the changed conditions.

Drawing up a balance-sheet of the war

The war was, first and foremost, synonymous with ruin. Whole regions which had served as battlefields were deserted and devastated. More than 2 million hectares of land were lost from agriculture. Almost everywhere farms were condemned to vanish. The conflict had the most profound human and material consequences for the future of the peasantry. It served, in particular, to accelerate a number of preexisting trends.

Estimates of the human costs vary.[12] The Marin report, presented to the Chamber in 1920, estimated that of the 3,700,000 of the agricultural population that was mobilised, 673,000 were killed and 500,000 wounded. But this can be considered as unreliable, because the occupational classifications were based on old declarations. Other sources have tended to reduce peasant losses. Depending on the author, the figures are in a range of about 500,000 to 700,000 killed or disappeared, together with 360,000 to 500,000 wounded. The latter figure is significant, given that invalidity posed major problems for farm work. For an active male agricultural population of 5,400,000 in 1913, this represented a loss of some 16 to 22 per cent. The villages were especially affected because they had supplied many of the infantry regiments that had suffered the most severe losses. In the canton of Montbrison, in the Loire, only one-third of those peasants that left for the front returned unhurt.[13]

From the start of the conflict, birth rates fell throughout the country. Even after a general increase in leave permissions in 1915, birth rates remained low.[14] In many regions, the demographic impact of the war was considerably greater than the rural migration of preceding years. In those areas where demographic dynamism had been low anyway, families that lost the father faced special difficulties. The departure of the widow was often the only solution. In areas of strong birth rates, the Bigouden region for example, many demobilised soldiers simply did not return to their villages. Hence the process of ageing and depopulation started in many areas. The large farms of the Beauce had difficulty recruiting agricultural workers. The population of the arrondissement of Montbrison fell by 9 per cent between 1911 and 1921. Some mountain communes lost 16 per cent to 20 per cent of their inhabitants.[15] In many of the poorest regions, social and economic evolution was blocked by these demographic processes.

Could it be said that the material advantages linked to the war helped to counterbalance the human losses outlined above? Many urban citizens thought as much, arguing that the peasant had made great material gains from price rises and was largely responsible for the high cost of living. It is, however, difficult to measure the evolution of farm incomes in the absence of any reliable farm accounts. It is certain that the financial allocations legislated for on 5 August 1914 for those families whose breadwinner had been mobilised brought valued monetary resources into the countryside.[16] They were certainly granted quite liberally. Thus, in one village in the Charente, fully half of the population received allocations. Such payments may have been small, but they provided an appreciable input into a family budget whose other sources of income continued much as before. They provided the possibility of purchasing previously inaccessible goods. The press was quick to stigmatise the peasant women who used make-up, who frequented the cake shop, or who aspired to the luxury of their own bicycle. Some, it was said, even had the temerity to wear silk stockings, symbols of waste and debauchery!

The pensions paid to widows and old soldiers played a similar role in the post-war years. These regular supplies of money permitted many peasant families to participate much more freely than before in the market economy. Inflation also increased the money supply in the countryside. If requisitioned cereals commanded only a low price, other products fared much better. This was especially the case for milk, eggs, poultry, vegetables and fruit. In general, agricultural prices rose fourfold between 1914 and 1920. But this increased money supply did not necessarily translate into greater wealth. In general, prices and agricultural wages evolved in the same way and the rises continued until the stabilisation of monetary conditions in 1928. Gains were perhaps more apparent than real. But, to those peasants who, for the first time, held quantities of liquid capital in their hands, this hardly mattered.

This abundance of money, coupled with inflation, led to a marked reduction in rural indebtedness. During the war, a general moratorium had been imposed on repayments. When they began again in 1920, they were based on the nominal levels and values of 1914. In 1928, the stabilisation of the franc set it at one-fifth of the 1913 level. Farmers were quick to take advantage of an inflation which increased their turnover three or four times whilst their rents remained fixed. The increased size of savings accounts at the end of the war was another sign of the more abundant monetary resources available to the peasantry.

These resources were used in part to finance the purchase of land. The war had initially interrupted land transactions. These recommenced in 1918. Sales of land multiplied in 1919 and 1920, both in terms of area and the value of land transacted. Farmers were the chief buyers. In the Montbrison arrondissement, more than one-half of all land transacted was acquired by peasants. In the Eure-et-Loir, many farmers bought up their previously rented land.[17] Because of the low level of land rents, landlords sold quite heavily. Up until 1920, the price of land rose less than the cost of living, increasing only by a factor of two. This represented something of a bonus for buyers, which lasted for as long as landowners remained unaware of the rate of monetary depreciation. After 1922, the situation changed, the price of land rose and transactions slowed. Even if the fever of land purchases had not lasted long in many regions, the phenomenon was fundamentally important for the peasantry.

Changes in habits and living conditions were no less important, both for those who had been mobilised and for the families left behind. The war created new habits, born especially of the need to keep in touch. In the countryside, the reading of daily papers increased as families sought out news from the front. Above all, soldiers and their families exchanged letters.[18] The amount of mail increased dramatically. In 1915, 4 million letters and postcards were sent daily. One estimate puts at 10 billion the final number sent during the conflict. A study of at least some of this correspondence reveals a good command of the French language. If the squaddies of the Midi spoke in dialect, this was to emphasise their provincial origins rather than their ignorance. In their letters, not surprisingly, they used French. For Bretons, on the other hand, the war, which obliged them to employ daily what was to many a foreign tongue, was a veritable cultural transformation. Many soldiers wrote home every day and received daily mail in return. Writing was a way of telling loved ones that all was well and of making the interminable waiting more bearable. The terrible struggle for survival in the trenches was eased by evoking in letters their farms and land, and the rhythms of the seasons.

Such exchange of letters, whilst helping to maintain links between soldiers and their families, did not prevent those soldiers from adopting new ways and values learnt during their four-year absence from home. They became accustomed to urban diets and meal times. On their return home they continued the habit of eating meat and drinking wine. In Brittany and Normandy, the consumption of cider fell after the war. The regular posting of supplies led many to discover the pleasures of conserves. In the Midi, people became accustomed to sealing up such containers to keep their contents fresh. The war created a whole new generation of peasants with different horizons. If, in many cases, this 'enforced tourism' was largely limited to the main railway stations, others discovered the sea and the delights of 'the East'. Yet others were captivated by technology, in particular, aviation.

For all these soldier-peasants, this period left an indelible mark on the rest of their lives. There is testimony enough to this in the rapid erection of so many war memorials as a way of remembering the dead and celebrating the survival of others, as well as the creation of countless associations of old soldiers in rural areas with a predominantly peasant membership.[19] These experienced a rapid growth, in part at least because they took up the links of many of the older, dying forms of rural sociability. The rural exodus and the falling birth rates had diminished the number of younger people who, in times past, had animated so many of the festive occasions. Old comrades and their families accounted for the majority of the population of many communes. Many of these groups were a throwback to the old brotherhood groups of earlier times; like them, they also helped with the burial costs and arrangements for their deceased members. The Armistice Day processions on 11 November took on an important communal role. But the banquet which followed, together with a dance at the end of the day, gave a festive note to the occasion.

Many returned from the front with a horror of war.[20] The general pacifism of the peasant was advanced by the press as a kind of universal value. Determined to defend his land to the last, the peasant nonetheless had an instinctive hatred of war, it was argued. Many local, rural politicians did not hesitate to refer to this pacifist streak in the peasantry, something which, it was said was deep-rooted in the peasant mentality. But there was not, it would seem, any specifically peasant form of pacifism.

The war years highlighted how poorly adapted socio-economic structures were to the needs of the nation. They also profoundly modified the old social equilbrium, a fact which created a certain unease. In other respects, however, the war reinforced a sentiment that nothing must change: it was the small peasant who had saved France with his ferocious defence of his land. Agricultural structures must, if only for political reasons, remain intact, whatever the ultimate price. But for many peasants, their experiences had served to highlight the hardships they faced in their daily lives, even if, for some, conditions had improved. This growing realisation was important: for Michel Augé-Laribé, 'the peasant in 1914 was largely a resigned fellow; the peasant in 1920 was an increasingly unhappy one. He had learnt the art of complaining'.[21]

2. The inter-war years

The war led to a reinforcement of the ideology of agrarianism. Its fundamental principles seemed unchallenged. Peasant property ownership continued to increase whilst landlords steadily disappeared from the countryside. But the reinforcement of the middle peasantry did not necessarily result in a more efficient agriculture during periods of prosperity. The peasantry, seriously affected by the depression years, became increasingly marginalised in society.

The rise of the family farm

A comparison of the agricultural census of 1929 with that of 1892, reveals that the number of farm units had fallen by around 30 per cent, from 5.7 million to less than 4 million.[22] Almost 2 million farms in the category of below 5 hectares had vanished. The fall was especially marked in those tiny units below 1 hectare – the number of these was halved over the period. The structure of the working population was likewise profoundly changed – much of the labour from these *minifundia* furnished the manpower necessary for the functioning of other farms. Day-labourers holding very small plots of land represented only 10 per cent of the active agricultural population in 1929. One thousand large farms of over 100 hectares also disappeared, largely because the fall in the real value of farm leases made them less profitable. Family farms of between 10 and 50 hectares were the chief beneficiaries of these changes. At the same time, 75 per cent to 80 per cent of all farms relied almost exclusively on family labour. Systems of tenure were fairly stable. Share-cropping, which represented 5 per cent of all farms, became increasingly marginal except in the west and the Bourbonnais. Elsewhere, family farming was the rule. Three-quarters of all farmers owned their farms. The myth of the small family farmer, a myth assiduously cultivated by the III Republic, began to approximate ever more closely to reality.

The increased rate of departure towards the towns explains much of this evolution in agricultural structures. It is legitimate to speak of a rural exodus or of the depopulation of the countryside when considering the migratory patterns of the inter-war period. Between 1921 and 1931, the rural population fell by 600,000. In 1931, it represented only 48.8 per cent of the total population; now, for the first time, the country popu-lation was a minority. In the poorer regions, the size of the exodus was considerable. Some upland communes in the Beaujolais lost around one-third of their populations.[23] This constituted a real depopulation which left clear marks in the countryside. Woodland and heath replaced cultivated land; deserted villages fell into ruin. It was also an agricultural as well as a rural exodus. The size of the active male agricultural popu-lation fell by more than 500,000 between 1921 and 1931. The proportion of the agricultural population in the total active population fell from 42 per cent to 36 per cent between 1921 and 1936.

The development of industry and the institution of the eight-hour day helped to accelerate the rate of departure. Sons of small farmers, not always younger ones, in any case less numerous with the fall in birth rates, moved to the towns. A very significant female exodus brought about an increase in celibacy rates, provoking, in its turn, the departure of the male population. The renewal of the next generation of farmers was now by no means certain on many farms. At the moment of succession, many inheritors based in the towns simply kept the farm as a secondary resi-dence or left their lands to go to waste. Others chose to sell, contributing to the growth in the size of the average property owned by peasant families who had profited from having larger families.

Government policies also helped to consolidate the place of the owner-occupier in agriculture. Such policies had as their cornerstone the necessity to maintain a sizeable peasantry. Becoming a property-owner, however modest, tended to put a brake on the desire to migrate. It was also perceived as a means of maintaining social order, an order regarded as threatened by the increasing size of the urban proletariat. The family owner-occupier was glorified by agrarians on the left because it was seen as symbolising an egalitarian society. This model of peasant proprietorship was seen as worthy of reinforcement.

The attentiveness of government to these small family farms was exemplified in a fairly light tax regime. Income taxes, voted in 1914, but not applied until 1917, were a growing element in government revenues. Yet, in 1929, the peasantry supplied only 5 per cent of total income-tax revenue. At the same time, the weight of land taxes continued to fall. There can be little doubt that the peasantry escaped the steady increase in taxes imposed in the post-war period.[24] More importantly, state support for accession to landownership was reflected in a series of measures. The law of April 1918 seeking 'to lend succour to those worst hit by the war' granted, through the Crédit agricole, twenty-five year loans at 1 per cent interest for the purchase or improvement of rural properties.[25] After the war, too, ex-soldiers benefited from loans at 2 per cent.

The success of these measures contributed to the growth of the Crédit agricole. The law of 5 August 1920, inspired by a radical administrator, Louis Tardy, created the Office national du Crédit agricole.[26] This public body had a wide degree of financial autonomy within state control. Its task was to group together existing credit groups in an umbrella organisation. The legislation also widened membership to include rural artisans and favoured the extension of medium-term credit for modernisation and the purchase of farm equipment. In the 1920s, more than half of its financial base was in the form of state credits. But the place of private investors steadily grew. The number of members increased from 241,000 to 417,000 in 1930. These members placed their savings with the Crédit agricole, encouraged by the high interest rates offered. Nevertheless, the use of cheques remained exceptional.

The peasants used the Crédit agricole primarily as a savings bank. Their interest was still largely as savers rather than borrowers. Can one, therefore, agree with the view that 'the agricultural sector remained largely a source of savings rather than a place for investments'?[27] Was there a major movement of capital from the agricultural sector into other parts of the capitalist system? For André Gueslin, the answer would be negative.[28] Few local banks used their funds to purchase outside investments. Those of Avignon and the Loir-et-Cher, for example, who placed considerable investments outside agriculture were, he argued, the exceptions. In the 1920s, the Crédit agricole served rather to transfer capital from other sectors into agriculture. The capital made available was used mainly for the purchase of land. Peasants, however, remained hesitant to go into debt in order to modernise their farms. The consequences of this failure to evolve modern production systems meant that the peasantry failed to reap the full benefits of prosperous times.

The limits of prosperity

An examination of production statistics would seem to suggest that the 1920s were excellent years for peasants. Production grew at around 2 per cent per year, an unprecedentedly high rate. At the same time, the cultivated area fell, especially for arable crops, as it had done at the end of the nineteenth century. But the area under pasture barely shifted. Fallow land, which occupied some 3 to 4 million hectares on the eve of the war, steadily decreased. Production, then, tended to be intensified. Because of the rural exodus, this intensification could not have been obtained through an increase in labour inputs. The use of immigrant workers was hardly sufficient to fill the gaps left by the departure of agricultural labourers and family workers. In 1927, there were between 250,000 and 300,000 foreign workers in agriculture, chiefly from Spain, Italy and Belgium. But it was an unstable source of manpower which was readily attracted into industrial rather than agricultural employment. The farm sector, then, could no longer rely on abundant supplies of poorly paid workers. One of the cornerstones of the production system was knocked away.

One consequence was that the use of more modern methods could no longer be put off. The consumption of fertilisers doubled between 1913 and 1936 and peasants became more and more skilled in their use of this resource. But much of this increase can be laid at the door of a major publicity drive by the chemical companies who made the product, and the railway companies who sought to transport ever-increasing quantities of the material. Ever-increasing numbers of card games, notepads and blotters were distributed to schoolchildren in these promotional drives.

The use of machinery became more widespread in medium-sized farms. The overall value of farm machinery doubled in real terms between 1925 and 1938. Henceforth, almost all farms of more than 5 hectares possessed a minimum of a modern plough and mowing machine, as well as one or more horses. The remainder continued to be under-equipped. Increasingly, farmers sought to use machines rather than labour, which was becoming more and more expensive, a trend which was to lead to modifications in traditional production methods. At the start of the 1930s, 100 combine harvesters were in operation but animals remained the main source of motive power. In 1929, some 27,000 tractors were recorded, but most were clumsy machines, unreliable and largely unsuitable for three-quarters of all farms.[29] Their running costs were considerably higher than the traditional animal teams. Mechanisation had barely made an impact in agriculture. The farm sector continued to prove incapable of meeting demand and, as urban consumption rose, the equivalent of one-quarter of all agricultural production still had to be imported.

In many respects, the slow pace of modernisation can be explained by the size characteristics of farms. Other reasons put forward include the lack of any sustained government interest in rural modernisation, except in the sphere of electrification. Under the influence of Etienne Clémentel, a new spirit aimed at diffusing technical progress into the smallest farms, spread through the Crédit agricole.[30] Rural electrification was a central priority of the Génie rural – the former service responsible for agricultural improvements within the Ministry of Agriculture. In 1919, 17 per cent of communes were connected to the national network. The diffusion of electrical power was viewed as one way of coping with the shortages of salaried labour, narrowing the gap between rural and urban living conditions, and therefore slowing the rural exodus. Under the management of Henri Queuille, and thanks to low-interest loans from the Crédit agricole, a considerable proportion of the costs of the programme came from state coffers.[31] Electrification progressed rapidly. In 1927, 48 per cent of communes had power and by 1938 only 5 per cent were not linked to the national network. But the effective use of such power was often limited and its employment in production was restricted. For many, the substitution of capital for labour was difficult: a kind of technical apathy carried the day. *Remembrement*, not yet obligatory, was undertaken at a snail's pace in most communes. Agricultural training remained embryonic. Almost all young peasants had no training other than the general advice given out by teachers and the practical education they received on the family farm.

Even if the transformation in production techniques was very limited, particularly in comparison with countries in north-eastern Europe, it at least had the effect, for better or worse, of creating closer links between farmers and the market. To produce more, farmers had to increase expenditure. These expenses increased as a proportion of the total agricultural product, from 10 per cent to 20 per cent between 1913 and 1938.[32] The agricultural market became an important outlet for many industrial products. In order to be able to make purchases, sales on the market had to be made. Nevertheless, most farmers continued to maintain a level of subsistence production. In 1938, fully one-quarter of farm production was consumed at home, although there were marked differences between regions and in different types of production.[33] In many respects, the figure was both too high and too low, depending on one's point of view. But the long-term evolution was fundamental. The growing commercialisation evident during the years of good prices in the 1920s did not benefit farmers alone. Many intermediaries drew considerable profit. Fairs tended to decline as the hold of merchants and wholesalers increased. The growing use of cars facilitated this change. For each product, a pyramid of intermediaries developed from the canton upwards. Several hundred producers would deal with a few merchants who then delivered the goods to the wholesalers of the nearest urban centre. For meat, it was by no means unusual to find four or five intermediaries between farmer and consumer. In the Lyonnais, meat-buyers circulated in lorries buying up produce.[34] Such intermediaries swallowed up much of the profit linked to rising prices.

As a result, peasant standards of living did not rise in any appreciable manner. Undoubtedly, diet became more diversified, drawing upon commercial products. The spread of cookers meant a lightening of domestic burdens for women, who could spend time on more elaborate preparation of food. Dress moved closer to urban working clothes. On Sundays, men would sport a hat and shoes, as in the towns. But, as far as incomes were concerned, the gap widened between the peasants and the rest of the population. According to the Dessirier index, farmers did not return to the real incomes they had enjoyed in 1913 until 1929. When in 1931, André Tardieu, the Minister of Agriculture, proposed measures to encourage farmers to keep more stringent accounts, his team at the Ministry quickly discouraged him, arguing that, if they knew their real incomes, the peasantry would be incited to revolution![35] At that time, a railway worker earned two and a half times the income of an agricultural worker, together with a number of additional social advantages and shorter working hours.

In fact, the peasantry was not slow to perceive just how inferior its position really was. This fact helps to explain the increased participation in agricultural syndicates. The two great central organisations were as powerful after the war as they had been before. One farmer in two was a member of at least one of the various groupings. Nevertheless, other organisations were not slow to solicit peasant support. The replacement of the old rural elite in rural associations by authentic farmers progressed in many advanced farming areas, as the memoirs of Ephraim Grenadou show.[36] At national level, the interests of the large producers were represented by newly founded groups such as the Confédération générale des producteurs de betteraves founded in 1921, or the Association générale des producteurs de blé established in 1924. They saw their task as ensuring that market conditions were favourable to the interests of their members. In other areas, Brittany, for example, the old landed elite refused to surrender control of agricultural organisations, notably the Office central de Landernau directed by Hervé Budes de Guébriant.[37] That organisation offered a whole range of services to farmers under the umbrella of a powerful paternalist ethos.

To compete with this group, a number of Breton clerics created a rival organisation of peasant syndicates, regrouped in 1920 into the Fédération des syndicats paysans de l'Ouest. But, from 1930, the clerics at its head were forced to withdraw under pressure from the church hierarchy, marking the apparent collapse of an organisation which laid important foundations in the countryside. The focus of the church shifted to youth movements. The Jeunesse agricole catholique (JAC), founded in 1929 following a series of such regional organisations, had a strong evangelising character. Its task was to rebuild old christian values in the village, as well as seeking to glorify agricultural work and encouraging technical innovation. In this respect, it helped to ease the spread of modernising ideas into the countryside and helped prepare young people for positions of responsibility.

Despite fervent efforts, the SFIO and PCF were never able to create powerful syndicates among the peasantry. After drawn-out strikes in the Paris Basin and the viticultural areas of the Midi in 1919–20, many agricultural workers chose to give vent to their frustrations by simply leaving the profession. To attract the support of farmers, communists relied largely on local initiatives. In Corrèze, Marius Vazeilles created the Fédération des travailleurs de la terre in 1922, which became the Fédération des paysans travailleurs in 1924. A year later it united with the Fédération de défense paysanne in Lot-et-Garonne, led by Renaud Jean. Overall, results were modest: some 13,000 members in 1926. The more traditional organisations could still lay claim to the right to represent the interests of their peasant members.

At the beginning of the 1930s, then, one of the principal characteristics of agriculture was its low level of economic efficiency. The agricultural sector could no longer provide a satisfactory living for the bulk of the peasantry. Peasants themselves accepted this condition with reluctance or anger. The economic crisis was to accentuate this basic malaise.

The peasantry and the agricultural crisis

It is customary to argue that France was less severely affected than other European countries by the crisis of the 1930s, primarily because of the important place that agriculture continued to occupy in the economy. In fact, the peasantry was profoundly affected by the collapse of prices. The impression that the crisis was not too severe was an illusion fostered by the fact that many farmers simply regressed to an almost subsistent economy. The peasantry was forced to suffer a massive reduction in income, a reduction which, ultimately, was to become unacceptable. This fact helps to account for the renewed importance that peasant organisations and the corporative ideology were to play.

World prices for agricultural produce stagnated from 1926, then fell from 1928.[38] Increased customs tariffs and a poor harvest brought some respite in 1930, but the following year there was a severe collapse. The price of wheat was especially hard-hit in 1932–3 and fell by more than 50 per cent between 1931 and 1935. Increased production can account for these price shifts. The steady improvement in techniques during the 1920s, coupled with a series of good wheat and wine harvests, persuaded farmers to produce more to compensate for price falls. Thus, the area under cereals increased slightly between 1931 and 1933. At the same time, demand fell as economic difficulties led to a tightening of purse strings amongst the population at large.

Government reaction to the situation was hesitant.[39] The poor quality of statistical data created particular difficulties for the authorities. Because some producer associations were especially fearful of increased government intervention, the first measures adopted were circumspect. After 1927, there was a small increase in customs tariffs. In 1931, import quotas were established. But produce from the colonies entered freely, further flooding the market. Protectionism was shown to be an inadequate and ineffective measure. Other measures to organise the marketing of more politically sensitive products were put in train. Viti-cultural pressure groups, in legislation passed on 4 July 1931, obtained a special viticulture statute which prohibited the planting of new vine-yards, limited irrigation and developed distillation methods. Legislation passed in December 1934 complemented the law by offering grants to those willing to uproot vines. Sugar-beet producers drew up a series of agreements with sugar refiners which helped to safeguard production. For wheat, a much more complex market meant that the first measures taken could not please everyone. In July 1933, a minimum price of 115 francs per quintal was established. But the government simply did not have the means to ensure the maintenance of this price. The size of the harvest was not known and possibilities for stockpiling were limited. Pressed to sell, many farmers accepted lower prices. These so-called 'gangster prices' were as low as 80 francs per quintal. In 1934, the mini-mum price was withdrawn.

These measures were incapable of stopping the headlong collapse of agricultural prices. Industrial prices, however, fell by only 25 per cent between 1931 and 1935. According to Alfred Sauvy, agricultural revenues fell by 24 per cent between 1931 and 1935. The Dessirier index of agricultural purchasing power moved from 100 in 1929 to 67 in the summer of 1935. Furthermore, the industrial depression put a brake on the rural exodus. Recent migrants, now unemployed, returned to their peasant households. A stable, perhaps even increased, agricultural population, found itself forced to cope with rapidly falling incomes. The situation meant that many farmers had recourse to loans to make ends meet during what they regarded as temporarily difficult times.[40] This was especially the case for regions where more speculative agricultural systems had developed. Credit banks often had difficulty in securing repayments; the fall in land prices also meant that the securities offered were not always sufficient. The Crédit agricole was able to survive thanks to exceptional grants from government. Other 'free' credit groups were less fortunate. Many banks affiliated to the rue d'Athènes experienced particular difficulties. The collapse of the Caisse régionale du Plateau Central in 1932 dealt a severe blow to some 7,000 depositers, chiefly small peasants, in Aveyron and Tarn. The only solution was to turn the clock back. The trend of purchasing machinery was halted in an effort to reduce expenditure. This return to a kind of subsistence economy was resented by many peasants whose life styles had been greatly modified since the war years. The money which had flowed in from the sale of their products on a buoyant market had been used both for saving and to satisfy daily needs. A return to the way of life of 1913 seemed unaccept-ably regressive.

A significant protest movement developed. It was not led solely by the rural elite who had sought to represent the peasantry at the end of the nineteenth century. Rather, many active farmers took part in the chal-lenges to agricultural policy. Traditional syndicalism was hard hit by the crisis. The Société des agriculteurs de France was renamed the Union nationale des syndicats agricoles in 1934, moving its headquarters from the rue d'Athènes to the rue des Pyramides, meeting-place of the Association générale des producteurs de blé. A further sign of the times was that there were now fewer landlords and more large cereal producers in its ranks. In 1937, it claimed to represent 1,200,000 peasant families. The Federation on the Bd Saint-Germain had, at the same date, about 1 million members.

Some syndical leaders sought ideological support in the doctrine of corporatism.[41] This was not simply a throwback to the old agrarian ideologies of the beginning of the century. Undoubtedly, a central aim was to further the social and economic interests of the peasantry. But it went well beyond that, weaving three threads of opposition: firstly, towards the policies of the state, which, it was argued, served urban interests. Incompetent politicians, serving monied interests had consistently failed to recognise the importance of the farming population. The second enemy was an economic liberalism which exploited peasant labour for the benefit of capitalism and the urban workforce. The third enemy was Marxism, which sought to collectivise society. To face such enemies, a unitary agricultural organisation was envisaged, the Corporation agricole, which would be endowed with some of the powers and authority of the state. Since the chaotic management of the crisis seemed to highlight how the peasantry had suffered from the incompetence of parliamentarians, the Corporation seemed to offer a sought-after order and stability. Louis Salleron, author of *Un Régime corporatif pour l'agriculture* (1937), was the leading theoretician of the movement. Professional organisations, seizing the occasion to try to increase their influence, were quick to place the corporatist idea at the heart of their programmes. The leaders of the Bd Saint-Germain, hostile at first, eventually approved in principle the idea of a corporatist organisation.

The crisis favoured in particular agrarian movements which placed action above ideological debate. Two especially had a success well beyond their regions of origin. The Parti agraire et paysan français, was founded in the Auvergne in 1927 by an ex-schoolteacher, Gabriel Fleurant, known as Fleurant-Agricole. The crisis brought him an abundant and enthusiastic audience. His aim was to unite all peasants because, as he put it: 'what do wheat, milk, wine, animals and the plough care for political opinions'.[42] There were, however, only eight deputies elected for the party in the legislative elections of 1936. The economic difficulties provided more propitious ground for a number of Comités de défense paysanne, founded in 1928 by a journalist Henri d'Halluin, who called himself Dorgères.[43] Initially based in Brittany, his committees soon spread to the Paris Basin and the north by the early 1930s. Dorgères, undoubtedly a talented demagogue, channelled discontent over the particular issues of taxes and social-security payments. The methods of direct action he used – violent demonstrations, commando operations to disrupt forced sales – gave militant peasants the impression that they were part of a powerful body capable of exerting real influence over events. The character of *dorgèrisme* is debatable. For Pierre Barral, it represented a kind of 'Pre-Poujadism' mobilising a frustrated small peasantry fearful of a crisis which threatened to proletarianise them. Despite the green shirts its members wore, and the paramilitary organisation and paraphernalia, they were simply loud and noisy conservatives. Pascal Ory, however, has shown that the movement evolved along fascist lines with its exaltation of virility and direct action.

Political parties were quick to appreciate the mobilisation of the peasantry. The right largely controlled the agrarian movement. The Dorgères committees received subsidies from the Worms Bank and large Parisian stores. To increase the political weight of peasant protest, the agrarian organisations united in a Front paysan in 1934. Regrouping the Union nationale des syndicats agricoles, the various producer organisations, the Parti agraire of Fleurant-Agricole and the Dorgères committees, it sought to oppose the electoral initiatives of the Popular Front. Its collapse after 1936 was largely the result of personal quarrels between its leaders.

The forces of the left had relatively little influence.[44] The syndicats des travailleurs de la terre, linked to the PCF, who had created the Confédération générale des paysans travailleurs in 1929, made little progress. Socialist groups helped to animate a number of local syndicates grouped from 1933 into the Confédération nationale paysanne. One of the most active departmental groups was that of Finistère, led by a local farmer, Pierre Tanguy-Prigent. Attempts to unite the syndicates of the left largely floundered. Nevertheless, it is worth noting that peasant membership of syndicates of the right did not necessarily preclude voting for the Popular Front. This dualism in attitudes was clear in the election of 1936. On the national scale, the stability of the peasant vote is striking. Nevertheless, the socialists made progress in the northern part of the Massif Central, the Aquitaine and the lower Rhône valley. The communists did well in the rural cantons of Corrèze, Haute-Vienne and Lot-et-Garonne. The main trend was a shift of the radical vote leftwards. There were few new voters on the left except in some cereal-farming cantons of the Paris Basin, which had been hard hit by the wheat crisis.

The manifesto of the Popular Front had included a proposal to create a government office to reorganise the wheat market. The instigator of the project, George Monnet, became Minister of Agriculture. He swiftly enacted legislation to create the Office national interprofessionel du blé (ONIB), which was responsible for all wheat imports and charged with controlling the internal wheat market.[45] It was able to fix wheat prices and control supplies to the market by creating a network of cooperatives to which wheat had to be delivered. Thanks to its actions, wheat prices recovered and a quintal of wheat sold at 180 francs in 1937 and 204 francs in 1938. The dominance of the old-established wheat merchants was broken. The cooperative movement, supported by the government, progressed rapidly. In 1939, 1,100 cooperatives collected 85 per cent of the wheat harvest which was paid for from Crédit agricole loans. The rise in cereal prices undoubtedly helped the recovery of farm incomes. Still, according to the work of Dessirier, the purchasing power of the peasant stagnated at around 80 per cent of its 1929 figure. This was certainly a better figure than at the worst phase of the crisis, but the peasantry still regarded a return to the 1913 level as unacceptable.

The other projects of George Monnet were less successful in their passage through the Chambers, primarily because of Senate opposition. The restructuring of commercial circuits for other products was never carried out. An insurance bank to deal with agricultural disasters was likewise frustrated. At the same time, a flood of social-welfare legislation seemed to many peasants to have little relevance to their lives. Dorgères argued that government policy was oriented primarily to the towns. Thus, farmers gained no family allowances until July 1939 and the extension of paid holidays to salaried farm workers, coupled with strike action in 1937, provoked the exasperation of many farmers. As a result, many were to lend passive or active support to the Vichy regime.

3. The tables are turned

In September 1940, the events of 1914 seemed to repeat themselves. The general mobilisation removed about one-quarter of the active agricultural population from their work. But the atmosphere in which these events took place was very different from that of 1914. Because the authorities anticipated a long war, many workers in specialised industries received exemptions. In the department of Loire, agents of the Information Office revealed that many peasants hurled abuse at urbanites walking in the country, fishing or collecting mushrooms, for having too easy a time of it.[46] The respite afforded by the phoney war meant that many farm workers received leave to complete the work of the autumn and spring agricultural calendars. The earlier hostility of the peasantry, which regarded itself as discriminated against in relation to urban dwellers, quickly dissipated. A few months later, the position was almost totally reversed as the Vichy regime glorified and exalted the peasantry, and economic circumstances placed it in a privileged position.

The peasantry, cornerstone of the Vichy regime

The agrarian theme was a constant motif in the Vichy government. The central imagery of the national revolution made Pétain, the 'Peasant-Marshall', proud of his country roots. In his speeches, which he liberally adorned with rustic metaphors, he drew on more simplistic agrarian themes. His pronouncement of 25 June 1940 typified his message: 'Our land doesn't lie. She demands your succour. She is the very heart of the nation.' Emmanuel Berl claimed responsibility for those famous words.

But it was the personality of the old marshall which gave it its real force. To him, the peasantry seemed to represent both a means of social organisation which allowed for the cultivation of the land, and a repository of moral and spiritual values at one with love of the nation. Exaltation of these values represented in many ways a sense of disdain and disgust for past policies which, by their identification with urbanism, were seen as ultimately responsible for the French defeat. The glorification of agriculture was also a reflection of the economic options that were imposed by Germany. These were formulated clearly in the project of constitutional revision: 'integrated in the new continental system of production and exchange, France will become once more a predominantly agricultural and peasant nation, and will reap the benefits from this return'.[47]

Agrarian themes dominated the press, with countless articles on such matters. The Ministers of Agriculture, Pierre Caziot and then Jacques Le Roy Ladurie, fervent agrarians, emphasised the rights and responsibilities of the peasant. A powerful regionalist literature was readily printed despite shortages of paper, and served to popularise peasantist themes. Henri Pourrat, whose eulogies of the Auvergne had already been exemplified and praised in *Gaspard des Montagnes*, obtained the Goncourt Prize in 1941 for *Vent de mars*. A flourishing popular literature was published in many catholic journals, popular in the countryside, as well as in almanacs and cheaply produced novels; much of it sought to persuade peasants of the essentially noble character of the work they did. Cinema, too, extolled the central themes of the national revolution.[48] Marcel Pagnol's *La Fille du puisatier* (1940) expressed the core of Vichy ideology: the return to the village home of children scarred by life in the corrupt town and their deepening attachment to the land.

The Corporation paysanne sought to create the necessary institutions designed to foster peasant unity and further peasant interests.[49] The Corporation was created by law on 2 December 1940, less than six months after the new regime took power. The new political situation should have meant that many pre-war agrarian projects would be swiftly put into operation, particularly since most of those in power were agrarians, such as Pierre Caziot, the Minister of Agriculture. But the legislation was vague. A commission established in January 1941 under Count Hervé Budes de Guébriant and consisting largely of the landed conservative elite, took nearly two years to draw up more precise legislative texts. The law of 16 December 1942 established a pyramid of groups with, at the base, a single unitary corporative syndicate, with a single leader and encompassing all social categories, from farmer to worker. It was endowed with the power to control many aspects of agricultural work in the commune. Membership was based on the whole family. It was, in theory at least, voluntary, but, because membership was required in order to receive family allowances, it was to all intents and purposes compulsory. At the departmental level, regional unions were established whose delegates sat on the national organising commission. Mutual-insurance groups, cooperatives and credit groups were under the authority of the syndicate. The Corporation was thus organised on a geographical basis – very different from those organisations which developed in Germany or Italy.

The objectives of pre-war corporatists were never fully realised in the Peasant Corporation. Their wish to see all agricultural organisations beneath the umbrella of a decentralised syndical structure at least, seemed to have been achieved. Hence, many peasants welcomed the Corporation because it seemed to represent some half a century of syndical aspirations. If many of the regional and national posts were in the hands of the old landed elite, those right-wing agrarian corporatists who now recovered much of their previous influence, the election of some 30,000 local syndical leaders meant that peasants did emerge into the ranks of the syndicate hierarchy. But the limitations imposed on the power of the Corporation ultimately reduced its overall importance.

While many corporatists sought a reduction in state power, the Minister of Agriculture was all-powerful in the Corporation, which, in any case, had no financial autonomy. The worsening of the political and economic situation in 1943 led it still further into the hands of the administration. The Corporation was given the task of organising the food-supply system and because local syndicates had to fix the level of individual requisitions, they inevitably either courted unpopularity or falsified statistics. Ultimately, many peasants came to view the Corporation as just one more cog in the administrative machine. Three-quarters of all salaried workers failed to join, seeing the Corporation as simply a farmers' association. For many members, the syndicate was simply a channel for obtaining fertilisers. They paid their subscriptions without great enthusiasm.

Beyond the Corporation, few other projects successfully saw the light of day. The law of 30 May 1941 instituted a series of grants for those wishing to return to farming. Its impact was slight. In four years only 1,516 candidates applied to take up vacant farms and of them only 600 lasted the course. Agricultural work was regarded as both hard and degrading by town-dwellers who were offered derisory sums to take up the profession. The failure of this policy serves to highlight the anachronism of policies designed to encourage a return to the land which had dominated since the crisis of the 1930s. Efforts to make agriculture and country life more attractive and to slow down the exodus required massive structural changes that simply could not be pursued in the particular circumstances of the time. What measures were taken were largely haphazard.

Legislation passed on 21 November 1940 and 17 April 1941 anticipated financial support for improvements to rural housing with grants of 25 per cent of the cost of improvements. More than 100,000 owners benefited from the aid. But, in the Forez, most demands for help came from non-residents.[50] Family-welfare legislation was aimed at ensuring the maintenance of the peasant family. Laws passed between July 1940 and January 1943 extended measures already adopted in 1938. The farm was henceforth considered not simply as a legal but also an economic unit that was to be kept intact if possible. Government also sought to reinforce the peasantry through the reorganisation of agricultural education and the development of rural apprenticeship schools, in which youngsters aged from fourteen to seventeen followed agricultural courses. Such meagre legislative efforts paled by comparison with the official rhetoric emanating from the government. In the event, it could do little other than concentrate on the immediate problems of food supply.

Agriculture in disarray

During the period of the 'phoney war', stocks accumulated during the crisis years helped to maintain food supplies in the country. Within a few weeks, however, the German victory had thrown the commercial circuits into disarray. The problem of food supply was exceptionally grave.[51] The division of France imposed by the Germans made food exchanges between the two territories impossible. The occupied zone, some 55 per cent of the national territory, had produced 62 per cent of the cereal and 70 per cent of the potato crop in the pre-war period. It produced little wine, however, and was separated from the unoccupied zone by a border that merchandise could cross only with difficulty. The occupied zone itself was further fragmented since Alsace-Lorraine was now distinct and the departments of the Nord and Pas-de-Calais were attached to German-controlled Belgium. Any excess produce from there went to other countries. In the Ardennes, where returning refugees were turned away, 170,000 hectares were farmed under German administration and the produce sent to Germany. In the southern zone, prefects strictly limited the movement of any produce outside departmental boundaries. In 1940, the free market in agricultural products vanished.

Production conditions also deteriorated rapidly. Manpower was less abundant: 500,000 of the farming population were imprisoned. Official volunteer groups from the *chantiers de jeunesse* or unemployed industrial workers were not always very efficient. The requisition of horses and shortages of petrol after 1941 deprived many farms of motive power. Fertiliser supplies were halved. Viticulturalists were unable to treat their vines, as shortages of lead arsenic prevented treatment against some diseases. Because sisal was no longer imported, harvesting machines had to use paper string which was not efficient and led to harvesting losses. Cumulatively, such shortages led to a drop in production. It is hard to gain precise estimates since, under the circumstances, many peasants misled the authorities, either out of a sense of patriotism or simple conservatism. From official estimates, the cultivated area fell by more than 2 million hectares between 1939 and 1943. In the department of Loire, prefectoral statistics showed a marked fall, but Monique Luirard has argued that many peasants made prodigious efforts to cultivate all the land they could.[52] Wheat production fell by 18 per cent to 20 per cent by comparison with pre-war. For milk and potatoes, the figures were 30 per cent and 40 per cent respectively. But, if estimates of wheat production were fairly easy for the authorities to make, the same did not apply to the whole array of horticultural and vegetable products.

At the same time, overseas trade was badly disrupted. Imports were reduced and, after 1942, virtually ceased. France found itself deprived of some 15 per cent of its food supply. For fats, the deficit reached 60 per cent. Whilst in 1914–18 the country could rely on food imports, consumers now had to depend on a declining national food-basket from which the Germans had already extracted their quota. Such quotas had been agreed at the armistice, but the actual quotas were well in excess of those required to feed the occupying forces. From 1941, German demands increased markedly, primarily because the supply of cereals from occupied Eastern Europe fell short of expectations. The Germans also secured supplies on the open market, a move facilitated by an especially favourable rate of currency exchange. Overall, the Germans appropriated between 10 per cent and 15 per cent of total production.[53] The internal market for food was therefore reduced by between 35 per cent and 40 per cent, an unprecedented collapse which put food producers in an especially commanding position.

Unscrupulous profiteers?

From the summer of 1940, the problem of finding enough to eat became an obsession with the French populace. Shortages were so acute that the authorities found themselves incapable of regularising the market in foodstuffs. The statistics they had available did not give realistic estimates of either production or consumption, particularly because the exodus from the occupied zone had led to considerable flows of people to the southern parts of the country. Nevertheless, from

September 1940, a system of organising food supplies was put in place. The haste with which it was developed meant, however, that it lacked cohesion. National offices of production, one for each area of specialisation, allocated production quotas on a departmental basis. Departmental committees in turn reallocated the quota, commune by commune. From 1942, Corporation leaders at local level were responsible for fixing the the level of individual quotas. Once the harvest had been gathered, deliveries were paid for at an official rate which was often very low. At some points in the chain, the division of production was left to the professions concerned. Thus, for meat, wholesalers were held responsible for putting controls into practice and had, therefore, considerable powers with which to influence producers.[54]

The system, far too complex, was basically inefficient. It depended on individual declarations of production by farmers – all too often the mayors or local Corporation leaders turned a blind eye to any falsifications. Many fought off the quota demands through sheer inertia and uncooperativeness. They sought to deliver as little as possible to the official market because prices, which took no account of burgeoning demand, were too low. As a result, the official rations for consumers were insufficient. An adult living in a large town could count on only 1,200 calories per day at the end of 1942 and less than 1,000 in 1944. Survival depended on searching out other outlets. Under such conditions, the temptations for profiteering were considerable.

The administration could not prevent the development of a parallel market to the official one and, powerless to prevent it, had to tolerate and accept it. Its growth was a social and economic response to the collapse of the national market; the growth of a black market was inevitable. Thus, for example, the fact that family parcels were permitted meant that those city-dwellers with rural roots benefited from regular supplies of foodstuffs. According to Henri Amouroux, 300,000 Parisians benefited from such parcels every day.[55] As the personal transportation of parcels up to 10 kilograms was permitted, many citizens spent their leisure hours 'touring' from one farm to another on their bicycles.[56] The railway served to widen their zone of movement. The station of Toury, in the Beauce, received 12,000 travellers a month in 1943 as against only 700 before the war.[57] Farmers were sometimes paid in kind: a ham for some cloth, or cheese in exchange for cigarettes. Prices charged depended on the degree of sympathy between the parties to the exchange. When they were double the official rate, it was the grey market. On the black market, official prices were multiplied by five. For certain products the place of such alternative commercial circuits was considerable. The departmental food-supply office of Cantal estimated in January 1943 that only 40 per cent of all butter produced was being delivered to the market. One-quarter was consumed by the household and the remainder went to parents, friends or the black market.[58]

Town-dwellers, forced to change into obsequious scroungers in order to survive, seethed with anger rather than gratitude towards the peasants whose lives appeared bathed in plenty in comparison with urban deprivations. Since purchases on the market were difficult, farmers turned increasingly to feeding themselves. Self-sufficiency doubled between 1940 and 1944. Careful husbandry of food increased. Ephraim Grenadou noted without shame that : 'We ate half as much again as before the war.'[59] He profited from the circumstances and from the proximity of the capital to alter his systems of production to cope with changed demand. Large quantities of carrots were produced; pigs were slaughtered secretly, with choice pieces for a compliant local police force. For many peasants, the boot was now on the other foot. By no means unhappy at being the object of so much solicitude, they lived from day to day, drawing as much advantage as they could from the situation, not knowing how long it might last. Opinion in the towns was that such behaviour typified the egotism of the peasants, unscrupulous in their desire to profit from the misery of others through their accumulation of massive profits.

Did the peasants enrich themselves as much as urban opinions would have us believe? It is impossible to judge since we have no way of knowing how much produce was actually traded clandestinely. Michel Cépède estimates that the figure was about 20 per cent for potatoes and farmyard products.[60] Fraud was more difficult for cereal producers, whose harvests were scrupulously counted. It is also important to bear in mind that gains from trading on the official market were small because of the low prices. For want of anything better, we can use other indicators. The banks of the Crédit agricole recorded a marked increase in deposits, especially in the poorer upland zones.[61] But the trend could equally be explained by the reduction in farm expenses because of the lack of investment opportunities, or by a better awareness of the Crédit agricole. Enrichment on the black market was not necessarily the prime cause. If profiteering did take place, it served to reinforce the tendency to save at a time when there were few spending options available and when savings were increasingly vulnerable to inflation.

Another criticism directed at the peasantry was its unconditional support for the Vichy regime. There were few peasants amongst the ranks of the resistance. The communists published *La Terre* and created the Comités de défense et d'action paysanne in 1943. It would appear that militancy in the resistance was largely occupationally defined. Workers and employers enrolled in much greater numbers than farmers.[62] Studies made of recruitment amongst the *maquis* seems to show the same peasant reticence. In the Hautes-Alpes and Isère, only one-third of those agricultural workers who refused compulsory labour service found their way into the resistance.[63] In some areas relations between the resistance and the local farming population were strained by the weight of resistance requisitions, which some peasants regarded as a form of robbery. Deportation statistics tell a somewhat more complex story. In the department of Finistère there were only 44 peasants amongst the 597 deportees. But in the Creuse – admittedly a predominantly agricultural department – there were 47 out of 158.[64] But the real diversity of peasant behaviour can only be grasped through further local studies.

4. The illusions of the post-war years

In autumn 1944, most leaders were of the opinion that a clean break with the agrarian policies of the past was necessary and that a radical modernisation of agriculture had to be undertaken. But the hasty creation of new professional organisations and a series of episodic structural reforms were insufficient to produce the anticipated changes. The continuation of the black market consolidated the view that the peasantry was hardly in need of financial aid. When the period of high prices ended in 1948, the mentality of the peasantry rapidly shifted from euphoria to uncertainty.

The creation of new professional organisations

On 13 October 1944, the provisional government disbanded the Corporation paysanne. Even if many subscriptions had been unpaid since the start of the year, there is little doubt that most local and regional organisations were at least functioning. The new Minister of Agriculture, the socialist François Tanguy-Prigent, the first authentic peasant to fill this post, had made a series of sharp attacks on the Corporation through his clandestine journal *la Résistance paysanne*. Nevertheless, in creating the Confédération générale de l'agriculture (CGA), he maintained the principle of a single syndical body which had underpinned both the Corporation and the aspirations of many pre-war syndicalists.[65] But the CGA excluded the non-peasant rural elite. Peasant unity was deemed to stem not from the old myth of a unity founded on ties to the land, but rather on the active participation in the same profession around which a series of social and economic interests converged. To break with the old syndicate/shops of pre-1940, the activities of syndicates and cooperatives were sharply separated. The mutuals, credit groups and cooperatives each had an autonomous place in the CGA with their own representatives. The Fédération nationale des syndicats d'exploitants agricoles (FNSEA) was regarded as simply one of several branches in the CGA. If it was the largest branch, it did not have a monopoly of control within the CGA, which was the primary means of negotiation with the Ministry. The socialists, traditionally powerful in the mutualist and cooperative groups, hoped this system would serve to counterbalance the conservatism of syndical representatives.

The founding congress of the CGA in March 1945 witnessed the apparent triumph of the 'democratic and humane control of the profession' that François Tanguy-Prigent had advocated. Nevertheless, one-third of the presidents of local syndicates were ex-syndics of the Corporation. The elections held in the winter of 1945–6 for posts of responsibility in the FNSEA brought little comfort to the team in charge of the CGA. The old Corporation activists triumphed in most regions, except the centre and south-east. René Blondelle, a large farmer from Aisne and an ex-member of the Conseil corporatif national, was elected to the post of secretary-general of the FNSEA. How, then, can one account for the return to power of so many ex-corporatists? Primarily because in so many communes only they had sufficient skill and standing to take up posts. Many had shown their fitness for office in the preceding period by functioning in a technocratic rather than a political fashion. By contrast, many regarded the Parisian team in charge of the CGA as too left wing. In the department of Rhône, 80 per cent of local post-holders and all the cantonal leaders of the Corporation were elected to positions of municipal or syndical responsibility after the war.[66] The clash between the national leadership of the CGA and the FNSEA, the inheritors of the pre-war syndical tradition, appeared inevitable.

In the event, the power struggle lasted eight hard-fought years. From 1947 onwards, the FNSEA demanded independence from the CGA, arguing that it, and it alone, represented the views of all peasants. The CGA lost much ministerial support when Pierre Pflimlin became Minister of Agriculture in November 1947. The CGA could no longer benefit from its monopoly of representation with government. In 1948, the directors of the FNSEA supported the revival of the Chambers of Agriculture. These elected, public bodies had an official function of con-sultation with the government and had considerable financial resources.[67] In many departments they supported the actions of the FNSEA. The victory of the FNSEA was assured in 1950. The CGA, whose statutes were modified, had no more than a symbolic existence before disappearing in 1953. The old traditions had won the day.

The kitchen boiler and the tractor

In the autumn of 1944, public opinion held that the end of rationing was in sight since the Liberation had freed the country from German requisitions. Nothing could have been further from the truth. Bread ration cards, hastily abandoned in October 1944, had to be reintroduced in January 1946. They were retained until February 1949. Numerous obstacles stood in the way of increased production. Soil exhaustion due to the chronic lack of fertilisers, coupled with unfavourable weather conditions, explained the succession of poor harvests between 1945 and 1947. Recourse to massive imports was hampered by the destruction of the transport infrastructure and the lack of foreign currency. As a result, agricultural prices increased even more rapidly than during the war. A quintal of wheat sold for 576 francs in 1945, 1,900 francs in 1948. The price of milk increased fourfold. Despite the admonitions of agriculture ministers, the black market continued to flourish. It was even more profitable than during the occupation, since the taxing of requisitioned goods diminished still further profit margins. Peasant enrichment took on the appearance of a veritable truth amongst town-dwellers, who propagated the myth of kitchen boilers in countless peasant homes being stashed full of money. The authorities were certainly of the opinion that peasant savings were considerable, an opinion which helps, in part, to explain the characteristics of post-war agricultural policy.

Because agriculture was at the root of inflation, it seemed essential to undertake a rapid increase in farm production. In keeping with the inspiration of Jean Jaurès, François Tanguy-Prigent did not envisage a profound structural change in the countryside. The law of 13 April 1946 which modified the status of both farmers and sharecroppers repeated much from an earlier text of 1942, reinforcing the position of the farmer at the expense of the landowner. The farmer now had the right of first bid for a farm should the landlord wish to sell it, and could also expect an indemnity at the end of contract if he had helped improve the farm. He also benefited from the right to unlimited extension of the lease both for himself and his inheritors. On the other hand, the owner could take over the farm if he wished to cultivate it himself. The disappearance of sharecropping, regarded as a socially backward form of farming, was encouraged by the legislation. Henceforth, the division of the product was to be two-thirds to the sharecropper instead of the more usual one-half. The sharecropper could, if he so wished, change his status to that of farmer. The 1946 legislation gave, above all, greater security to the farmer, who could embark on farm modernisation with an easier mind.

The agricultural policies of the post-war period can be described as productivist: production increases were essential if shortages were to be overcome and exports developed. Such policies represented the consensus opinion with, for example, the support of both Marcel Braibant, a right-wing agrarian and René Dumont, an agricultural adviser with the ear of the Ministry of Agriculture.[68] Machinery was considered the means *par excellence* to increase the unit productivity of agriculture and the tractor became the symbol of farm modernisation. The tractor, too, would help to integrate agriculture into the economic system. This change of direction was fundamental. The first version of the Monnet plan, drawn up in 1946, emphasised the importance of mechanising agriculture and the manufacture of farm machinery was made an industrial priority. The plan anticipated 200,000 tractors by 1950. Because the authors of the report largely shared a belief in the prevailing myth of peasant boilers piled high with money, it was thought that two-thirds of the finance for this immense programme of mechanisation should come from the peasants themselves. It was for this reason that, in terms of government financing, agriculture was not regarded as a priority sector. The only real novelty was a scheme for loans to young farmers introduced on 24 May 1946.[69] Loans were granted for fifteen years at a special interest rate of 2 per cent – a very low figure considering the rate of inflation. The Marshall plan further accentuated the productivist tendencies of agricultural strategy. Agriculture was regarded as a priority sector in the new plan, which replaced the Monnet plan in 1948. Thirty-year loans at 3 per cent interest were established to help finance modernisation and equipment purchases.

Farmers, it would seem, responded well to the production demands of the authorities. The number of tractors rose from 35,000 in 1938 to 98,000 in 1948. However, because of the paucity of supplies, many farmers were required to obtain a quota from the Génie rural in order to buy one. Because coopératives d'utilisation du matériel agricole (CUMA) were given priority, they multiplied throughout the country.[70] This new fashion for mechanisation can be explained, in part at least, by the desire to dispose of savings quickly at a time of rapid inflation. Peasants were much more conscious of the rapid erosion of their capital than they had been in 1919–20. It is also important to emphasise the social prestige attached to owning a machine. Driving a tractor seemed much more prestigious than walking beside a plough team. It is worth noting, too, that the use of fertilisers, by comparison, remained low in this period.

Nevertheless, the figure of 200,000 tractors by 1950 anticipated by the plan was not reached. Variations in the supply of domestic farm machinery and the unsuitability of much imported material partly account for this. Above all, after 1948, as food shortages tailed off, the years of high prices and easy profits came to an end. Simultaneously, the property market became more active.[71] Farm sales, which had been very sluggish since 1940, as people clung on to land as a refuge and, for urban-dwellers, a possible source of food, took off again in 1948. In the department of Loire, peasant ownership increased. The purchase of land, always a high priority for the peasant, became both possible and attractive, since inflation made savings in liquid assets less attractive.

Overall, the post-war transformations were fairly limited. When, in 1948–9, René Dumont travelled through the countryside to examine how much progress had taken place, he painted a picture of technical backwardness even if, here and there, he found signs of progress.[72] In the Limagne, thanks to mechanisation, three men could farm 35 to 50 hectares whereas, in 1932, two men were needed for a farm of only 12 hectares. Still, in 1950, most peasants remained disquieted at the gap which seemed to separate them from the national economy and society. For many, the temptation to turn in on themselves was too great.

The inheritance of the past

At the start of the 1950s, the peasantry, still one-third of the active population of France, seemed to live in an introverted way, relying on increasingly archaic materials which hardly seemed to have changed for half a century. But, despite appearances, the first studies in rural sociology portrayed the countryside as highly unstable. Two monographs on village life in southern France are particularly valuable. Henri Mendras described the village where he was born, Novis in Aveyron, whilst Laurence Wylie, after a long period of residence in the village, wrote about a Roussillon commune he called Peyranne to conceal its true identity.[73]

The structures of material life appeared timeless. Patterns of ownership were long established. Except in areas affected by the two world wars, the only new buildings erected tended to be farm buildings. Inside the home, there were some signs of change. Except in the poorest areas, extra rooms had been created. But as they were not heated they were used only for sleeping. Heating was reserved for the main living-room, where a wood or charcoal stove served for cooking as well. A beaten-earth floor was now increasingly covered by tiles or floorboards. The odd bits and pieces of furniture were usually factory-made. Amongst the better-off farmers, a rarely used front room with a collection of family photographs and the better items of furniture would exist. But the home could hardly be described as comfortable. In 1946, fewer than 20 per cent of rural homes had running water and only 4 per cent were connected to the mains sewage system. Two-thirds of farms in Savoie had no proper toilets.[74] Hygiene standards undoubtedly suffered. At both Novis and Peyranne, children's hands and faces were washed daily only because of the demands of the village teacher. To most peasants a weekly wash continued as the norm. If 83 per cent of households were connected to the electricity grid, in most it was used simply for lighting. A dim 25-watt bulb suspended in the middle of the room was regarded as sufficient.

At Novis, the diet was monotonous, based as it was on what the farm produced. Bread and soup were the basis of most peasant meals. Still, in some families, this diet was supplemented by purchases from the grocer which introduced a little more variety.[75] The introduction of travelling stores helped to facilitate such buying. Wartime shortages had helped to show how difficult it was to do without such 'extras'.

Techniques of preserving fruit and vegetables and making jam spread rapidly in the countryside and helped to vary the winter diet. Wine consumption increased in most areas. At Novis, Henri Mendras detected a recent increase in alcoholism. As far as dress was concerned, urban models were widespread, except for the elderly women of the community. Leather shoes, suits and overcoats were an accepted part of the men's Sunday dress. Young women quickly adopted the latest urban fashions. Peasants could no longer avoid the market economy.

Patterns of social interaction also took on a more modern form except in the most isolated areas. In imitating urban models, dances and the like triumphed over more traditional festive celebrations. Travelling fairs and cycle races replaced more local traditions. They became festivals held at the village, rather than village festivals. Sometimes, the JAC would organise specifically agricultural gatherings. But, in the immediate postwar period, these tended to celebrate the triumphs of the new technological age rather than a respect for the past. Overall, religious fervour became less ostentatious, even in areas still strongly religious. Increasingly, social life became atomised. In many places, the only time when the whole community celebrated together was at harvest festivals. At Novis, communal activity no longer existed. Friendship was rarely manifested externally. Laurence Wylie came to similar conclusions at Peyranne: children of neighbouring families were rarely allowed to play together except in the school playground. Families increasingly turned in on themselves.

The loss of cohesion within peasant society was linked to the rural exodus which restarted with a vengeance in the post-war period. At Novis, in 1948, all the young people without exception wanted to leave. Their aims were for a less difficult life with the possibilities of greater enjoyment and leisure facilities. The full insertion of the countryside into national life meant that the town no longer represented an unknown quantity. In areas close to towns commuting began to develop. Many families had at least one of their number based in town whom they could visit and stay with. They served as a kind of halfway house.[76] Bus services, sometimes aided by grants from the Conseil général, developed in the 1930s. They opened up many areas that were not linked to the local rail network. A surprising number of peasants had access to cars. In 1953, 29 per cent of farmers had a car, against only 8 per cent of workers. Their access to cars was about the same as middle-grade office workers. Undoubtedly, possession of and use of a car are not the same thing. Still, the idea of long journeys became much more common. At Novis, youngsters went on honeymoon, often to Paris. The Lourdes pilgrimage became a kind of social norm, accepted and respected by peasant families. In many regions contacts with the towns increased. Life there seemed a little easier, the work of an employee in factory or town less demanding. It was an important illusion of the post-war years.

The attraction of the towns reflected in some ways a loss of confidence by many peasants in the land, a land which no longer seemed capable of securing their future. Added to this was a sense of inferiority *vis-à-vis* town-dwellers, whom, at the same time, they despised. Low levels of educational attainment accentuated such sentiments. In 1954, more than one-third of young peasants left school without their certificates of primary education. The productivist atmosphere of post-war agricultural strategy increased the sense of disarray among a peasantry to whom the extent of change was both dramatic and rapid.

Between 1914 and the early 1950s, the peasantry seemed to turn in on itself. It formed a kind of separate world which was ageing and which appeared to resent the impress of the subsistence economy forced upon it by the crisis of the 1930s and the war. As village sociability declined, so the role and place of the family grew. The tensions between town and country grew steadily after the First World War. By the end of the 1940s, consciousness of the need for rapid agricultural change was brutally clear. The transformation of production structures, up till then resisted on ideological grounds, could no longer be postponed. But both government and the syndical organisations continued to argue that farm modernisation could be achieved without throwing into question the very identity of the peasant.

5

A spectacular transformation: 1950 to the present

After 1950, the peasantry was confronted by a series of changes which deserve to be described as revolutionary. A sharp break with the slow pace of change of preceding periods was instituted. A rapid modernisation of agricultural techniques permitted huge increases in productivity. In order to keep in step with the pace of economic change, farmers had to become more fully integrated in the national economy, with, as a necessary corollary, rapid increases in total production as well as much greater recourse to borrowing. The social changes that accompanied this agricultural revolution were, for their part, no less spectacular. The peasant population, smaller in size and increasingly marginal in rural structures, had, through its command of complex techniques and methods, an important place in that society. Access to increased revenues led many peasants to adopt life styles and habits not dissimilar from those of the middle class. Increasingly, they seemed to have lost that identity which had been shaped by economic and cultural isolation. Had the 'end of the peasant', to use the controversial phrase of Henri Mendras, finally come about?[1]

1. Peasants and modernisation

At the beginning of the 1950s, most peasants planned their lives 'day by day'. But, within a few years, fundamental changes were brought about. These changes were the responsibility of the voluntary and progressive action of an activist minority at the very heart of the peasantry. Their modernising ethos quickly imposed itself and created the necessary psychological conditions for change. This modernisation led to a sharp increase in both production and productivity and, ultimately, to a chronic instability in the rural world and a deep-seated sense of unease amongst the peasantry.

The agents of change

JAC militants played a major part in this transformation of attitudes.[2] In the post-war years, the organisation continued to grow and, in

1955, could count some 440,000 members. Undoubtedly, it did not form a homogeneous block. In conservative areas, it tended to appear rather left wing, whilst in radical anti-clerical areas, it struck moderate positions. But, taken as a whole, the JAC embraced modernist themes. It borrowed from Emmanuel Mounier the guiding theme that economic and social structures had to be changed. Technical advances coupled with organisation would, it was argued, lead to the promotion of the peasant. 'The best form of charity is technical progress' was the guiding motto.[3] Popular training sessions helped to spread new methods of farming and gave many youngsters an aptitude for things mechanical. It gave them, too, the conviction that farm modernisation would eventually lead to improvements in the conditions under which they lived and worked. The JAC broadened the horizons of many of its members. Study and educational programmes took place outside the confines of the village and were not confined solely to agricultural matters. At them talks might equally range over economic, sociological and political matters. A central aim was to persuade youngsters that farming was a worthy and worthwhile pursuit. A greater openness to society was accompanied by the desire to create common bonds within the farming world that would help to secure its advancement. Such achievements could not be made in isolation. The organisation of dances, sometimes with the opposition of the local priest, was encouraged by Canon Fernand Boulard, because it meant that all young people could meet together.[4] As a result of these efforts, the JAC was able to ensure the emergence of a new generation of militants who would act as the agents of technical, social and moral change in the countryside.

It was soon realised that this action had to extend into syndical affairs. To achieve this many militants joined the Cercle national des jeunes agriculteurs (CNJA), part of the CGA which had largely been left moribund. Here they advanced modernist views: the state, they argued, should elaborate a policy on landownership which favoured the creation of an elite of young farmers capable of turning family farms into economic enterprises. In this, they opposed the FNSEA, where an ageing elite defended the traditional canons of syndical activity. In 1956, some 70 per cent of the members of the administrative council of the FNSEA were aged over fifty. The youngsters of the CNJA seemed to threaten that peasant unity which the FNSEA had defended with such force. This explains why, in 1956, the latter sought to absorb the CNJA with the creation of the Centre national des jeunes agriculteurs. But, instead of being quietly absorbed, its members began, bit by bit, to impose their particular views.

It would be too simplistic to put responsibility for the transformation of the rural world solely at the door of the JAC. One should not ignore many less disinterested forces fuelling the process of modernisation.[5] Representatives of industrial firms were important propagators of new techniques, especially in the use of fertilisers and animal feedstuffs.[6] Agricultural cooperatives, anxious to improve the quality of the goods they received, played a similar role. Rural shopkeepers and merchants also played their part. Their numbers had increased considerably in rural areas between 1945 and 1950. Economic circumstances, generally unfavourable to salaried workers, encouraged many to become shop-keepers. As the costs of installing a shop in town was high, many took their chance in often thinly populated villages. To make ends meet, they acted as grocers, stationers and chemists, and went to great lengths to persuade women to consume more. Thus, they provided bottled butane gas, thereby encouraging the spread of gas cookers which made meal preparation simpler. Garage owners, increasingly numerous in the countryside, addressed themselves to male purchasers. They served as agents for the sale of agricultural machinery, especially tractors, and looked after any repairs. In offering such temptations to peasants, they pushed them into an increasing involvement in the market.

The spread of 'urban civilisation' had similar effects. It was facilitated by the spread of the mass media into the countryside.[7] In the 1950s, the peasant read more and more regional daily newspapers. These, fewer in number than pre-war, tended to contain relatively little local news. They no longer reflected the old, dominant image of rural society. Radio also pushed the peasantry out of its isolation. In 1961, 77 per cent of farm households had a radio receiver. Peasants were even quicker to equip themselves with televisions. At the start of the 1960s, such was the cost of a television that most regarded purchasing one as virtually undreamt of. At Plodemet, Edgar Morin tells the story of some owners hiding the aerial in the attic. But the gap that had opened up with other social groups was quickly bridged. In 1973, 75 per cent of households owned a television. Television, radio and the press shared a common emphasis on urban models and fashions. At the same time, they proclaimed, albeit haphazardly, the basic elements of modernity.

The presence of more and more urban citizens in the countryside also changed rural society. Improvements in the standards of living of salaried workers in the 1950s led to an increase in the numbers of holidaymakers in the countryside. At first, they were regarded with dis-trust, because of their relaxed standards of behaviour. But they provided images of other, undoubtedly more agreeable, life styles. Rural shop-keepers were attentive to the needs of this new clientele. Improvement to the home, stimulated by the influx of tourism, was also an important factor in rural change. In some areas, speculative activity developed. Thus, in the Aigues district of central Provence, olive orchards in many areas, destroyed by the frosts of 1956, were not replanted, but divided into housing lots.[8] The influx of town-dwellers undoubtedly varied from region to region, depending on the proximity of large urban centres. But, all the same, few villages were left untouched.

Within ten years, the peasantry made a complete break with the old, self-sufficient, self-centred past. Of course, urban penetration was hardly a new phenomenon. But, henceforth, it largely submerged all aspects of rural life, which found itself bereft of any system of values with which to oppose it. Most peasants were convinced that modernisation represented the only way to bridge the gap between themselves and their fellow citizens.

The tractor revolution

The increase in the number of tractors was in many ways symbolic of farm modernisation after 1950. At that date, there were an estimated 140,000. By 1955, the number was 305,000: 13 per cent of all farms had one. In 1963, numbers were just below 1 million: more than one-half of all farms had tractors. The use of animals for motive power was disappearing. In the space of a decade agriculture had become mechanised. The use of tractors was accompanied by the development of complementary mechanisation, the need for which only became apparent rather late. A number of other innovations were introduced at the end of the 1950s. Maize cultivation was extended beyond the Aquitaine Basin thanks to the use of hybrid plants from the United States. The Institut national de la recherche agronomique (INRA) developed a new wheat variety, 'Etoile de Choisy', which greatly improved yields in departments south of the Loire. Improvements in grasses and the development of silage techniques ensured the continued development of pastoral farming.

The rapid and widespread adoption of mechanised farming was all the more remarkable, given the very slow pace of innovation which had previously existed. Why then, did farmers, previously so reluctant to adopt any kind of innovation, fall headlong into adopting mechanisation? The American sociologist Laurence Wylie, returning to Peyranne-Roussillon in 1959 after an eight-year absence, was struck by the changed mentality of the peasants.[9] Now, farm modernisation was seen as essential by a large number of peasants. It seemed the best means of remaining on the land and participating in a more abundant society at a time of general economic uncertainty. The purchase of a tractor became a symbol of the social progress that was at the heart of the aspirations of many

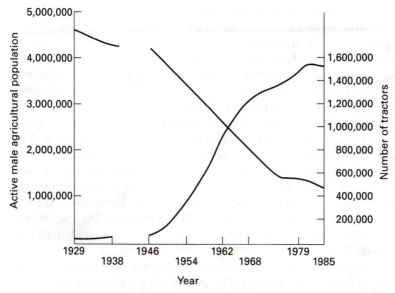

Figure 6 Mechanisation and agricultural employment levels. (*Source:* Jean-Paul Girard, Monique Gombert and Michel Petry, *Les Agriculteurs*, vol. I, Paris, INSEE, 1977; and *Annuaire statistique de la France*, Paris, INSEE, 1987.

young peasants. It could be a decisive step for parents who feared the departure of their children to the town. Technical reasons are also important in explaining the rapid development of mechanisation. American firms, whose domestic markets were saturated, keenly sought European outlets. They marketed 25 horse-power tractors which were well adapted to small family farms. The fact that diesel for agricultural purposes was exempt from tax was a further argument in favour of purchase that the marketing men did not hesitate to employ.

The seemingly unstoppable drive towards modernisation brought abut a change of attitude towards credit. Undoubtedly, the tractor 'brought many people to the doors of the Crédit agricole'.[10] To obtain credit, an account had to be opened; by 1959, two-thirds of farmers were members. The Crédit agricole became the peasant bank. Many farmers borrowed 'because everyone else did'. Pressures for social conformity imposed mechanisation even if its economic justification was lacking. On the upland areas of the Massif Central, small farmers with considerable areas of arable land, rapidly equipped themselves with machinery.[11] There can be little doubt that most of these tractors were under-utilised. But at least they served many other varied and useful functions. They allowed an intensification of agricultural systems as well as speeding the journey from home to field. Many became as much a piece of household equipment as an item of farm machinery.

Mechanisation and an increasing recourse to science brought about major changes to production systems. Whereas previously these had been based on manual work, they were now increasingly oriented around the tractor. It represented much greater motive power than could previously be obtained from animals. One man on his own could accomplish tasks that previously had to be carried out in a team. This feature transformed the whole nature of both agricultural work and, subsequently, of rural society as a whole. As a consequence, too, farmers were now much more reliant than in the past on commercial circuits and often found themselves with considerable debts. Those who failed to follow suit were castigated as backward. The French economy, wedded to the mystique of ever-spiralling production since the war, pulled agriculture along in its wake.

The strong increases in agricultural production were a direct consequence of farm modernisation. The rate of growth was more than 3 per cent per year, compared with less than 1.5 per cent in the inter-war period. Such rates were unprecedented in the history of the French countryside. Between 1950 and 1967, total production increased by more than two-thirds, whilst the agricultural area fell by 10 per cent and the active agricultural population dropped by one-third. Such results were reflected in the improvement in yields: wheat yields, for example, rose from 18 quintals per hectare in 1950 to 29 quintals per hectare in 1960. But the greater efficiency of production systems was best reflected in the spectacular gains in productivity. According to Paul Bairoch, these rose by an average of 6.8 per cent per year between 1950 and 1980, a rate higher than that of industry.[12]

In the space of a few years, French agriculture became both more fertile and productive. Such rapid changes inevitably had consequences for the peasantry. Up till then, the peasantry had remained within the rural world. The mechanisation of agriculture brought opportunities for choice.

The destabilisation of the peasantry

Two sorts of reaction to the modernisation of agricultural techniques could be detected amongst peasants. The increasing rural exodus resulted from essentially individual decisions, whilst those who wished to stay made clear their collective unease. The rising anger amongst peasants forced government to act.

The rural exodus accelerated rapidly after 1950. Whilst the rate of exodus exceeded by some considerable margin rates in the past, only a few authors expressed disquiet.[13] Novelists between 1950 and 1960 described villages overflowing with life and animation, whilst in fact many had already been transformed by the exodus.[14] For agricultural technicians, the fall in the agricultural population was a necessary accompaniment to its modernisation. Public opinion was made aware of the size of the phenomenon when the 1962 census results were compared with those of 1954. Farmers, as well as non-farming country-dwellers and agricultural workers, were leaving. Between these dates, the size of the active agricultural population fell from 3.5 to 2.6 million, a reduction of more than 3.5 per cent per year. Between 1955 and 1963, more than 400,000 farmers left agriculture. The link between mechanisation and the rural exodus was clear and unequivocal. But it is far from easy to determine the direction of the relationship. Was a tractor purchased to make up for the departure of a family member? Or did the purchase of a tractor create underemployment on the farm and hence encourage migration? The fall in production prices after the easy post-war years coincided with an increase in purchasing power for many salaried workers which may well explain many individual decisions.

The consequences of these departures varied regionally. In the Limousin, the southern Alps and Landes, where the exodus was already a well-established phenomenon, some villages were totally depopulated and abandoned. Male celibacy became a major problem. The thinly scattered population threatened the survival of many communes and led to communal regroupings after 1959 in order to use collective services more efficiently. From the start of the 1960s, between 2,000 and 4,000 rural schools closed each year. At the end of the 1950s, the church authorities were forced to leave many of the smallest parishes without a resident priest.[15] Even in the west, a region which had always been demographically buoyant, the agricultural population was ageing, and the succession of farms no longer certain. For those who decided to stay, it was necessary, depending on farm size, to either struggle to survive, or attempt to finance the costs of farm modernisation.[16] A massive recourse to credit had, as a corollary, the fear of bankruptcy. This fear was real because the fall in prices threatened repayments. From 1949, the supply of agricultural products largely exceeded demand. The prices of wine and animal products fell very sharply, whilst those of cereals, protected by ONIC, were less subject to fluctuation. State intervention appeared to many the only solution.

Faced with this situation, René Blondelle, president of the FNSEA, decided to play the politicians at their own game by supporting the election to the Assembly of representatives of the peasant world. For him, the action was not political but rather civic: there was no question of the FNSEA engaging in party-political activity.[17] The electorate sent twenty-seven 'peasant' deputies, members of the FNSEA, to the Palais-Bourbon in June 1951. Together with sympathetic senators, they formed the Amicale parlementaire agricole, which became a powerful pressure group with around 100 members. Paul Antier, president of the peasant party, became Minister of Agriculture; the aims of the FNSEA seemed to have been achieved. But the apparent gains were deceptive. The purchasing power of viticulturalists and pastoral farmers fell sharply in 1952. Because it looked as if there had been collusion between the government and syndical leaders, membership of the FNSEA tailed off sharply south of the Loire. Discontent also took a more violent form. The revolt against both the government and national syndical leaders broke out initially in the wine-producing zones of the Midi in July 1953. It soon spread to the Massif Central, Poitou and Charentes where many small pastoral farmers had been hard-hit by price falls. The Comité de Gueret was created on 22 September by the socialist Roland Viel, an old colleague of Tanguy-Prigent, and a number of delegates from dissident departmental syndical federations. In October, a series of road blocks was created with tractors playing their full part. They were the symbol of peasant indebtedness but, for many citizens, seemed to represent peasant wealth. Some road-users called them grasping and greedy and spat on them. The old antagonisms of the black-market days were far from over.

The sharp reaction of those who had been shunted aside in the race for economic growth forced the government to intervene. On 22 October the president of the Council, Joseph Laniel, sprang to the defence of the peasants in front of the Assembly: 'We have told them to produce as much as they can and they have done what we asked. It is grossly unfair to penalise them now for that very success.' A more careful regularisation of the agricultural markets coupled with a degree of price support seemed the inevitable consequence of the push for modernisation. The Société interprofessionnelle du bétail et des viandes (SIBEV) was created in December 1953. A few months later Interlait and the Société nationale interprofessionnelle de la pomme de terre were established. These three private limited companies were charged with buying and stocking excess agricultural stocks when prices were low. Intermediaries held half of the shares of the groups and were the chief beneficiaries. The measures taken at least avoided a catastrophic fall in prices, but could not provide any durable stability to the markets.

This political intervention was both costly and inefficient, but, at the smallest sign of a threat to their continued role, there was strong reaction. In 1954, for example, Pierre Mendès-France was obliged to cancel a decision to suppress certain rights given to farm distillers after massive protests, especially in western France where distilling brought considerable profit. A profound malaise remained within the peasantry, which helps to explain the peasant support for poujadist candidates in 1956, when independent peasants lost one-quarter of their seats. The leaders of the FNSEA, no longer closely associated with government, and supported by the militants of the CNJA, organised a series of mass demonstrations. In September 1957, they succeeded in getting agricultural prices indexed to farming costs. This marked the triumph of a farm-price strategy, which gave much greater advantages to the larger producers, regardless of the conditions under which farmers worked. Very quickly, however, the financial cost to the government of this strategy spiralled. The actions of the IV Republic thus helped to pave the way for the much more selective modernisation strategy that was developed under the Vth.[18]

2. The peasantry and state intervention

Within the space of three years, from 1959 to 1962, a radically new agricultural strategy had been elaborated. With the often-controversial cooperation of part of the peasantry, the state decided on a more active intervention in the evolution of agricultural structures.[19] Although these policies were the subject of great debate and dispute over the following decade, the measures adopted at the start of the 1960s were never profoundly reshaped. The close links established between the peasantry and the authorities explain to a large extent this status quo.

Elaborating a new agricultural strategy

At the start of the V Republic, many of the leaders of the FNSEA were at a loss as to their future path. They had supported De Gaulle's accession to power and had been encouraged by his often nostalgic comments about the peasantry which appeared little different from those of his predecessors. But the weakness of parliament meant that the peasant pressure group which had obtained the indexation of farm prices at the end of the IV Republic was without teeth. Then, at the end of 1958 the Rueff and Armand reports drew up a bleak picture of French agriculture. They argued that its backwardness put a serious brake on French economic growth and that agricultural prices tended to be inflationary. Price indexation was thus ended in February 1959. There then began a long period of violent demonstrations and opposition, in a political climate which was especially difficult for the government. The Gaullists, lacking any means of exercising influence on the peasantry, turned to the CNJA. It was given equal status with the FNSEA in terms of representation and was given generous government grants. Rather than supporting price policies which mainly favoured large farmers, the CNJA argued that the state should intervene to modify farm structures and release more land for younger farmers.

The Debré government sought to calm tempers by quickly proposing a special Orientation Law, largely inspired by the demands of the CNJA. It was voted in on 5 August 1960, despite lengthy discussions and opposition from the Senate. The text was replete with declarations of intent. It was necessary, it argued, to establish 'parity between farming and other sectors of the economy' and to make it competitive in Europe. Agricultural strategy should be aimed at providing the means for such a transformation. A central aim of the government was to create some sort of compromise between the conservatives and reformists within the FNSEA. The Fonds d'orientation et de régularisation des marchés agricoles (FORMA) was established with this in mind. In response to the requests of the CNJA, a number of sociétés d'aménagement foncier et d'établissement rural (SAFERs) were created to buy up land on the market in order to distribute it to those farmers seeking to increase their farm size. But, crucially, they were not given priority of purchase. The decrees to make these policies operational took some time to appear. On 25 January 1961, sickness benefits were extended to farmers, but covered only limited risks. The younger members of the CNJA felt themselves betrayed, while the 'old guard' of the FNSEA feared yet more new proposals from government. The Debré government, preoccupied by the Algerian crisis, was surprised at the harsh reaction to a problem it believed it had solved, or at the very least, successfully delayed.

Demonstrations recurred once more in the spring of 1961, with much more virulence than in 1959, especially in Brittany. On 4 June, during cantonal elections, the ballot boxes at Pont-l'Abbé were seized and burnt. At Morlaix, the sub-prefecture was occupied and barricades erected. Roads and railways were cut. The demonstrations spread to the Massif Central and the Midi in July. To try to defuse peasant anger, the Minister of Agriculture, Henry Rochereau, was replaced by Edgar Pisani. He did not hesitate to bypass Ministry red-tape and collaborate directly with the CNJA. His complementary Orientation Law was passed on 8 August 1962.

The two laws of 1960 and 1962, the products of long discussions, were largely compromise documents.[20] Despite this, they did contain several important themes. The need to speed up the modernisation of agriculture, which employed too many people in too many small farms, was recognised. It was seen as essential to ensure the survival of the more dynamic farmers and encourage the departure of the rest. In a significant policy shift, the rural exodus was regarded as a trend to be encouraged. It was important, the laws argued, to favour the creation of 'a family farming structure capable of utilising to the full the most modern production methods'. The ideal 'model farm', then, was envisaged as a family farm able to support two full-time workers (Unité de travail-homme, UTH) per year, that is, a farming couple. An increase in farm sizes together with the use of modern methods was seen as the best way of ensuring the parity of farm revenues with other economic sectors. Such policies implied the need for selectivity of support. But, it was argued, all those who wished to modernise and adapt to increased European competition would be allowed to do so. If they failed to take their chance, they had no one to blame but themselves.

To ease the social consequences of this strategy, a number of new organisations were created. The Fonds d'action sociale pour l'aménagement des structures agricoles (FASASA) was given the task of encouraging the retirement of farmers aged over sixty-five, by offering financial help in the form of an indemnity (*Indemnité viagère de départ*, IVD) provided they ceded at least 3 hectares of land. The size of the IVD was, however, modest.[21] Nevertheless, its success was considerable. Between its establishment and 1987, the IVD freed 12.9 million hectares of land and contributed to the reduced average age of the farming population. The SAFERs were empowered to intervene on the property market to ensure that increases in farm size did not occur in an anarchical fashion.[22] They had, from 1962, the right of preempting sales, which allowed them to buy up any land that came on to the market. The land that they disposed of went to carefully selected farmers anxious either to obtain a first farm or increase their holding size. These powers were extensive and, given the sensitive nature of such transactions, it is not surprising that their role has often been criticised. Between the creation of the SAFER and 1986, some 24 per cent of the total land market was acquired by the SAFER. One-third of the land bought was resold to farmers wishing to establish their first farm. The SAFERs were especially active in the west and southwest.

The legislation also encouraged many types of cooperation. It permitted the formation of groupements agricoles d'exploitation en commun (GAEC), which were an enlarged and modernised form of family farm. These associations could be formed between as many as ten associates and developed widely in Brittany. From 1975, father–son associations were allowed under the GAEC formula. In 1985, 34,000 such associations were recognised. The Crédit agricole was charged with the task of funding these structural reforms.[23] From 1963 onwards, it was able to offer thirty-year loans at 3 per cent interest – such conditions were especially advantageous to farmers wishing to expand and modernise their farms. However, to benefit from the loans, they had to have a minimum farm size which varied from region to region. In some areas as many as one-half of all farms fell below this threshold figure.

A lasting strategy

The success of the strategy of structural reform in the 1960s rested on three factors. Firstly, it was developed at a time when there was a growing awareness within the peasantry itself of the need for change. Secondly, demographic factors had disrupted the transfer of farms from one generation to the next, meaning that many sons were having to wait longer and longer to take over the running of farms. The place of the young in society was also being fundamentally reevaluated and the pressure for change was strong within the syndical movement. The arrival of Michel Debatisse as secretary-general of the FNSEA in 1964 illustrates the pressure exerted by the young. Thirdly, the syndical movement played an active part in elaborating the new structural strategy, helping to make it more acceptable to peasants as a whole, and making its application more efficient. The state decided, by and large, to allow the profession to regulate its own, specific affairs on the spot.[24] Thus, for example, the public body set up to decide on the allocation of retirement grants was composed of an equal number of administrators and farmers. The development of the agricultural policies of the EEC gave an added impetus to agricultural growth and held out the hope of wider markets for French farm produce at guaranteed prices. The creation of the EEC also transferred some of the powers of state intervention to the community. The implications of such a shift were of central importance.

The success of these structural policies depended, then, on the climate of the times; once this had changed, the policies tended to stagnate. The high hopes placed on the creation of the EEC had, by the end of the 1960s, largely disappeared. The vice-president of the European Commission, Sicco Mansholt, made public a report in December 1968 which threatened the stability of the Common Agricultural Policy. In it, the practice of high farm prices was attacked, and a minimum threshold of 40 hectares as an economically viable size for farms was suggested. There were, it was argued, some 5 million excess farmers in the community. A few months later the Vedel report on French agriculture suggested reducing the farmed area by one-third and encouraging the departure from farming of 300,000 farmers. The two documents led to violent peasant demonstrations aimed at ensuring that government treated the reports with great prudence. Condemnation of these theoretical views came from all sides. Nevertheless, such points of view were reflected in the measures adopted during the 1970s. Lower product prices and the struggle to prevent overproduction meant that growth margins for farmers were reduced. The trend was accentuated with the greater competition consequent upon the enlargement of the community. Milk quotas brought in in 1984 greatly reduced the possibilities for developing agriculture in upland areas, whose only option was diversification. The economic environment, too, was drastically altered. The rise of unemployment since 1974 has made a policy of encouraging the rural exodus more difficult to sustain.

Problems which could not have been anticipated at the start of the 1960s have also come to the fore. The emptying of parts of rural France has begun to cause serious disquiet. This in part explains the policy, held since 1974, of maintaining a duality of farm structures. Peasants maintaining their activities in more marginal areas should be able to coexist with much more efficient farm units. Because an increasing number of farmers have no secure successors, after 1973 the installation of young farmers became a major priority. A grant for young farmers (Dotation aux jeunes agriculteurs, DJA) was created through which, provided applicants had sufficient professional training, grants varying from 52,000 francs in lowland areas to 162,000 francs in upland zones, were made. Applicants could also obtain special low-interest loans. The new Orientation Law of 4 July 1980 continued the previous policies, elaborated in 1960 and 1962, of encouraging the family farm. But it also sought to give particular support to maintaining agriculture in upland areas and sought to provide a range of legal options through which younger farmers could gain access to land. Since 1981, the emphasis on structures has not been greatly modified with the left in power.[25] The hostility of the FNSEA has led to the abandonment of many of the policy proposals of Edith Cresson. The offices set up to control the evolution of production structures are largely somnolent. Is it possible, then, to change agricultural strategy in the present socio-economic context? There can be little doubt that, since the end of the 1970s, more and more people are reflecting seriously on the future.[26] The necessity for a change of orientation is widely recognised, but no clear consensus has yet emerged on the type of productive unit that should be favoured. A large number of farmers are simply not prepared to be regarded as the guardians of nature, charged with the task of keeping the countryside beautiful for the benefit of other citizens. The peasantry continues to search out its future role.

Peasants and power

Although the peasantry is numerically far less important than it was, and despite the fact that its contribution to Gross National Product is now relatively small, the attitude of politicians to the peasantry has not fundamentally altered.[27] The old 'peasant values' of stability and harmony continue to feature in political discourses and in electoral propaganda.

Farmers benefit from quite considerable financial transfers from the state. More than 10 per cent of state expenditure goes on the agricultural sector, a good deal more than its demographic importance.[28] According to one estimate in 1981, between 40 per cent and 60 per cent of gross farm revenues comes from the state.[28] One-half of the resources of the farm sector comes, not from the activity of farmers, but from decisions made by the parties in power. These figures frequently give rise to heated discussions as to the advisability of such policies. The expression 'state support', of course, covers a varied and complex reality which is difficult to measure. Financial intervention by the state in farming does not come solely through the Ministry of Agriculture. Some of this aid, for rural improvements for example, benefits the non-farm sector as well. In terms of social security, the agricultural sector is inevitably in deficit, since the size of the active, contributing population is falling whilst the number and cost of retirements increases. Only one-quarter of its financial cost is met by the farm community itself. If one focuses solely on the economic budget of the Ministry of Agriculture, more than 50 per cent of expenditure goes on supporting prices. But such policies disproportionately favour the large producers. It would seem especially difficult to help farmers in need without creating such anomalous situations.

Why, then, has such heavy financial support for the peasantry continued, when the peasantry is no longer the dominant force in France it once was? Perhaps it can be argued that its marginal position gives it a key role in many rural constituencies. The peasant vote can make all the difference, hence the careful attention paid to farm matters by many elected rural members. Such representatives are rarely slow in letting the regional press know of their personal interventions in parliament on peasant issues. Only thus can a solid local vote be maintained. The career of Jacques Chirac in Corrèze (now Mayor of Paris) followed in the steps of Henri Queuille, and was built on a careful attention to peasant problems and issues.

Above all, farmers are strong because they are organised. In many ways, the FNSEA is a powerful pressure group able to bring influence to bear on public authorities at all levels. The state, in associating the FNSEA with its decisions and the execution of policy, has thus helped to reinforce its power. Thus, departmental and national leaders of the FNSEA have a major say in the policies of the SAFER or the Crédit agricole. This form of cooperation with the state has allowed the FNSEA to increase its support in previously hostile regions. The fact that the 1985 FNSEA national congress was held in a stronghold of the left-wing viticulturalists, Narbonne, was highly symbolic. On any issue, the FNSEA demands the right to speak in the name of all peasants and to occupy the most important place in discussions with the authorities. Despite the fact that the peasant population is more diverse, more heterogeneous than it ever was in the past, syndicalism continues to reinforce the appearance of unity. With economic crisis, however, has come budgetary constraint, making this form of syndical–government cooperation more difficult. The complicity of syndical leaders in difficult government decisions appears more and more obvious at branch level.[30] This has led to debate and dissent at the heart of the FNSEA and to the emergence of a number of dissident syndical movements.

The first to be organised was the Mouvement de défense des exploitants familiaux (MODEF). Established in 1959, it sought to unite all those who were unable to tread the path to economic progress. It separated from the FNSEA in 1975 to create an independent syndical movement, many of whose leaders were close to the communist party. Still on the left of the FNSEA, the Confédération nationale des syndicats de travailleurs paysans (CNSTP) was created in 1981 out of the move- ment created by many peasant-workers who were militants of the CNJA and FNSEA, sympathetic to the socialist party. The Fédération nationale des syndicats paysans (CNSP) was formed by two departmental feder- ations excluded from the FNSEA in 1982 for their opposition to syndical policy. On the right, the Fédération française de l'agriculture was estab- lished in 1969 by a group of farmers who refused the path of integrating farming with the rest of the economy. As a means of compromising the hostility of the FNSEA, Edith Cresson gave official government recog- nition to all these groups. But their implantation was hardly solid enough to be able to disturb the hegemony of the dominant syndicalism. The elections to the Chamber of Agriculture in 1983, in which most farmers participated, provided a test of support. Of the eligible electorate, 70 per cent voted, an exceptionally high figure. The FNSEA, in gaining 71 per cent of the vote, showed that it continued to maintain its dominant position.

Action on the part of farmers is not limited solely to the negotiating power of its representatives. Their ability to react to events is greater than that of many other social groups.[31] Demonstration provides another means of representing their views. A range of episodic, localised and often violent demonstrations is the hallmark of many small groups, victims of economic circumstances. Amongst the loudest and most violent are the viticulturalists of Languedoc and the market-gardeners and pig farmers of Brittany, for the most part small producers, victims of modernisation, who see no role for negotiation. The geography of peasant protest is located primarily to the west of a line from le Havre to Marseille. Set apart from these demonstrations where the participants represent only themselves, are the massive, united demonstrations organised by the leaders of the FNSEA. Designed to impress both public opinion and the government, they often take on the form of a quasi-military demonstration, with tractors replacing tanks in the procession. The peasants themselves become actors and spectators in a form of action that becomes almost a theatrical event. The rules of the game are clearly understood. They have to make themselves heard in high places. The attitude of the peasants towards government remains ambiguous. They both resent and yet rely on government. Farmers regard the state almost as their employer, such is their dependence on state revenues. They demand help without wishing to undermine the basis of power.

Is there, any more than in the past, a specifically peasant vote?[32] It is not easy to identify precisely the voting patterns of particular socio-professional categories. One can barely identify the rural and peasant vote, because it forms such a small element of so many constituencies. It can be argued that regional contrasts have become less important since the 1960s. The rural constituencies of the west are no longer the bastions of the right they once were; the 'red' areas of the centre and south-east have also weakened. It may be argued that, with the disappearance of large numbers of agricultural workers and sharecroppers, support for the communists in the countryside has diminished. As for the old influences on voting, these are no longer what they were in the nineteenth century.

According to opinion polls carried out in 1981, farmers, who constituted 7 per cent of the national electorate, constituted only 3 per cent to 5 per cent of the communist electorate and 5 per cent to 8 per cent of the socialist vote. The RPR took 11 per cent to 19 per cent of its votes, the UDF between 10 per cent and 13 per cent. A majority of farmers voted on the right. According to a post-electoral poll, 33 per cent of farmers voted for François Mitterrand and 67 per cent for Valéry Giscard d'Estaing in the second round of presidential voting in 1981. Since 1962, Gaullism has been able to take over the place of radicalism amongst a peasantry which strongly believes that the efficiency of a deputy is all the greater if he or she belongs to the party in power.

The evolution of the peasantry over a period of twenty-five years has reinforced the place of the family owner-occupier and simplified peasant society by removing many marginal groups. It has also had the effect of reducing peasant participation in local civic life. In 1985, 37 per cent of mayors were engaged in farming, compared with 44 per cent in 1974. Yet local institutions have become, even more so than in the past, very important in deciding the outcome of power struggles between the increasingly minority farming groups and those other social groups anxious to install themselves in rural areas.

3. The farm unit in search of a new equilibrium

In the space of a quarter of a century, farmers have had to face dramatic and unprecedented social and economic changes. Their improved production has created a series of ancillary problems that many were not ready to face. The strategy of structural reform has, furthermore, not always had the desired results. There still remains a large proportion of essentially marginal farms, whilst others which should be viable are on the point of disappearing.

Modernisation and its problems

Agricultural production has grown at an unprecedented rate, increasing by 64 per cent in terms of volume between 1959–61 and 1979–81.[33] In view of the fact that the active agricultural population has halved in the same period, the productivity gains are clearly considerable. They remain considerably higher than those of industry. In 1983, a farmer provided food for, on average, forty people as against seven in 1960. Most estimates suggest that the value added per worker tripled between 1959 and 1981. In terms of yields, the gains have been equally spectacular. Wheat yields rose from 25 quintals per hectare in 1959–61 to 65 in 1984, a record year. In the Paris Basin, yields of 80 quintals per hectare have become the norm. In animal production, the adoption of the Holstein breed has meant that milk yields rival those of Denmark. France became in 1981 the second largest world exporter of food products after the United States. Despite this, the importance of agriculture in the national economy continues to diminish, chiefly because agricultural prices have risen less quickly than those of industry and services. In 1987, agriculture represented 4 per cent of Gross Domestic Product, as against 6.7 per cent in 1970. It is also important to take account of the growing importance of the food-processing industry, linked to the greater integration of agriculture into the economy. Even if agriculture alone accounts for only 7 per cent of the active population and 4 per cent of value added, the food-processing industries employ 16 per cent of the active population and account for between 10 per cent and 15 per cent of value added.[34]

Systems of cultivation have changed in a spectacular manner, shifting from traditional polyculture to a focus on two or three speculative products. Monoculture, considered somewhat risky, remains rare. Production methods have also radically changed. The capital required for farming has spiralled: at least a threefold increase since 1960. Now, almost all farms are mechanised and many possess several tractors. In 1985, an average-sized dairy farm of about 30 hectares required an investment in modern machinery of between 1 and 1.5 million francs. Intermediate expenditure on such things as goods and services essential to production increased from 22 per cent of sales in 1960 to 45 per cent in 1984 (35 per cent).[35] For intensive, factory-farming the figure reaches 80 per cent. The increasing integration of agriculture into the global economy can be analysed in terms of dependency. Thus, farmers are required to purchase fertilisers and fuel whose prices have generally increased more rapidly than those of agricultural products, thereby calling into question the profitability of farms. Equally, however, a number of farmers have very close links with the food-processing and commercial sectors. Their often-generous contracts give them privileged access to innovations and commercially secure markets. But such contracts can be destabilising. Thus, in the case of animal factory-farming, companies provide all the necessary feedstuffs and also buy up all the animals. The farmer provides nothing more than his labour. Some milk cooperatives have also begun to refuse to collect the milk of small producers distant from the major routeways; such action both undermines their supposedly 'social' role, and threatens the survival of the small producers. Farmers are forced to constantly seek new types of products as the markets evolve. Thus, in the plain of Valence, polyculture was largely abandoned and replaced by peaches. Overproduction soon engendered a shift to apples which, before long, were uprooted and replaced by kiwi fruit. Following the same logic, in Cantal, traditional Cantal cheese which was selling badly was replaced first by English cheddar-type and, later, by Italian- and Greek-style cheeses.[36] Evidently then, despite the pace of modernisation, the basic economic situation has changed little.[37] Farmers continue to compete with one another in markets in which they exercise little control. Lacking any real autonomy, they can hardly be considered entrepreneurs in the modern sense of the term.

Increased indebtedness is a further form of dependence linked to modernisation. This increased fourfold between 1960 and 1973.[38] It has slowed down somewhat since the economic crisis, as farmers are more reluctant to make long-term investments when economic circumstances are none too promising. But the role of the Crédit agricole has undoubtedly increased. In 1986, 70 per cent of all farm debt was incurred to the Crédit agricole. Overall, producers were spending 20 per cent of the value added on the farm in servicing debt. Young farmers, viticulturalists and factory-farmers had the highest debts. Can one thus speak of overindebtedness? The notion has to be qualified in time and space. Thus, an acceptable debt level for a cereal farm in the Paris Basin does not apply to a Breton pig-farmer. It may well be that lower interest rates have persuaded some farmers to take risks by moving into areas of agriculture that are unlikely to yield high returns, particularly because the consequences of bad decisions in farming need not always be fatal. It is rare, for example, for the Crédit agricole to call in the bailiffs. The farmer in difficulty tends to reduce investments, to tighten his belt rather than declare bankruptcy. To the extent that the farm budget and the domestic budget can overlap, many farmers are able to face financial crises in ways which would be impossible for other social groups.

The evolution of agricultural structures

The strategy of structural reform had as its basic premise the notion that modernisation should be accompanied by an increase in average farm size.[39] Between 1955 and 1988, almost 1.3 million farms, 56 per cent of the total, disappeared. There remained 1.0 million farms in 1988. The rate of decline, over 2.5 per cent per year prior to 1973, has subsequently slowed down. Since the early 1980s, the rate has once more risen. The average farm size has grown from 15 hectares in 1955 to 28 hectares in 1988. Since 1970, an average increase of 9 hectares has occurred. The decline in the number of farms has been size-dependent. A rapid rate of decline has been evident for farms below 20 hectares. Numbers of farms between 20 hectares and 35 hectares, fairly stable until the early 1970s, have now begun to fall, whilst those between 35 hectares and 50 hectares have remained stable. Only farms between 50 hectares and 200 hectares have increased at a rapid rate since 1963. They now occupy almost a half of the agricultural area compared with 28 per cent in 1963.

There are clear regional patterns to these changes. An especially rapid decline in farm numbers has been the case in the Massif Central and the north. In Languedoc-Roussillon, there continues to be a wide range of farms, large and small. The largest farms, over 200 hectares, have increased only on the margins of the Paris Basin and in thinly settled areas with low agricultural potential, such as Lozère and the southern Alps. The size of the 'average' farm has steadily grown over the years. Currently, it has been the farms between 35 hectares and 100 hectares that have dominated, rather than the very large farms. Such a trend almost certainly reflects the outcome of deliberate government strategies to favour the medium-sized farm. Gaps between the regions still remain high, however. In 1988 farms in the Pyrénées-Orientales were on average about 8 hectares. Those in Seine-et-Marne were 79 hectares.

However, the other facet of farm strategy, the favouring of owner-occupation, has not been realised. Despite legislation to encourage its development since 1938, it is currently declining. In 1988, it characterised only 45 per cent of the farmed area. Sharecropping is almost insignificant; in 1988, it occupied only 174,000 hectares, some 0.7 per cent of the farmed area. According to the agricultural census of 1979–80, fewer than 7,000 farms were held under this system. In some areas – the viticultural farms of the Beaujolais, for example – it continues to be important. Overall, mixed forms of tenure have been most important: two-thirds of all farmers rent some of their land. The extent of such land is difficult to estimate precisely, because verbal agreements and free renting of land are by no means uncommon, especially in areas where the rural exodus has created a group of urban plot owners. In poor, depopulated areas, small owner-occupiers can often amass quite large areas of land to farm. This trend is exemplified, for example, by the peasant-merchants of the Alps of upper Provence, or the transhumant entrepreneurs who move sheep from the lowlands of Languedoc, exploiting large areas of land at little cost.[40] The availability of land remains more important than its ownership. In areas where owner-occupation is the norm, the core of the farm will pass in direct ownership from one generation to the next, whilst the area farmed tends to be increased by renting land. Where renting is the norm, farmers often use the right of pre-emption to ensure secure access to at least some of the land they farm. It is the farmer, then, who shapes the farm. It is modelled by him to a much greater extent than by his predecessors. The farmer regroups his fields often on an *ad-hoc* basis, which is more widespread than *remembrement*, which, by the end of 1985, had been effected on only half of the national farmed area. The pace of simplification of the rural landscape cannot always be explained simply by reference to the cadastral documents.

The obsession with land ownership seems to be in decline, although the change is a recent one. Up until 1979, the price of land was rising rapidly. In real terms, there was a rise of 32 per cent between 1965 and 1980. Faced with the necessity of increasing farm size, farmers competed avidly with each other to buy land. The relative ease with which loans could be obtained from the Crédit agricole further increased competition. Since farmers accounted for three-quarters of the land market, their behaviour had a key influence on the market. However, with the

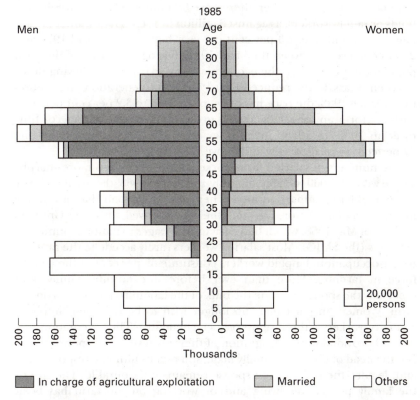

Figure 7 Age-profile of the familial agricultural population. (*Source: GraphAgri* 87, p. 25, after SCEES, structural enquiry.)

economic crisis, farm revenues have fallen. Almost at once, land prices have fallen. For arable land and meadows, the fall was of the order of 5 per cent in 1987. At that date a hectare of such land sold for, on average, 19,750 francs There were marked regional variations from 12,500 francs in the Limousin to 30,100 francs in Alsace. Farmers appear increasingly prudent in their land purchases. Have they, then, ceased to subscribe to the ideal of owner-occupation? It is probably necessary to wait for a marked recovery in farm revenues before deciding if a real change in behaviour has taken place.

An ever-smaller agricultural population

The transformation in the agricultural population has been spectacular. In 1985, according to INSEE, the active agricultural population was just under 1.6 million, 7 per cent of the total active population[41] Of this number, there were 1.3 million heads of farm households or family workers, as against 3 million in 1962. Their numbers have fallen at a rapid rate: 4.4 per cent per year between 1962 and 1975 and 2 per cent a year between then and 1982. The age structure of the farm population, rather than the economic crisis, explains the slowing down in recent years, as the reduced First World War generation takes retirement. Since 1983, the pace has once more risen to 3.2 per cent per year. Farmers form an especially ageing group with an average age of fifty-three in 1983. In 1988, only 13 per cent were below thirty-five while 27 per cent were aged sixty and above.

The numbers of salaried farm workers have fallen even more sharply. There were 600,000 in 1955, but only 156,000 in 1988, the great majority of them elderly, unmarried men. Their pay, lower than that of workers in the secondary sector, has nonetheless improved since the Grenelle accords of May 1968, which tied agricultural wages to national minimum pay rates (the SMIG). Most salaried workers rarely accede to the ranks of owner-occupation. Unpaid workers constitute 85 per cent of the labour-force in farming. More than ever before, the farming family, and especially the spouse, provide the bulk of the labour requirements on the farm. Women, in particular, no longer wish to be regarded simply as auxiliary workers without rights or social benefits.[42] The Orientation Law of 1980 provided some recognition of their professional responsibilities. But the head of the farm, usually male, still retains ultimate responsibility and, legally, the place of the spouse remains unfavourable. The size of the family population living and/or working on the farm has been estimated by the Ministry of Agriculture at 3 million. Today, all family members working in some capacity on the farm are regarded as family workers. Among them, the number of full-time workers is fairly small, which complicates still further estimates of the manpower used in agriculture.

Part-time activity outside farming, far from having vanished, applies to a large number of farm workers.[43] In 1980, 21 per cent of farm heads were involved in some form of outside paid employment. Two-thirds of all farm households benefited from at least one source of outside revenue. More than one-third of these part-time workers have industrial jobs. Only 14 per cent have middle-rank white-collar posts and 7 per cent higher executive posts in commerce or industry. Regional distributions of such work have also altered. Whereas twenty years ago, such employment was concentrated in the east, Normandy and upland areas, today it is found throughout France. Such an important phenomenon is, inevitably, highly complex. Outside activity might be regarded simply as a sign of the insertion of the peasant household into global society in which part-time work is widespread. If, rather, it results from the condition of the farm household itself, it would seem to be closely linked to farm size. Mechanisation, too, has released more time on the farm. Viticultural work allows more leisure time than in the past, especially if membership of a cooperative means the manufacture of the wine is carried out elsewhere. Many urban-dwellers have thus been able to keep the family farm. Teacher-viticulturalists are by no means uncommon in the south-east. The desire to keep the family inheritance and traditions explains in large measure such situations in which agriculture becomes a subsidiary activity. For farmers themselves, part-time work can help the farm to survive as minimum threshold sizes of farms increase. Perhaps, too, it serves to help them through the early years of a new venture. This can provide additional resources, as in the case of young modernist farmers in the ski-station areas who work as ski instructors or lift operators to help finance their farms.[44]

This multiple activity permits many farms to survive where otherwise they would go to the wall. It also explains how some 600,000 farmers maintain farms of below 20 hectares, still 55 per cent of the total farms of France. Does it damage the agricultural profession? Professional groups have for many years condemned such practices, regarding them as an excessive human load. Their current attitude is rather more qualified. Full-time farmers are not really competing with part-time ones, who are largely engaged in farming to meet subsistence needs and rarely demand financial support. For government, they at least fulfil the useful function of helping to maintain farming in poorer regions.

Farms without a successor?

Young farmers must be installed on the land if French agriculture is to have any future.[45] More and more of the young farmers of the 1950s are close to retirement, but new entrants into the profession are rare. At the start of the 1970s, some 50,000 new farmers appeared each year; in 1988 only 30,000 did so. The fertility of farming families remains very low. In 1982, farming households had, on average 0.9 children compared with 1.4 children in workers' families. The rapid ageing of the farm population because of the rural exodus explains in large part this trend. Thus, peasant families have fewer and fewer potential successors and, of course, not many expect to follow in their parents' footsteps. In 1988, 73 per cent of all farmers aged over fifty thought that they would not have any successors to the enterprise.

Educational patterns amongst the children of farming families reveal stark choices. Only 15 per cent of them enrol for agricultural education and only 11 per cent actually become farmers.[46] They represent under half of the student population at agricultural colleges, whence only a minority of students anyway goes into farming. The majority follows educational courses similar to its rural peers, which allow it to contemplate careers outside farming. Today, children have much more opportunity to make comparisons between life styles, for families tend to be more geographically and socially dispersed than was the case one or two generations ago. College education, in particular, seems to play a crucial role. According to a survey made in 1985, children of farming families are attracted to two professions in particular.[47] One-third of all lorry-drivers are sons of peasants; 8 per cent of peasant sons go into this profession. The other main attraction is working for the Post Office; 41 per cent of such workers are of peasant origins. Such choices perhaps reflect the desire to remain in the countryside and work largely in the open air. These are also jobs with which such children are familiar from an early stage in their lives. With the exception of these two professions, farmers' children follow a similar range of professions to those of workers' children.

The profession of farmer appears to hold few attractions. To become a farmer, it is necessary to be a farmer's son. Of those young farmers who receive state help to establish a farm, 94 per cent come from peasant families, an exceptionally high figure. Inheriting land remains the commonest way of gaining a foothold in farming. But, when youngsters start to decide on their future careers, the prospects of rapidly taking over the family farm are often remote. They must also rely on help from their families or some kind of gift to help with creating a farm. The financial conditions imposed by co-inheritors can also be a disincentive. Some might demand their share of the inheritance in order to build a second home or to make other investments. At each generational change, the one who stays behind on the farm has to find money to purchase the land. As a result, really viable successions are few and far between. Groupements fonciers agricoles (GFA) which help prevent the division of the land, often provide only temporary solutions although they do at least allow the purchase of the land to be spread over a longer period of time.

The central importance of recruiting family labour to take over the farm is not simply a consequence of it being the most efficient strategy. Young people coming from other walks of life usually find it very difficult to amass sufficient capital to control a farm and benefit from state aid. The efforts of 'utopian migrants' after May 1968 usually failed for this reason.[48] Because they lacked capital, many established themselves in thinly peopled regions – Ardèche, Lozère, the southern Alps – where land was cheap. Harsh economic reality quickly disenchanted many. The more enterprising survived through drawing on other sources of revenue: the sale of honey and cheese or putting on craft courses. Once they had shown their determination to survive, they were able to benefit from state help and from the action of SAFER.

If it is necessary to inherit in order to become a farmer, inheriting alone is rarely enough. The state, too must play its part. To obtain the young farmer's grant, a sizeable sum, and benefit from low-interest loans, it is necessary to obtain at least a diploma in agricultural studies. The size of the proposed farm must be above a certain threshold. Perhaps not surprisingly, entrants into farming are later, better prepared and more secure than in the 1960s. But they are still too few to ensure the renewal of the generation of farmers who will retire over the next few years.

4. The reinvention of the peasantry

In a quarter of a century, farmers have lost their preeminent place in a rural world now shaped in the image of urban society. The improvement of incomes has created greater conformity in ways of life. But can one therefore argue that the peasant no longer exists, although many farmers still declare that they are members of the peasantry? Perhaps the diversity of farming situations means that such generalisations require modification?

Peasants, country-dwellers and urban citizens

Between 1975 and 1982, the census has revealed a spectacular renaissance of the rural world. For the first time in more than a century, the population of rural communes has increased more rapidly than urban ones, corresponding to a reversal of past migratory trends. But this does not imply some sort of return to the land. Farmers are no longer in a majority in the countryside. In 1982, they represented only 23 per cent of the rural population although a further 19 per cent depends on agriculture in some way for a living.[49] There are no more than ten or so cantons in the whole country where farmers and their families are in the majority. Rural and agricultural can no longer be regarded as one and the same. Today there are as many blue-collar workers in rural communes as there are in the towns. By the same token, some 350,000 farmers or salaried agricultural workers lived in towns in 1982. Can one thereby conclude that the peasantry is now marginal in rural regions? Initially, it is perhaps helpful to distinguish peri-urban and tourist areas from what Roger Béteille called 'an emptying France'.[50]

This emptying rural France embraces an economically diverse set of regions: the east and south of the Paris Basin, the Massif Central, the Pyrénées and the Alps. Almost one-third of the national territory falls within its boundaries. Those living in such areas are primarily peasants – either active or retired. But they are less and less numerous and increasingly elderly. In some communes of the Beauce or the Grands Causses, almost all land might be in the hands of one farmer. Where small farms do survive, they are poor and without any future. As the social structure of village life is simplified, so the traditional systems of social relations break down. To break out of their isolation, some farmers have sought to establish cooperative networks. Positive demographic changes come about primarily from the arrival of new activities linked to urbanism and built on the foundations of a rapidly declining rural civilisation.

Such areas contrast dramatically with those zones influenced by urban growth, which tends to cast its influence ever wider around the main towns. There rural territories become subsumed in the urban economy. Land is divided into building plots sold, not by the hectare, but by the square metre. This 'rur-urbanisation', an ugly if expressive term, results in the parcelling out of the countryside into ever-more extensive housing lots, each in the middle of its garden.[51] In tourist areas, the proliferation of second homes has had much the same effect. Their numbers have increased from 330,000 in 1954 to 2,500,000 by 1985. Increasingly, urban citizens are investing in territories in which farmers have become a minority. In many communes a rump of two or three farmers share what little land the *plan d'occupation des sols* (POS) has left them. Rural society, then, is no longer dominated by farming: occupational diversity has become the norm. Managers, employees, blue-collar workers, the retired are now neighbours to the farming population. In a short space of time, social relations are no longer based on the economy. Cooperation can no longer be based simply on geographic proximity and, in many areas, informal networks of cooperation have disappeared. Only in Brittany, formerly a region renowned for its individualism, have networks of association flourished.[52] No doubt because they have had to confront such harsh economic realities as farmers modernised, Bretons have become avowed cooperators. Here, the maintenance of dense farming populations has allowed systems for sharing work tasks and machinery to develop. The links between farmers with similar farm areas have developed strongly, but have not really altered basic hierarchies in the farm community.

Old traditions of village social life have greatly altered as the character of rural populations has changed. Increasingly, they have followed urban models. The shift of the clergy from rural areas was accentuated with the effects of the rural exodus. Even in the west, the end of the 1960s was marked by a precipitous decline in religious practice. Many priests had to look after whole cantons: often they could not even maintain a weekly mass in some villages and were unable to participate in traditional celebrations, which soon vanished. Village fêtes increasingly developed into commercial events designed to attract people from other communes.[53] The range of events on offer tends to be a rather bland, standardised imitation of urban fêtes and TV variety shows. The Saturday-night dance has taken on major importance. Drum majorettes in hats and miniskirts or groups of folkdancers parade without enthusiasm in front of passive crowds of spectators. In some tourist communes, professional organisers have sought to recreate the old 'traditional' celebrations. On occasions, farmers will act out the old agricultural tasks, common in the 'old days', that is, prior to mechanisation, with all the contradictions that such performances imply. With a few, poorly executed gestures, such actions symbolise a whole way of life abandoned, without regret, by their parents in the 1950s. Play-acting the part of peasants, they slip into the role that urban-dwellers expect of them.

Once again, it seems, one can identify a reversal of the values attached to being a peasant.[54] The devaluing of the peasant *métier* in the 1950s was increasingly replaced by a growing taste by town-dwellers for things peasant and, ultimately, the triumph of the peasantry. Many of the themes reemerging at the end of the 1960s were part and parcel of agrarian discourse at the turn of the century. In addition is the notion that farmers are especially privileged because of the quality of their lives: for countryside read nature. Many citizens thus seek to recover their roots out of sheer nostalgia. They transcend the past, creating their own, idealistic collage of memories. Advertisers play to such tastes. They were quick to grasp that 'village' themes sold better than suburban ones, that 'rustic' cheeses were a better bet than standardised products from a dairy factory. Urban daydreams are fed by the representations of farming advanced by the media. Cinema and television have turned their backs on the present to indulge the values of the past. Other productions seeking to qualify such representations of the peasantry have created, instead, yet further stereotypes: the young farmer, brave victim of modernisation is one of the more recent themes.[55]

Even if they are fewer in number, it is the presence of farmers that makes the rural world distinctive. Frequently, however, they are invisible in this world made anew by town-dwellers. The countryside is hardly perceived by them as a place primarily for agricultural production. Most new arrivals in the country seek an escape from the constraints of the town, without adapting to those of the country.[56] Such contradictions go some way towards explaining the conflicts that often develop between these neo-rural dwellers and the other inhabitants of the countryside. The noises and smells of agricultural work inconvenience country residents seeking peace and quiet. Hunting often provokes considerable argument. Long-established members of hunting associations often resent newcomers, whom they regard as something of an invading army. The drawing up of the POS is often the cause of ferocious municipal electoral struggles. Generally in the minority, farmers often have difficulty in making their voice heard. Recent arguments over the reform of the statutes of the Caisse nationale de crédit agricole, whose clientele is increasingly rural rather than agricultural, have revealed the defensive attitudes of professional organisations anxious to keep at least some of their control over rural territories.

Undoubtedly, village society has greatly altered and evolved, with farmers now rarely occupying first place. Where they do, they rule, by and large, over something of a desert. Their ability to resist urban influences is all the weaker in part, at least, because they have adopted so much of the urban way of life.

The peasantry – part of the middle class?

There can be little doubt that, within the span of a quarter of a century, the standard of living of the farming community has risen considerably. Has it then, achieved that parity, which was promised by the Orientation Law of 1960? It is much more difficult to evaluate the revenues of farmers than of other socio-professional groups. Most farmers are still reluctant to reveal information for statistical surveys out of fear of the Inland Revenue. The system of tax allowances also means that agricultural revenues are often under-estimated. Furthermore, in 1979, only 37 per cent of farmers kept proper accounts.[57] The place of subsistence consumption is also difficult to evaluate. The complexity of the annual *Comptes de l'agriculture* published by INSEE hardly helps to clarify such questions.[58]

Between 1965 and 1974, the annual available revenue of farmers increased by about 10 per cent, approximately the same as the figure for salaried workers. In terms of purchasing power, the rise was of the order of 3 per cent to 4 per cent per year. The oil crisis abruptly ended this long period of progression. Through the operation of the price 'scissors', the rising costs of production, much higher than those of agricultural prices, brought about a fall in farm revenues.

1980 was especially unfavourable for farmers, with a 7 per cent fall in gross farm revenue. In 1981, there was some recovery but, since then, it has fluctuated: rises in 1981, 1982, 1984 and 1987, a fall in 1983, 1985 and 1988, stagnation in 1986. This temporal irregularity is paralleled by considerable differences between farm types. For comparable farm sizes, the revenues of pastoral farmers are markedly lower than cereal farmers.

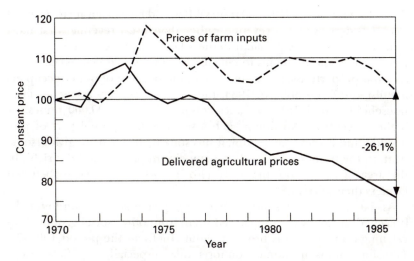

Figure 8 The price 'scissors' – the divergence in the prices of farm inputs and outputs. (*Source: Les Cahiers du BAC*, February 1987, p. 42, from INSEE.)

Those farms integrated in the food-processing sector have also been more seriously affected. By the same token, regional revenues vary considerably. In 1985, the average revenue per family worker was five times higher in the Champagne–Ardennes region than in the Limousin. At the departmental level, revenue was eleven times higher in Marne than in southern Corsica. If the size of farm is considered, perhaps the simplest form of discrimination, farms of 50 hectares and over have on average revenues eight times higher than those below 5 hectares. The crisis has also meant that physical variations, whose effects had perhaps been smoothed out by technical progress, again reasserted their importance. Property improvements were more costly in a period of dear money. Marginal land, sometimes brought under cultivation in the relatively euphoric period of the 1960s, made farms all the more susceptible during leaner times.

Out of gross revenues, the farmer has to pay his own salary and those of his family workers, social-security contributions, loan repayments and investment costs. This gross revenue cannot thus be directly equated with available household income, although often the two are regarded as the same. According to an INSEE enquiry, the available household income for a typical farming family was 164,580 francs in 1983.[59] The figure is well below the average for the professions (280,780 francs) but higher than that of middle-executive groups (151,600 francs) and well above the figure for employees (121,300 francs). It would be inaccurate to argue, if one considers available revenue rather than fiscal revenue, that most farmers are at levels equivalent to the salaried working class. In revenue terms, the peasantry seems to fall clearly into the middle-class category. As far as property assets are concerned, the position of owner-occupiers is still more favourable. In 1984, the average property assets per farm household were 1,750,000 francs compared with 1,400,000 francs for higher executives. No doubt such assets are an essential part of production and require large capital investments by farmers, giving some truth to the traditional view that many 'live in poverty and die rich'. In the area of assets, too, there are also important differences between farmers themselves.

As far as life styles are concerned, peasants have undoubtedly breached the gap which separated them from other social groups. This catching-up process was brought about chiefly in the period 1965–75. Transformations in home comforts were especially significant, and exemplified the promotion of the nuclear family and changes in means of production.[60] Because the old rural houses were often ill adapted to modern living and in poor repair, new houses have multiplied. Modern detached houses have been built for younger couples, whilst their parents have been content to remain in the old house. In the 1960s, many new houses were modelled on suburban lines, with a garage beneath the house, kitchen, dining room and first-floor bedrooms. Where families were content to remodel the old house, the large living room was often subdivided. A dining-room was created together with a living area with comfortable chairs from which to watch the television. Previously, social life had largely relied on upright chairs arranged around the table. Some of the various farm buildings and barns, now empty and largely useless because farm animals have gone and wheat is sent straight to the local silo after the harvest, were abandoned or turned into rural *gîtes*. Pre-fabricated farm buildings made of metal are better adapted to the storage of machinery. In viticultural regions, the growth of cooperative *caves* has meant that many domestic *caves* and cellars are no longer used. The peasant house no longer represents a work-place in which home comforts are reduced to a minimum. The farmyard, no longer an economic space, has been transformed into a garden. The home environment, then, has become a means of affirming an equality of status between the farmer and the rest of society, a way of representing the break with the past.

Domestic comforts are another index of the triumph of urban household images. The rapid development of mains water and sewage systems since the mid-1950s has permitted major improvements in sanitation. In

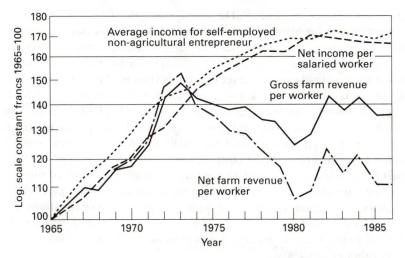

Figure 9 The decline of agricultural revenue. (*Source: Les Cahiers du BAC,* February 1987, p. 41, from INSEE, Comptes de la nation.)

1984, 78 per cent of farmhouses had a separate bathroom; only 18 per cent had no toilet. Such figures are still worse than the average, but the gap has been very considerably narrowed between farmhouses and the rest of the housing stock. By contrast, in terms of domestic goods, farmers have a range at least as good as that of the rest of the population. They possess rather more cars and freezers than average. The latter are important for fully utilising garden produce – in 1987 more than 83 per cent of farm households had freezers, compared with a national average of 38 per cent. In terms of diet, farm households are increasingly adopting urban patterns. Even if one-third of everything consumed in farm households is produced on the farm, a considerable amount of buying is done at supermarkets. The timing and composition of meals increasingly reflect urban ways, except for the more elderly households.

But this 'normalisation' is not total. In many areas, the gaps between farmers and other social groups remain. In terms of dress, urban fashions have dominated the countryside for some considerable time. Nevertheless, purchasing practices for farmers differ from those of other groups.[61] They spend only half the national average on clothing. They buy few articles, but choose the most durable. A considerable financial input is made for children's clothes, primarily because they go to school and mix with their peers. Farming households continue to spend little on leisure and recreation. According to INSEE, in 1987 only 25 per cent of farm households went on a summer holiday, compared to 54 per cent of the population as a whole.[62] The average length of holiday was below seventeen days, compared to the average of twenty-four days. The number taking winter holidays is much lower than average. But the development of replacement programmes for farmers wishing to go on holiday has meant a steady improvement in these figures. Thus, in 1974 only 12 per cent of farmers took a summer holiday. The constraints of looking after animals continue to be powerful on at least half of all farms. The conditions of farm work and the range of cultural practices which surround it might also explain the small number of medical consultations that farmers make.[63] Distance constraints do not seem to play a part in such patterns, since GPs are rarely consulted in spite of the fact that they are distributed in a network designed to cater for all parts of the country. At certain times of the year, journeys for consultations are simply considered too costly in terms of time. An INSEE enquiry in 1985–6 found that, on average, farmers worked two hours a day longer than other citizens.[64]

Is the farming population, then, to be regarded simply as another component of the middle class? Much of the sociological distinctiveness of the peasantry has undoubtedly disappeared. It is not easy to speak of, or to define, a peasant culture. This process of normalisation does not mean that farmers do not continue in some respects to be very different from their fellow citizens. Farm work creates its own particular way of life. The tremendous diversity of living conditions also means that the social position of the rural population is not homogeneous. Capitalist farmers coexist with a multitude of small producers whose tiny incomes are out of all proportion to the weight of property assets they bear.

From peasant to entrepreneur

In 1950, peasant society was largely dominated by the family owner-occupier. That society had become much simplified after a long process of secular evolution, marked by the departure of the poorest and the diminution in importance of the large landlord.

Social hierarchies were based, first and foremost, on control of land. In less than a quarter of a century, the disappearance of a large number of farms has been accompanied by a reinforcement of the inequalities at the heart of peasant society. New rifts have developed alongside older ones, complicating the hierarchies which exist at the core of the peasantry.

The old split between modern and traditional farmers has become, over time, rather too simplistic: the machine has triumphed throughout. Differences between farmers increasingly reflect aptitudes and abilities to adapt to rapid technical shifts. The age of the farmer is important, as well as the presence or absence of a potential successor to the farm. Some farmers have been able to increase their holdings before really fierce competition between farmers for land has set in. In the same commune, large farms coexist with smaller farms at the very limits of their viability. Sometimes powerful 'village Yaltas'[65] are held, leading to agreements between the more dynamic farmers to agreed bids for certain plots of land before they even become vacant. The SAFER and syndicates have been accused of favouritism towards the 'land eaters' at the expense of smaller farmers. The very choice of production systems is far from neutral. The traditional farmers often opt for a system of polycultural-pastoral farming; the more modernist for profitable specialities which require investments and, hence, debt. But the economic crisis, in hitting especially hard the more intensive farms, has overturned the rules of the game.

Modernisation, however, has not destroyed all the traditional differentiating factors within the peasantry. Individual initiatives can still run up against the difficulties of a local milieu which can enhance or curtail that initiative. Regional traditions can be very significant, creating a diverse geography of mentalities.[66] Two examples appear apposite. The high income farms of the Paris Basin contrast markedly with the smaller, indebted farms of Brittany, which provide mediocre or inadequate revenues for their occupants. The large-scale mechanised cultivation methods of the Paris Basin continue to benefit, as in the past, from considerable advantages. The production system, eliminating animals, is a simple one. Cereal prices are guaranteed, and one or two other crops complete the picture. In the Beauce, two workers can manage a farm of 150 hectares. This dynamic, capital-intensive model has developed in the Champagne, from Marne to Berry, as well as in the flat, poorer areas of Gascony. Migrant farmers from abroad – often those repatriated from North Africa – have played a part in taking the risk to set such systems in motion.

In Brittany, the pace of evolution has been even more rapid. In the space of a single generation, it has become the most important agricultural region in France. As André Fel suggests, some of the explanation for this lies in a kind of 'defiance of existing farm structures',[67] in the dynamism of an area richer in men than in land. Progress has been achieved through an intensification of the basic polycultural–pastoral farming systems. The average farm size remains small, at about 18 hectares in 1980. The farmers, many of them young, have tried to overcome this constraint with their dynamism. A powerful cooperative and food-processing sector has encouraged them to take financial risks. But, with the crisis in the Common Agricultural Policy, based as it is on high prices, these Breton farms have become especially vulnerable.

Such a diversity of situations makes it tempting to distinguish not one but many peasantries. Depending on the author and the mood of the times, typologies have varied. In the 1960s, a modernist agriculture was juxtaposed with a traditionalist peasantry condemned to poverty. With the economic crisis, the number of groups in these typologies has increased. Perhaps four major groups have crystallised. 'Fossil' peasants, to use the expression of Maryvonne Bodiguel,[68] are in the process of disappearing. In charge of small polycultural farms dominated by animal production, their efforts at modernisation have often been limited to the purchase of a tractor. Their influence on syndical organisation is negligible: their interests are barely given consideration. Because their farms are not regarded as viable, they can expect little state aid. Such farmers work without ambition, knowing that no one will succeed them. Many are forced to work well beyond retirement age because of their meagre financial resources. These groups, the cast-offs of the period of expansion, are especially numerous in 'empty France', such as Ardèche where they form the majority of farmers. They should not be confused with part-time farmers. These are, like them, farming small, unmechanised farms, largely exempt from the hand-outs and constraints of the structural strategy. But part-time farming often represents a positive choice by farmers who are young and dynamic.

The category of middle peasants has tended to fragment under the combined impact of the market and shifts in community agricultural policy. Some farmers, generally on small farms with few capital resources, have tended to specialise in forms of intensive production, relying heavily on credit. Their efforts at creating viable farm sizes seem endless for, as they accumulate land, so the minimum threshold seems to rise. Today, many are indebted and over-equipped, and always at the mercy of market fluctuations. They furnish a large contingent of determined syndical troops, especially in Brittany. To try to cope with a difficult situation many take on second jobs and hence suffer from overwork. This is the 'farming of overwork and anguish' to use the expression of Ronald Hubscher.

A part at least of this middle peasantry had been able to cross the threshold of profitability by the end of the 1960s, when the politics of high prices allowed them to take risks. Certain of them chose the right form of specialisation because they had a good level of technical education. They benefited, too, from the support of the cooperative and syndical network that they themselves helped to create. These farmers are forced to adapt continually to the rising threshold of profitability.

Access to land is for them a fundamental priority. A cereal farm of over 100 hectares can provide an income equal to that of an executive and can create a sense of confidence in the future. A further key distinction relates to the employment of salaried workers. A small minority of bourgeois farmers exploits, with the help of salaried workers, very large farms devoted to the production of cereals and wine. This 'agricultural success-story' provides most of the leadership of the FNSEA.[69] Many of them are the representatives of veritable peasant dynasties who have been active in the professional organisations for several generations. The image they give the public is of competent and responsible technicians. A majority of peasants supports them because they identify with, and value, such qualities. It is for that reason that they continue to speak in the name of the peasantry, although, realistically, few could call themselves peasants.

In a quarter of a century, a spectacular series of changes has been accomplished. Are the farmers today still peasants? The 'disappearance of the peasantry' is first and foremost reflected in the massive reduction in the agricultural population, such that it is now a minority in rural regions dominated by other groups. It has also lost that identity which was shaped by a quasi-autarkic economy and a system of values which gave it coherence *vis-à-vis* society as a whole. Farmers today form a heterogeneous group whose divisions are a reflection of divergent economic interests. Their individuality within French society increasingly stems from the powerful economic position they occupy by virtue of their ownership of land. That individuality stems, too, from their attitude to government. Many still feel that they belong to the peasantry. In this, public opinion often concurs. It is that nineteenth-century peasantry, one which persisted through to the 1950s, that has now vanished forever.

Conclusion

In the long term, the French peasantry has undergone a unique evolution, one which marks it off from the rest of society. The dramatic changes of 1950–60 obscured from view the slow pace of change that had taken place in the nineteenth century, giving the impression that peasant society was immobile and unchanging. Increasingly, farmers have been able to secure their access to land. The rapid development of new agricultural techniques has helped to considerably improve working conditions. Social and economic emancipation has been achieved, however, at the cost of cultural absorption into the rest of society. The peasantry has been able to throw off the control of the old rural squirearchy and has created its own elite. The image of the peasant has also been transformed in spectacular fashion. In less than a century, the peasant has passed from that lowly, despised individual to someone seeming to inculcate, at least for urbanites, all the very best values. He has become someone to be envied, not despised. Such a flattering image is, of course, as unrealistic as earlier, rather different ones. Too simplistic, it fails to take account of diverse reality. Today, the peasantry can hardly be said to exist as a coherent group. There is precious little in common between the large farmer of the Brie and Beauce, endowed with great economic influence and, in terms of income, integrated into the upper echelons of society, and the indebted Breton small farmer making ends meet with a second job. Peasants, there still are, but the peasantry has gone.

Appendix 1

Demographic change: 1801–1907

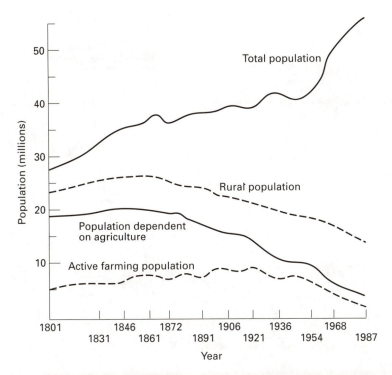

Source: Jean-Claude Toutain, 'La population de la France de 1700 à 1959', *Cahiers de l'ISEA*, no. 133, January–March, 1963; Jean-Paul Girard, Monique Gombert, Michel Petry, *Les Agriculteurs*, vol. I, *Clés pour une comparaison sociale*, Paris, INSEE, 1977, pp. 15–25; *Annuaire statistique de la France*, Paris, INSEE, 1987.)

Appendix 2

The price of corn in France: 1760–1980

(Prices standardised on the basis of values as of 1 January 1960)

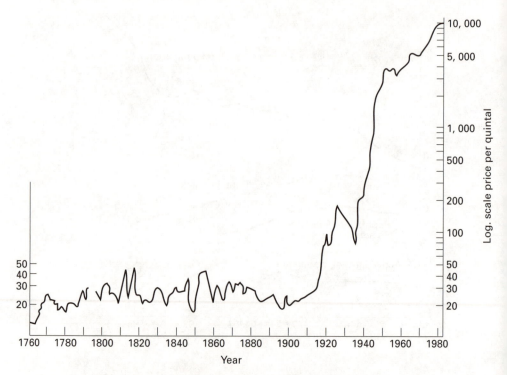

(*Source:* From Ernest Labrousse, *Histoire économique et sociale de la France*, vol. IV (3), pp. 1712–13.)

Appendix 3

Farm categories by size: 1882–1985

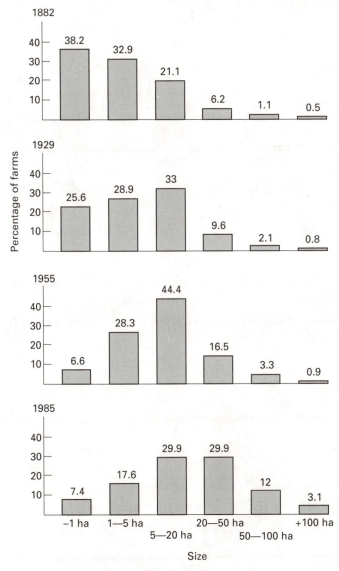

(*Source:* INSEE and SCEES.)

Appendix 4

The price of agricultural land: 1850–1985

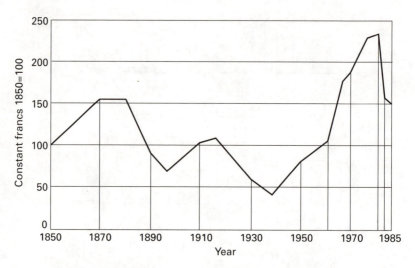

(*Source: L'Agriculture française,* in *La Documentation photographique,* no. 6084, 1986, and *GraphAgri 87.*)

Appendix 5

Revenue generated by agricultural labour: 1882 and 1986

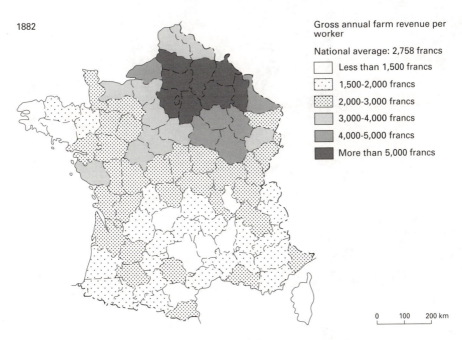

1882

Gross annual farm revenue per worker

National average: 2,758 francs

	Less than 1,500 francs
	1,500-2,000 francs
	2,000-3,000 francs
	3,000-4,000 francs
	4,000-5,000 francs
	More than 5,000 francs

0   100   200 km

(*Source: Histoire économique et sociale de la France*, vol. III (2), p. 732.)

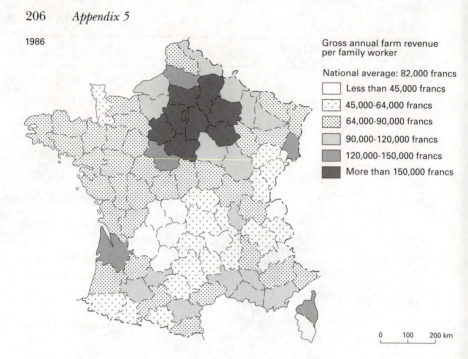

1986

Gross annual farm revenue
per family worker

National average: 82,000 francs

☐ Less than 45,000 francs
▦ 45,000-64,000 francs
▦ 64,000-90,000 francs
☐ 90,000-120,000 francs
☐ 120,000-150,000 francs
■ More than 150,000 francs

0   100   200 km

(*Source: Comptes de l'agriculture*, 1986, INSEE, pp. 80–1.)

Notes

Introduction

1 See bibliography, reference (11).
2 On the changing sense of the word peasant since the beginning of the nineteenth century, see P. Barral, 'Note historique sur l'emploi du terme "paysan"', *Etudes rurales*, 1966, pp. 72–80.
3 See, for example the definition given by P. Richelet in his *Dictionnaire de la langue française ancienne et moderne* in 1728: 'The peasant: someone who comes from a village in the country. Peasants are not as cultured as city people . . . Adj. Used as a term of abuse signifying rustic, crude, impolite, dishonest.'
4 Quote from the late-eighteenth-century dictionary, the *Littré*, to illustrate the sense of the word peasant.
5 H. Mendras, *Le Monde*, 13 September 1977.

1 From the ancien régime to the Restoration: 1789–1815

1 See bibliography. A summary of some of the problems of interpreting the history of this period is given in A. Soboul (128); and J. Nicholas (121).
2 J.-P. Jessenne (114), p. 705.
3 J.-M. Sallmann (88), pp. 73–7.
4 F. Sigaut (148), pp. 631–43.
5 Lavoisier, 'Mémoire lu à l'Assemblée provinciale de l'Orléanais'. Quoted in O. Festy, *L'Agriculture pendant la Révolution française*, vol. II, *L'Utilisation des jachères (1789–1795)*, 1950, p. 14.
6 See M. Lachiver (83), p. 400.
7 A.-G. Haudricourt and M. Jean-Brunhes Delamarre (37).
8 Quoted in P. Houée (14), p. 20.
9 A. Young, *Voyages en France pendant les années 1787, 1788, 1789*, Paris, Colin, 1931, reprinted 1976. The parliamentarians of Aix showed little interest in agronomic work. Their libraries had few specialised works on the subject. In 1785, the *intendant* noted that the agronomic society of Aix met only infrequently. Cf. M. Cubells, *La Provence des Lumières. Les parlementaires d'Aix au XVIII siècle*, Paris, Maloine, 1984.
10 J. C. Toutain (44).
11 M. Morineau (40).

12 E. Le Roy Ladurie (11), vol. II, p. 580.

13 Cf. J.-C. Asselain (29), p. 30; and E. Labrousse (30), vol.II, p. 476.

14 For Auvergne, see A. Poitrineau (86), vol. I, pp. 153–62. For the Beauce, cf. M. Vovelle (109), p. 217.

15 J. Péret (85), p. 533.

16 J.-P. Jessenne (114), p. 720.

17 J. Péret (85), vol. II, p. 533.

18 P. Bois (56), vol. I, p. 459. On the question of rent see also: B. Garnier, 'Structure et conjoncture de la rente foncière dans la Haut-Maine au XVII et XVIII siècles', *Cahiers des annales de Normandie*, no. 1, Caen, 1979, pp. 103–36.

19 On the nobility at the end of the eighteenth century see J.-P. Gutton (104), pp. 155–70; and G. Lemarchand (117), pp. 536–58.

20 On the level of seigneurial rents see J. Nicolas (84), p. 210; J. Godechot (113), p. 39; A Poitrineau (86), vol. I, pp. 341–51; J.-P. Gutton (104), p. 165; R. Secher (125), pp. 62–3; J.-N. Luc (119).

21 A. Poitrineau (86), vol. I, pp. 355–74.

22 A. Poitrineau (97).

23 On the position of domestic farm workers see J.-P. Gutton, *Domestiques et serviteurs dans la France de l'ancien régime*, Paris, Aubier, 1981, pp. 101–32.

24 J. Péret (85), p. 538.

25 See J.-M. Boehler (100), pp. 93–116.

26 J.-M. Moriceau, 'Les baccanals ou grèves de moissonneurs en pays de France (deuxième moitié du XVIIIe siècle)' (54), p. 421.

27 J.-L. Flandrin (95).

28 E. Claverie and P. Lamaison (101).

29 J.-M. Boehler (100), pp. 103–4.

30 B. Derouet (94), pp. 54–5.

31 See A. Collomp (93).

32 In the countryside *seigneurie*, parish and community constituted three separate territories, often similar in area but not always coexisting. See J.-P. Gutton (104), pp. 69–88.

33 By edict in June 1787, the monarchy reformed the so-called 'community of inhabitants' in order to make them more responsive to central control. A form of representation based on a tax census was instituted. A minimum tax payment of 10 pounds was required to be able to vote and 30 pounds to be eligible for election to a municipal assembly comprising between three and nine members. Priests and the nobility were members of this council by right.

34 See J.-P. Gutton (104), pp. 226–54; and F. Roudault, 'Le message politique des sermons en Breton à la fin de l'ancien régime' (53), pp. 143–5.

35 It is perhaps permissible to use the term *notable* in the sense that it took on under the monarchy, that is, those groups with comfortable incomes, the respect of the community and a local and national political influence, whilst still retaining personal links with the local community.

36 On this question see F. Furet and J. Ozouf (203); and B. Grosperrin (103).

37 A number of recent works have dealt with the subject of fêtes. See especially J.-P. Gutton (104), pp. 238–45; Y.-M. Bercé (99); M. Vovelle (108).

38 N. Pellegrin (106).

39 On violence and disorder in the countryside see O. Hufton (105).

40 D. Martin, 'Justice parisienne et justice provinciale au XVIII siècle. L'exemple de l'Auvergne', *Bulletin de la société d'histoire moderne*, 1976, no. 15, pp. 3–12.

41 See E. Le Roy Ladurie (11), vol. II, p. 5750 and R. Dupuy, 'Sociologie et politique de la contestation' (54), pp. 727–30.

42 J. Nicolas, 'Le paysan et son seigneur en Dauphiné à la veille de la Révolution' (81), vol. II, p. 506.

43 See the works of E. Labrousse (82). Recent researches in quantitative history (J. Marczewski, T. Markovitch and J.-C. Toutain) have supported the notion of strong economic growth at the end of the ancien régime. But industry and commerce played the central role and for agriculture the position remains far from clear.

44 On the procedure for convocation see the thesis of R. Robin, *La Société française en 1789: Saumur-en-Auxois*, Paris, 1970. On the contents of the *cahiers de doléances*, P. Goubert and M. Denis, *Les Français ont la parole*, Paris, Juillard, coll: 'Archives'; R. Chartier (111), pp. 68–93.

45 J. Nicolas (121), p. 25.

46 His work still retains its value. G. Lefebvre, *La Grande Peur*, Paris, 1932; new edn, Paris, Ed. Sociales, 1953; new edn, Paris, Colin, 1988.

47 M. Vovelle (109), pp. 236–69.

48 On this controversial question see P. Massé, 'Les survivances des droits féodaux dans l'Ouest', *Annales historiques de la Révolution française*, 1965, pp. 270–93; and A. Soboul (127), pp. 147–66.

49 O. Festy, *L'Agriculture pendant la Révolution française*, vol. I, *Les Conditions de production et de récolte des céréales (1789–1795)*, Paris, 1947, pp. 67–86.

50 On the progress of enclosure see J. Merley (69), p. 308; and G. Gavignaud, 'La propriété privée des terres en Roussillon: respect et contestations de 1789 à 1849' (54), pp. 253–9.

51 See O. Festy, *L'Agriculture pendant la Révolution française*, vol. I, pp. 168–9; and H. Luxardo (17), pp. 209–10.

52 P. Goujon (200), p. 126.

53 G. Garrier (62), vol. I, p. 123.

54 The question is considered in a number of regional monographs dealing with the period. See especially G. Lefebvre (115), pp. 414–510; G. Garrier (62), pp. 120–5; M. Vovelle (109), pp. 204–7; R. Marx (131).

55 A. Soboul (128).

56 *Ibid.*

57 C. Petitfrère (124), pp. 36–7.

58 There is a huge bibliography on this subject. Among the more recent works see P. Bois (110); C. Petitfrère (122); R. Dupuy (112); J.-C. Martin (120).

59 These estimates are controversial. See J.-C. Martin (120), p. 315; and the thesis of R. Secher (126).

60 P. Bois (56).

61 C. Petitfrère (122).

62 G. Lefebvre (115), pp. 11 and 536.

63 M. Vovelle (109), p. 222.

64 A. Soboul (128), pp. 36–7.

65 M. Vovelle (109), pp. 279–99.

66 The phrase is from A. Soboul (30), vol. III (1), p. 132.

67 J. Merley (69), pp. 334–5.

68 M. Agulhon (196).

69 J. Godechot (130), pp. 279–301.

70 *Ibid.*, pp. 516–20.

71 J. Tulard, 'Problèmes sociaux de la France napoléonienne' (132), pp. 643–5.

72 The work of A. Chabert published in 1945 has since been followed up by L. Bergeron, 'Problèmes économiques de la France napoléonienne' (132), pp. 469–505; and by A. Soboul (30), vol. III (1), pp. 86–7.

73 J. Tulard (132), p. 660.

74 Cited by A. Soboul (30), p. 97.

75 M. Morineau, 'La pomme de terre au XVIII siècle', *Annales ESC*, 1970, no. 6, pp. 1767–85.

76 L. Bergeron (129), pp. 187–8.

77 J. Dupaquier, 'Problèmes démographique de la France napoléonienne' (132), pp. 339–58.

78 C. Rollet, 'L'effet des crises économiques du début du XIXe siècle sur la population' (132), pp. 391–410.

79 M. Agulhon (222), pp. 47–106.

80 On the anti-Napoleon legend see J. Tulard, *L'AntiNapoléon, la légende noire de l'Empereur*, Paris, Juillard: coll. 'Archives', 1964. On the Imperial Legend the key reference remains A. Tudesq, 'La légende napoléonienne en France en 1848', *Revue historique*, 1957, pp. 64–85.

2 A slow transition: 1815–1870

1 M. Lévy-Leboyer, 'La croissance économique de la France au XIX siècle', *Annales ESC*, no. 4, July 1968, pp. 787–807; and J.-C. Toutain (44). A synthesis of their conclusions can be found in (30), vol. III (2), pp. 713–35.

2 On the evolution of viticulture see R. Pech (146), pp. 35–7; R. Laurent, 'Les quatres âges du vignoble du bas Languedoc et du Roussillon' (34), pp. 11–18; G. Garrier (62), pp. 173–5 and 366–7.

3 B. Garnier, 'Comptabilité agricole et système de production: l'embouche bas-Normande au début du XIX siècle', *Annales ESC*, no. 3, March–April 1982, pp. 320–43.

4 See the paper by J. Mulliez (145).

5 Regional disparities and their evolution have been examined in J. Pautard,

Les Disparités régionales dans la croissance de l'agriculture française, Paris, Gauthier-Villars, 1965.

6 See R. Hubscher (65), pp. 193–270.
7 Numerous examples have been cited by E. Weber (21), pp. 183–8.
8 On the diffusion of techniques see J.-C. Farcy (137), pp. 163–70.
9 *Ibid.*, p. 176.
10 R. Hubscher (155), pp. 10–12.
11 P. Lévêque (67), p. 355.
12 A. Gueslin (141), pp. 109–15.
13 G. Garrier (62), vol. I, pp. 310–11.
14 On the slow pace of diffusion of the heavy plough in Limagne see P. Coutin, 'Evolution de la technique des labours dans le nord de la Limagne depuis le début du XIXe siècle jusqu'en 1938', *Folklore paysan*, 1939, pp. 30–9.
15 J. Heffer, J. Mairesse, J.-M. Chanut (143), p. 1275.
16 R. Hubscher (65), vol. I, p. 59.
17 On the route network at the beginning of the nineteenth century see B. Lepetit, *Chemins de terre et Voie d'eau. Réseau de transports et organisation de l'espace en France (1740–1840)*, Paris, EHESS, 1984.
18 Cited by E. Weber (21), p. 288.
19 Cited by Y. Lequin (16), vol. I, pp. 113–15.
20 M.-L. Aubry-Lebreton (134), pp. 169–74.
21 M. Segalen (201), pp. 163–4.
22 For an analysis of the method of using the *cadastre* see R. Hubscher (65), vol. I, pp. 75–92.
23 R. Laurent (30), vol. III (2), pp. 637–8.
24 *Ibid.*, pp. 740–4.
25 Estimates of the level of property rents can be found in (11), vol. III, pp. 252–3; G. Garrier (62), vol. I, pp. 281–3; M. Denis (58), p. 343.
26 See M. Denis (58), pp. 156–60.
27 See the paper by G. Postel-Vinay (157), pp. 27–50.
28 See G. Garrier (62), vol. I, pp. 137–40; R. Hubscher (65), vol. I, pp. 120–4.
29 M. Agulhon (222), pp. 254–8.
30 Figures cited by A. Rowley (43), p. 244. They are no more than estimates because the 1862 census did not take farms below 1 hectare into consideration.
31 J.-C. Farcy (61), p. 514.
32 J. Heffer, J. Mairesse, J.-M. Chanut (143), p. 1277.
33 F. Braudel (30), vol. III, p. 176.
34 Estimates from J.-C. Toutain (44), pp. 54–5.
35 See M. Agulhon (11), vol. III, pp. 60–1.
36 See the thesis of E. Thibault (168), p. 29.
37 M. Segalen (26).
38 See R. Hubscher (65), vol. I, p. 148.
39 On medical developments in the countryside see J. Léonard (187), pp. 503–54.

40 The article by Y. Rinaudo (176) is a good summary of the question of multiple occupations and also provides a typology.

41 On rural artisans see J.-C. Farcy (171), pp. 473–90.

42 The *Revue du Nord* published two special issues on the subject of proto-industrialisation in 1979 and 1981. See (169).

43 See also the thesis by Y. Lamy (173), p. 511.

44 Migration patterns in the nineteenth century are well covered. See the theses of A. Châtelain (170) and A. Corbin (57).

45 Y. Rinaudo (176) has argued that agricultural migrations should not be considered as part of multiple-occupation patterns since they did not involve any change in the employment sector.

46 E. Weber (21) records a range of curious activities, pp. 327–8. See also Y. Rinaudo (176), p. 285.

47 The expression 'rural exodus' would seem to have first been used in France in 1903. See on this subject J. Pitié (24), p. 3.

48 H. Mendras suggests in (19) p. 141 that the term should be restricted to the large-scale movement of peasants into industrialised villages.

49 G. Garrier (62), vol. I, pp. 104–13.

50 *Ibid.*, vol. I, p. 106.

51 This is the classification suggested by R. Hubscher in (16), vol. II, p. 98.

52 On this subject see the contribution of G. Désert in *Le Bâtiment. Enquête d'histoire économique, XIV, XIX siècles*, Paris-La-Haye, Mouton, 1971, pp. 35–69. See also (11), vol. III, pp. 277–305.

53 Example cited in F. Dubost (179), pp. 45–60.

54 The tax on doors and windows was abolished in 1917.

55 On peasant diet see E. Weber (21), pp. 195–206.

56 The 'recycling' of textiles is considered by N. Pellegrin (189).

57 Study led by M.-T. Larroque (185), pp. 275–84.

58 Calculations by M. Garden (16), vol. I, p. 387.

59 Thesis put forward by J.-L. Flandrin in (102). The work is based on statistical data relating to premarital conception and illegitimacy.

60 With regard to sexual practices outside marriage see M. Segalen (107), pp. 44–8; and Y.-M. Hilaire (215), vol. I, pp. 76–7.

61 On family structure in the nineteenth century see J.-R. Lehning (164); F. F. Mendels (165); J.-C. Peyronnet (166).

62 Regional examples drawn from G. Augustin, R. Bonnain, Y. Péron, G. Sauter (160); J.-C. Farcy (61), p. 761; P. Bourdelais (161), pp. 21–38.

63 M. Segalen (201), pp. 30–46.

64 *Ibid.*, pp. 90–111.

65 A detailed study of the *fruitières* can be found in J.-L. Mayaud (228), pp. 101–19.

66 On patterns of female sociability see M. Segalen (201), pp. 150–1. The *couvige* (*covize* or *covedis*) is described by Ulysse Rouchon, *La Vie paysanne en Haute Loire*, vol. II, *Les Travaux et les jours rustiques*, Le Puy, 1935, pp. 140–1.

67 On this topic see M. Agulhon (222), pp. 207–34.
68 Numerous studies have examined popular religion in the nineteenth century. See the proceedings of the conference on this theme (219); the thesis of Y.-M. Hilaire (215); and the paper by P. M. Jones (216).
69 Statistics given in E. Weber (21), p. 319.
70 E. Weber devotes a chapter to this topic in (21), pp. 108–45.
71 Analysis drawn from M. Agulhon (222), pp. 192–5.
72 The picture industry expanded at the end of the nineteenth century. On the spread of the written media see P. Ory (16), vol. I, pp. 212–17, and A. Corbin (57), vol. I, pp. 382–90.
73 There is an enormous bibliography on this topic. The key reference remains F. Furet and J. Ozouf (203).
74 F. Furet and J. Ozouf (204), p. 490.
75 *Ibid.*, p. 494.
76 M. Agulhon (222), pp. 263–4.
77 On the post of mayor in France, consult the study undertaken in M. Agulhon, L. Girard, J.-L. Robert and W. Serman in (52), which deals primarily with rural communes.
78 H. de Balzac, *Les Paysans.* Cited by G. Garrier (62), vol. I, p. 314.
79 Y.-M. Hilaire (215), p. 664.
80 See the paper by J. Beauderot (219), pp. 159–69.
81 G. Garrier (62), vol. I, pp. 318–19.
82 M. Agulhon (222), pp. 472–81.
83 In the Doubs, the republican commissioner promised to let communal lands to the poorest members of the community, arousing thereby the hostility of many mountain villages. See J.-L. Mayaud (228), p. 215.
84 A. Corbin (57), vol. II, pp. 734–43.
85 An electoral map is given in M. Agulhon, *1848*, vol. VIII of the *Nouvelle Histoire de la France contemporaine*, Paris, Ed. du Seuil, 1974, p. 174.
86 See R. Ponton (243), pp. 103–7 and (244).
87 On the portrayal of peasants in painting see J.-C. Chamboredon (242); M.-T. Caille (241); C. and R. Brettell (240).
88 A. Corbin (57), vol. II, p. 852.
89 M. Vigreux (239), pp. 443–69.

3 The difficult years: 1870–1914

1 On the crisis in silk cultivation see C. Mesliand (70), vol. I, pp. 199–210.
2 *Ibid.*, p. 210.
3 See (11), vol. III, pp. 395–7.
4 On how the crisis was perceived by contemporaries see G. Dupeux (60), pp. 490–501; R. Hubscher (65), vol. II, pp. 591–5; and (30), vol. IV (1), p. 365.
5 J.-C. Toutain (44), p. 64.
6 G. Dupeux (60), p. 279.

7 On the viticultural situation see R. Laurent, 'Les quatres âges du vignoble du bas Languedoc et du Roussillon' (34).

8 The phylloxera crisis has been examined in depth in the theses of G. Garrier (62); R. Pech (146); Y. Rinaudo (71).

9 R. Pech (146), pp. 153–84.

10 G. Garrier (62), vol. I, pp. 498–9.

11 Numerous studies have examined the viticultural crisis. See the paper by J. Sagnes (235) or his book (234).

12 A detailed biographical note on Marcellin Albert is found in J. Maitron, *Dictionnaire bibliographique du mouvement ouvrier français*, vol. 10, Paris, Ed. Ouvrières, 1973, pp. 122–3.

13 See the paper by G. Désert, 'La production cidricole français face à la crise de la fin du XIXe siècle', *Colloque de la Société française d'économie rurale*, 23–4 September 1987. Published in *Economie rurale*, 1988.

14 See (11), vol. III, pp. 421–9.

15 On credit see G. Garrier (62), vol. I, pp. 507–11; R. Hubscher (65), vol. II, pp. 587–8.

16 See M. Hau, 'Pauvreté rurale et dynamisme économique: le cas de l'Alsace au XIXe siècle', *Histoire, économie et société*, no. 1, 1987, pp. 113–38.

17 G. Garrier (62), vol. I, p. 474.

18 *Ibid.*, vol. I, p. 477.

19 The standard work on the subject is P. Barral (46), especially pp. 104–40. A number of regional examples are given in G. Garrier (62); R. Hubscher (65); and Y. Rinaudo (71).

20 G. Garrier (62).

21 Y. Rinaudo (233), pp. 11–12.

22 See P. Gratton (48).

23 Recently republished (327).

24 On the action of Méline and the development of 'mélinism' see P. Barral (46).

25 See. A. Gueslin (141).

26 Statistics cited by P. Barral (46), vol. IV (1), p. 353.

27 R. Hubscher (155), p. 8.

28 R. Hubscher (65), vol. II, pp. 639 and 768–89.

29 J.-C. Farcy (61), pp. 514 and 567.

30 G. Garrier (62), vol. I, pp. 459–60; R. Hubscher (65), vol. II, pp. 691–702.

31 See the polemic between J.-N. Luc, R. Grew and J. Harrigan in *Annales ESC*, no. 4, July–August 1986, pp. 887–922.

32 On the pivotal role of the school in the process of social and political change during the second half of the nineteenth century see Thabault (320).

33 R. Hubscher (65), vol. II, p. 820.

34 J. Ozouf (210), pp. 63–85.

35 On newspapers see the *Bibliographie de la presse française*. A project to publish departmental volumes is currently being undertaken by the Bibliothèque nationale.

36 Cited by E. Weber (21), p. 437.
37 See the special number of *Ethnologie française* devoted to French diet (194), notably the papers of J. Lalouette and R. Bonnain.
38 See T. Fillaut (180) and (181).
39 On the chestnut see R. Bruneton-Governatori (178).
40 Y. Rinaudo (71), vol. II, p. 936.
41 See E. Weber (21), pp. 331–3.
42 This paragraph draws on the innovative paper by Guy Thullier (193).
43 On the growth of associations see M. Agulhon and M. Bodiguel (195); and P. Goujon (200).
44 E. Weber (21), pp. 669–79.
45 See C. Bertho, 'L'invention de la Bretagne", *Actes de la recherche en sciences sociales*, 1980; and F. Raison, *La colonie auvergnate de Paris au XIXe siècle*, Paris, Commission des Travaux Historiques, 1976.
46 R. Ponton (243), pp. 67–8; P. Barral (46), pp. 130–7.
47 On painting see M.-T. Caille (241); C. and R. Bretell (240).
48 On the early days of the III Republic see A. Corbin (57), vol. II, pp. 917–94; Y. Rinaudo (71), vol. II, pp. 650–722.
49 On methods of voting see J.-M. Mayeur, *La Vie politique sous la IIIe République*, Paris, Ed. du Seuil, 1984, pp. 22–7.
50 Cited by M. Agulhon (11), vol. III, p. 357.
51 A. Corbin (57), vol. II, pp. 936–7.
52 On the advance of republicanism, the standard work remains J. Gouault, *Comment la France est devenue républicaine*, Paris, Colin, Cahiers de la FNSP, 1954. See also P. Barral (46), pp. 36–9.
53 See J.-M. Mayeur, *La Vie politique sous la IIIe République*, pp. 84–5.
54 *Ibid.*, pp. 74–81.
55 On the *cercles*, see Y. Rinaudo (71), vol. II, p. 997.
56 See the paper by C. Mesliand (229).
57 See the contribution of M. Agulhon, 'La mairie' (231), pp. 167–93.
58 Architectural books offered a range of standard plans to builders which could be modified depending on the number of inhabitants in the commune.
59 M. Agulhon (223).
60 (52), p. 41.
61 A. Corbin (57), vol. II, p. 977; Y. Rinaudo (71), vol. II, p. 958.
62 Statistics cited by R. Hubscher (65), vol. II, p. 108.
63 J.-C. Bontron (224), p. 148.
64 These regional examples are taken from A. Corbin (57), vol. II, pp. 979–80; and C. Mesliand (70), p. 208.
65 On examples of such action see A. Rivet, *La Vie politique dans le département du la Haute-Loire*, Le Puy, Ed. des Cahiers de la Haute-Loire, 1979.
66 See M. Burns (225), who defends the argument that there was a decline in the political role of rural-dwellers at the end of the nineteenth century.
67 See the article by P. Boutry (213), pp. 25–31.

68 Cited by Y.-M. Hilaire (215), vol. II, p. 451.
69 This section draws heavily on the work of Louis Pérouas, especially (220), pp. 94–134.
70 See J. Ozouf (210); and F. Muel (209).
71 P. Barral (46), pp. 41–66. The typology suggested by Barral has been used, with some modifications, by M. Agulhon in (11), vol. III, pp. 512–15; and J.-M. Mayeur, *La Vie politique sous la IIIe République*, pp. 205–8.
72 L. Pérouas (220), pp. 80–3 and 200–4.

4 Towards a separate world: 1914–1950

1 The works of Augé-Laribé (247) are still a fundamental reference for agricultural questions. On the question of public opinion see J.-J. Becker (249) and (250).
2 The theses of G. Garrier (62); G. Gavignaud (63); C. Mesliand (70); and J.-C. Farcy (61) are exceptions.
3 Cited by J.-J. Becker (250), p. 105.
4 On the way in which mobilisation was organised in the countryside see J.-J. Becker (249), pp. 269–76; and, by the same author, 'Voilà le glas de nos gars qui sonne . . . ', *1914–1918. L'Autre Front*, no. 2, *Cahiers du mouvement social*, 1977, pp. 13–33.
5 On the involvement of women in agricultural work during the First World War see M. Segalen (201), p. 186; and (11), vol. IV, pp. 165–6.
6 See A. Cochet (251), p. 42.
7 J.-C. Farcy (61), p. 574.
8 *Ibid.*, p. 582; and H. Gerest (253), p. 135.
9 On the decline in production see P. Barral (30), vol. IV (2), p, 825.
10 On requisitioning see H. Gerest (253), p. 120; and (11), vol. IV, p. 45.
11 Cited in H. Gerest (253), p. 129.
12 A. Prost has outlined some of the problems posed by the statistics on war victims in (254), vol. II, pp. 2–4.
13 Estimate by H. Gerest (253), p. 169.
14 On these demographic problems see P. Festy, 'Effets et répercussions de la Première Guerre mondiale sur la fécondité française', *Population*, November–December 1984, pp. 977–1010.
15 See J.-C. Farcy (61), p. 185; and H. Gerest (253), p. 149.
16 On this question see J.-J. Becker (250), pp. 22–5.
17 See H. Gerest (253), p. 185; and J.-C. Farcy (61), p. 600.
18 An increasing number of wartime correspondences have been published recently. See, for example, P. Raybaut (255); G. Baconnier, A. Minet, L. Soler (248); J. Lovie, *Poilus, savoyards. Chronique d'une famille tarentaise, 1913–1918*, Chambéry, coll. 'Gens de Savoie', 1980. See also R. Chabert, *Printemps au tranchées. Notes de campagnes de Joseph Astier, soldat de la Grande Guerre*, Lyon, Bellier, 1982.

Soldiers' letters can also be studied by examining the archives of the postal service. See, for example, A. Cochet (251). On living conditions at the front see S. Audoin-Rouzeau (246).

19 See A. Prost (254), especially vol. II, pp. 128–200. On war memorials see, by the same author, 'Les monuments aux morts. Culte républicain? Culte civique? Culte patriotique?' (231), pp. 195–225.

20 On pacifism amongst the peasantry see I. Boussard, 'Le pacifisme paysan' (257), pp. 59–75.

21 Cited by P. Barral (46), p. 191.

22 The census of 1929 was not, in fact, completed until after 1931. The only real point of comparison should be with the census of 1892.

23 G. Garrier (62), vol. I, pp. 619–25.

24 This question excited considerable controversy in the inter-war period. Because peasants paid a considerable tax upon inheritance, their defenders minimised the fiscal immunities they benefited from.

25 Cited by A. Gueslin (35), vol. I, p. 55.

26 On the reorganisation of the Crédit agricole in 1920 see A. Gueslin (35) vol. I, pp. 58–69. The renamed Caisse nationale de crédit agricole replaced the old Office in 1926.

27 See (11), vol. IV, p. 72.

28 See A. Gueslin (35), vol. I, pp. 140–2 and 507–8.

29 Their numbers increased rapidly in the Paris Basin. See in this regard the experiences of Grenadou (325), pp. 155–8.

30 See A. Gueslin (35), vol. I, pp. 131 and 314.

31 On the financing of the electrification programme see *ibid.*, p. 131.

32 Estimates from (11), vol. IV, p. 64.

33 See (11), vol. IV, p. 78.

34 G. Garrier (62), vol. I, p. 592. Grenadou started to sell meat direct to the butchers after he had purchased a car. See (325), p. 184.

35 Cited by J.-C. Bonnet in (13), p. 416.

36 See (325).

37 On the Office at Landernau see S. Berger (256).

38 A. Sauvy (260), vol. II, pp. 67–9; and P. Barral (30), vol. IV (2), pp. 834–6.

39 On the policies pursued between 1928 and 1935, see P. Barral (30), vol. IV (2), pp. 841–2; and A. Sauvy (260), vol. II, pp. 73–4.

40 On this question see A. Gueslin (35), vol. I, pp. 343–71.

41 On the rise of corporatism before the Second World War, see, *inter alia*, S. Berger (256), pp. 157–67; and (11), vol. IV, pp. 426–30.

42 *La Voix de la Terre*, 1 March 1929. Cited by P. Barral (46), p. 237. The Parti Agraire was seen as a left-wing party by Grenadou: see (325), p. 176.

43 See P. Ory, 'Le Dorgèrisme, institution et discours d'une colère paysanne', *Revue d'histoire moderne et contemporaine*, April–June 1975, pp. 168–90; and P. Barral (46), p. 240.

44 On left-wing syndicalism see (11), vol. IV, pp. 409–12; and P. Gratton (48), pp. 123–94.

45 On the creation of the ONIB see P. Barral (30), vol. IV (2); and A. Gueslin (35), vol. I, p. 504.
46 From M. Luirard (258), p. 554.
47 Cited by R. Estier (13), p. 430.
48 On this subject see R. Hubscher (16), vol. II, pp. 143–4.
49 On the Corporation see I. Boussard (262).
50 M. Luirard (258), p. 554.
51 On the difficulties of food supply see M. Cépède (263); and P. Barral, 'La soudure du blé en France en 1942 et 1943', (10), pp. 221–33.
52 M. Luirard (258), p. 559. On the problems of agricultural statistics relating to the war years see M. Augé-Laribé, *Situation de l'agriculture française*, Paris, Berger-Levrault, 1945, pp. 259–62.
53 Estimate from INSEE, *Mouvement économique de la France de 1938 à 1948*, Paris, INSEE, 1950, p. 69.
54 M. Luirard (258), p. 545.
55 H. Amouroux, *La Vie des Français sous l'Occupation*, Paris, Fayard, 1961, p. 154.
56 M. Luirard (258), p. 545.
57 J.-P. Azéma, *De Munich à la Libération*, vol. XIV of the *Nouvelle Histoire de la France contemporaine*, Paris, Ed. du Seuil, 1979, p. 164.
58 Cited by J.-C. Bonnet (13), p. 435.
59 E. Grenadou and A. Prévost (325), p. 205.
60 M. Cépède (263), p. 333.
61 See A. Gueslin (35), vol. I, pp. 602–3.
62 H. Rousso examines this question in 'Où en est l'histoire de la Résistance' (264), pp. 113–37.
63 *Ibid.*, p. 122.
64 Data from J.-C. Bonnet (13), pp. 436–7.
65 On the creation of the CGA see I. Boussard (262), p. 357; and J.-C. Bonnet (13), pp. 439–41.
66 Calculations made by E. Morfin (267), p. 44. G. Wright, from a sample of case studies, estimated that one-third of regional syndics from the Corporation gained their old posts in the post-war groupings. See (261), p. 137.
67 On the Chambers of Agriculture see (11), vol. IV, pp. 459–60.
68 *Ibid.*
69 On the financing of post-war agricultural modernisation see especially (35), vol. I, pp. 656–64.
70 There were some 10,000 CUMAs in 1948. They largely disappeared once machinery became more widely available on the market.
71 On the department of Loire see M. Luirard (258), pp. 811–16.
72 R. Dumont, *Voyages en France d'un agronome*, Paris, Génin, 1951. On the Limagne see M. Derruau (74).
73 H. Mendras (301); and L. Wylie (303). The daily life of a peasant family in Aveyron was traced in the film *Farrebique* directed by G. Rouquier in 1945.
74 On the privations of domestic life in 1946 see (11), vol. IV, p. 213; and J.-C. Bonnet (13), p. 443.

75 On changes in diet see R. Bonnain, 'Les transformations de l'alimentation paysanne dans les Baronnies depuis l'entre-deux-guerres', *Ethnologie française*, no. 3, 1980, p. 312.
76 On town–country relations see R. Schwab (167), p. 455.

5 A spectacular transformation: 1950 to the present

1 See H. Mendras (274), 1967. The author reaffirms his interpretations made in that volume in a chapter entitled 'Réflexion vingt ans après' in the new edition of his book published in 1984.
2 On the role of the JAC see D. Barres, F. Colson, H. Nallet (305).
3 Taken from the *Cahier de formation de la JAC*, December 1954. Cited in (11), vol. IV, p. 467.
4 F. Boulard, *Problèmes missionaires de la France rurale*, Paris, Ed. du Cerf, 1945. Dances provided the opportunity for young men and women, normally carefully segregated, to meet.
5 These networks of modernisation have been studied by the sociologist E. Morin in (302).
6 See M. Besnault, 'Le rôle respectif du public et du privé dans la fourniture d'informations aux agriculteurs', *Economie rurale*, no. 171, January–February 1986, pp. 16–25.
7 See the paper by H. Tudesq given to the meeting of the Société française d'économie rurale, 'Cent ans d'histoire agricole française', September 1987, published in *Economie rurale*, 1988.
8 M. Marié and J. Viard, *La Campagne inventée, ou ce qu'il advient des rapports entre les paysans, leurs communautés et l'environnement urbain dans quatre villages d'un pays de moyenne Provence*, Le Paradou, Actes/Sud, 1977, p. 85.
9 L. Wylie (303).
10 Cited by A. Gueslin (35), vol. I, p. 819. On the role of the Crédit agricole in agricultural modernisation see *ibid*, vol. I, pp. 807–24.
11 A. Fel (76), pp. 206–7.
12 Statistics given by P. Bairoch at the conference of the Société française d'économie rurale, September 1987. See note 7.
13 This was the case, for example, for Lucien Gachon. See J. Pitié (25), p. 134.
14 On the rural novels of the 1950s see R.-M. Lagrave, *Le Village romanesque*, Le Paradou, Actes/Sud, 1980. The films of the same period have been considered in *Cinémas paysans*, special issue of *CinémAction*, 1982.
15 On the regrouping of parishes and communes see (11), vol. IV, pp. 368–71.
16 For an examination of the efforts at agricultural adaptation made by medium-sized farmers in Aude see P. Collomp (291).
17 On this initiative see G. Wright (261), p. 177; and (11), vol. IV, pp. 460–2.
18 The financial implications of the agricultural policies of the IV and V Republics are considered in P. Alphandéry, 'Les concours financiers de l'Etat à l'Agriculture de 1945 à 1984', paper presented to the conference of the Société française d'Economie rurale, September 1987. See note 7.

19 A detailed study of how the new structural policies of the 1960s were put in place can be found in M. Faure (12), pp. 126–36; in (30), vol. IV (3), pp. 1441–3; and in (11), vol. IV, pp. 586–97.

20 The future of the structural policies is considered in J. Astruc (278), pp. 27–31; and R. Groussard (280), pp. 5–10.

21 The age at which indemnities could be granted was lowered to sixty in 1967 and the sums paid were increased at the same time.

22 On the SAFER see B. Villain, 'Histoire des SAFER', communication to the conference of the Société française d'économie rurale, September 1987. See note 7.

23 See A. Gueslin (35), vol. II, pp. 183–94.

24 On the development and problems posed by the joint management by the state and unions see P. Muller, 'La politique agricole entre corporatisme et management', *Pour*, no. 102, September–October 1985, pp. 31–40.

25 On the difficulties faced by the left once they gained power see P. Muller, 'Les obstacles au changement: peut-on changer de politique agricole', *Economie rurale*, no. 171, January–February 1986, pp. 48–51.

26 See the books by M. Debatisse, *Le Projet Paysan*, Paris, Ed. du Seuil, 1983; F. Guillaume, *Le Pain de la Liberté*, Paris, J.-C. Lattès, 1983; L. Lauga, *Agriculture: le présent dépassé*, Paris, Economica, 1985.

27 On peasant–state relations see (15), pp. 68–71.

28 Estimate from R. Chapuis (289), p. 162. On the same theme see P. Le Corroler, 'Agriculture: 100,000F par exploitant et par an', *Le Nouvel Economiste*, 19 October 1981.

29 See C. Royer, 'Les aides de l'Etat a l'agriculture: une parte croissant du revenu agricole', *Economie rurale*, no. 145, September–October 1981, reprinted in *Problèmes économiques*, 17 February 1982, pp. 12–18.

30 On recent developments in agricultural syndicalism see F. Colson, 'Diversité de l'agriculture et pluralité syndicale', *Pour*, no. 102, September–October 1983, pp. 72–5.

31 On peasant demonstrations see in particular P. Champagne (312), pp. 9–41; C. Grignon, 'Le paysan inclassable', *Actes de la recherche en sciences sociales*, no. 4, July 1975, pp. 82–7; A. Guillemin (313), pp. 42–8.

32 Amongst recent studies see I. Boussard (311), pp. 3–11.

33 On recent agricultural change see J. Klatzmann (272); A. Fel (270); P. Roudié (276). See also L Bourgeois, 'L'expansion de la production agricole française', *Problèmes économiques*, 7 April 1983, pp. 14–19. Recent documents can be found in (275).

34 Statistics cited by P. Coulomb and H. Delorme, 'L'agriculture, les agriculteurs et la crise', *Pour*, no. 102, September–October 1985, p. 12.

35 *Ibid.*, p. 13.

36 Examples are to be found in the paper by A. Fel (270), pp. 10–11.

37 This idea is taken from a paper by P. Coulomb, 'Les paysans immergés dans la politique", *Pour*, no. 102, September–October 1985, p. 5.

38 Statistics from A. Gueslin (35), vol. II, p. 179. On the level of farmer debt see

also P. Trebiou, 'Pourquoi l'agriculture s'est-elle endettée?', *Economie et finances agricoles*, August–September 1985, and reprinted in *Problèmes économiques*, 2 January 1986, pp. 24–9.

39 On property structures see F. Houillier (281); and D. Boscheron and C. de Cirsenoy, 'De l'usage du sol agricole: la propriété contre l'exploitation', *Nouvelles Campagnes*, July 12983, reprinted in *Problèmes économiques*, 15 February 1984, pp. 17–25.

40 Example cited by R. Béteille (286), p. 91.

41 The Ministry of Agriculture, using rather different criteria, estimated the agricultural population in 1985 at 2,241,000 full- or part-time workers, representing some 1,499,000 UTA (a unit representing one full-time worker per year). See *GraphAgri*, 87 (5), p. 26.

42 See A. Barthez, *Famille, travail et agriculture*, Paris. Economica, 1982. See also C. Denisse, 'Les femmes dans l'agriculture', *Pour*, no. 93, January–February 1984, pp. 49–55.

43 A number of recent studies have looked at the importance of pluriactivity in farming. See in particular (174); E. Régnier, 'La pluriactivité en agriculture en 1981', *Archives et documents*, INSEE, April 1986; A. Brun, 'Aspects macro-économiques de la pluriactivité des familles agricoles', *Economie rurale*, no. 171, January–February 1986, pp. 38–74.

44 On farming/tourism see D. Ciavaldini and G. Novarina, 'Ni paysan, ni perchman, ni moniteur' (299), pp. 150–6.

45 On the problems faced by young people wishing to enter farming see F. Guillon, 'S'installer et moderniser l'exploitation agricole', *Economie rurale*, no. 171, January–February 1986, pp. 32–7; M.-C. Becouam, 'Le poids de l'héritage', *Pour*, no. 102, September–October 1985, pp. 8–10. On the sociological problems posed by successions to farms see P. Champagne, 'La reproduction de l'identité', *Actes de la recherche en sciences sociales*, November 1986, pp. 41–64.

46 See H. Hannin, 'L'enseignement agricole: évolutions contemporaines et spécificité', *Economie rurale*, no. 180, July–August 1987, pp. 37–42. See also no. 97 of the journal *Pour* (September–October 1984), which focuses on agricultural training.

47 See the dossier, 'Mobilité sociale', *Economie et statistique*, no. 199–200, May–June 1987, pp. 83–99.

48 The nature of such experiences is detailed in D. Léger and B. Hervieu, 'Les immigrés de l'utopie' (299), pp. 48–70. See also, by the same authors, *Le Retour à la nature. Au fond de la forêt . . . l'Etat*, Paris, Ed. du Seuil, 1979.

49 See R. Chapuis (289), p. 157; and J.-C. Bontron, 'Population et espace rural vers une nouvelle dynamique', *Pour*, June 1985, pp. 10–23. See also D. Dumain, 'Déconcentration urbaine', *Population et société*, February 1983, reprinted in *Problèmes économiques*, 7 April 1983, pp. 3–5.

50 This was the title of his book (286). See especially pp. 83–90 and 136–8.

51 See (285); and A. Fel (292), pp. 16–17.

52 T. Barthélémy de Saizieu (294), pp. 362–76.

53 B. Hervieu, 'Le village mort-vivant' (299), pp. 227–8. See also P. Champagne, 'La fête au village', *Actes de la recherche en sciences sociales*, 1977, pp. 73–84.

54 See M. Jollivet, 'Les pièges de la mère Denis' (299), pp. 22–30; R. Hubscher in (16), vol. II, pp. 500–2.

55 On the recent development of peasant themes in the cinema see R. Hubscher, 'Regards sur le monde agricole: les archives filmiques', paper presented to the conference of the Société française d'économie rurale, September 1987. See note 7.

56 On this point see N. Eizner, 'Sociologie composite, besoins contradictoires', *Pour*, June 1985, pp. 36–8.

57 Estimate from the Gouzes report (271), p. 111.

58 The gross agricultural revenue (RBA) is calculated by subtracting from agricultural revenue (both production and subsidies) intermediate inputs (fertiliser, energy, etc.), as well as social-security contributions. The gross farm revenue (RBE) carries out the same kind of calculation at the level of the individual farm. It equals the difference between receipts to the farm and expenses (intermediate inputs and charges). More details are given in P. Roudié (276), p. 47.

59 M. Gombert, 'Estimation du revenue des ménages par catégorie socials pour 1983', *Premiers Résultats*, INSEE, no. 77, November 1986, pp. 1–4. At that date the taxable revenue of farms was, on average, only 83,700 francs.

60 See F. Dubost (179), p. 4; and F. Zonabend (45), p. 41.

61 See the research of N. Herpin, 'L'habillement, la classe sociale et la mode', *Economie et statistique*, no. 188, May 1986, pp. 35–54.

62 See C. and C. Samy, 'Les départs en vacances de l'été 1986', *Premiers Résultats*, INSEE, March 1987, pp. 1–4.

63 See the study by P. Morniche, 'Pratiques culturelles, profession et consommation médicale', *Economie et statistique*, no. 189, June 1986, p. 44.

64 See 'Les emplois du temps en France en 1985–1986', *Premiers Résultats*, INSEE, no. 100, June 1987, p. 4.

65 The expression comes from R. Béteille (286), p. 95.

66 On the geographical patterns of farms see A. Fel (270), pp. 318–21; and V. Rey (275), p. 7.

67 A. Fel (270), p. 320.

68 On the diversity of the peasant world see B. Kayser, 'Face au "déménagement rural", quels paysans, quels espaces?' (299); M. Bodiguel, 'Du paysan à l'éternel paysan' (15), p. 6; R. Hubscher, in (16), vol. II, pp. 503–22; R. Béteille (286), pp. 94–9.

69 On the background and recruitment of agricultural leaders see S. Maresca (308), pp. 35–61, where he shows the family background of F. Guillaume. See also his book (307).

Bibliography

It is not the intention here to attempt to provide a complete bibliography of works on the peasantry. Instead, only a listing of works published after the appearance of volumes III and IV of the *Histoire de la France rurale*, under the general editorship of Georges Duby and Armand Wallon (published by Ed. du Seuil) has been provided. Much more detailed bibliographic material is contained in those two volumes noted above. Amongst the numerous journals devoted to agriculture and rural matters, *Etudes rurales* and *Economie rurale* deserve particular study. For the recent period, INSEE publishes a range of valuable material, especially in *Economie et statistique*. Publications by professional groups are also a useful source of material.

1. General

General sources

The major agricultural censuses have all been published. See in particular:
1 Gilbert Garrier, 'Les enquêtes décennales du XIXe siècle: essai d'analyse critique', *Pour une histoire de la statistique, Journées d'études sur l'histoire de la statistique (1976)*, vol. I, Paris, INSEE, 1977, pp. 269–81; new edn, Paris, Economica, 1987.
2 *Propriétaires, Fermiers et Métayers au XIXe siècle. Les enquêtes décennales, mode d'emploi*, vol. I, Paris, INRA, 1982.

These can be complemented by an examination of material in Series M of the departmental archives, Series F10 of the national archives and the archives of the Ministry of Agriculture. On the latter see:
3 Isabelle Richefort, 'Les archives du ministère de l'Agriculture', *Institut d'histoire du temps présent*, no. 23, March 1986, pp. 16–30.

For the recent period, as well as the INSEE studies, the publications of the Ministry of Agriculture repay careful study. On the problems of using agricultural statistics see:
4 Gérard Théodore et Michel Volle, 'Les statistiques agricoles', *Pour une histoire de la statistique*, vol. II, *Matériaux*, Paris, INSEE, 1977; new edn, Paris, Economica, 1986, pp. 501–32.

Recent agricultural data has been usefully summarised in an annual publication:

5 *GraphAgri 87, Annuaire de graphiques agricoles*, Paris, Ministry of Agriculture, SCEES, 1987.

General works

6 *Atlas de la France rurale*, Paris, Colin, 'Cahiers de la FNSP', 1968.
7 Michel Augé-Laribé, *Politique agricole de la France de 1880 à 1940*, Paris, PUF, 1950.
8 Marc Bloch, *Les Caractères originaux de l'histoire rurale française*, Oslo, Aschehoug, 1931; new edn, Paris, Colin, 1976.
9 Monique Clavel-Levêque, Guy Lemarchand and Marie-Thérèse Lorcin, *Comprendre les campagnes françaises. Précis d'histoire rurale*, Paris, Ed. Sociales, 1983.
10 'Conjoncture économique, structures sociales', *Hommage à Ernest Labrousse*, Paris-La Haye, Mouton, 1974.
11 Georges Duby and Armand Wallon (under the general editorship of), *Histoire de la France rurale*, Paris, Ed. du Seuil, 1975–6, vols. II, III and IV.
12 Marcel Faure, *Les Paysans dans la société française*, Paris, Colin, 1966.
13 Jean-Pierre Houssel (under the general editorship of), *Histoire des paysans français du XVIIIe siècle à nos jours*, Roanne, Horvath, 1976; new edn, 1987.
14 Paul Houée, *Les Etapes du développement rural*, 2 vols., Paris, Ed. Ouvrières, 1972.
15 'Le monde paysan', *Cahiers français*, no. 187, July–September 1978.
16 Yves Lequin (under the general editorship of), *Histoire des Français (XIXe–XXe)*, 3 vols., Paris, Colin, 1983.
17 Hervé Luxardo, *Les Paysans. Les républiques villageoises (Xe–XIXe siècle)*, Paris, Aubier, 1981.
18 Hervé Luxardo, *Rase Campagne. La fin des communautés villageoises*, Paris, Aubier, 1984.
19 Henri Mendras, *Sociétés paysannes. Eléments pour une théorie de la paysannerie*, Paris, Colin, 1976.
20 Jean Vidalenc, *La Société française de 1815 à 1846*, vol. I, *Le Peuple des campagnes*, Paris, Marcel Rivière, 1970.
21 Eugen Weber, *Peasants into Frenchmen: The Modernization of Rural France (1870–1914)*, Stanford University Press, 1976.

The evolution of the rural population

22 Philippe Ariès, *Histoire des populations françaises et de leur attitude devant la vie depuis le XVIIIe siècle*, Paris, Ed. du Seuil, 1979.
23 Philippe Ariès and Georges Duby (under the general editorship of), *Histoire de la vie privée*, vols. IV and V, Paris, Ed. du Seuil, 1987.
24 Jean Pitié, *L'Exode rural*, Paris, PUF, coll. 'Que sais-je?', no. 1747, 1979.
25 Jean Pitié, *L'Homme et son espace. L'exode rural en France du XVIe siècle à nos jours*, Paris, CNRS, 1987.

26 Martine Segalen, *Quinze Générations de bas Bretons*, Paris, PUF, 1985.
27 Martine Segalen, *Sociologie de la famille*, Paris, Colin, 1981.
28 Françoise Zonabend (under the general editorship of), *Histoire de la famille*, vol. II, *Le Choc des modernités*, Paris, Colin, 1986.

The socio-economic context

29 Jean-Charles Asselain, *Histoire économique de la France*, 2 vols., Paris, Ed. du Seuil, 1984.
30 Fernand Braudel and Ernest Labrousse (under the general editorship of), *Histoire économique et sociale de la France*, Paris, PUF, 1970–80, vols. II, III (1–2), IV (1–3).
31 Fernand Braudel, *L'Identité de la France*, 3 vols., Paris, Arthaud-Flammarion, 1986.
32 André and Danielle Cabanis, *La Société française aux XIXe et XXe siècles*, Toulouse, Privat, 1986.
33 Georges Dupeux, *La Société française (1789–1960)*, Paris, Colin, 1964; new edn, 1972.
34 'Economie et société en Languedoc-Roussillon de 1789 à nos jours', *Colloque de Montpellier* (25–6 September 1976), Montpellier, 1978.
35 André Gueslin, *Histoire des crédits agricoles*, 2 vols., Paris, Economica, 1984.
36 André Gueslin, *Le Crédit agricole*, Paris, La Découverte, 1985.
37 André-G. Haudricourt and Mariel Jean-Brunhes Delamarre, *L'Homme et la Charrue à travers le monde*, Paris, Gallimard, 1955.
38 *Hommage à Robert Laurent*, Montpellier, Université Paul Valéry, 1980.
39 Pierre Léon (under the general editorship of), *Histoire économique et sociale du monde*, vol. II, *La Domination du capitalisme*, Paris, Colin, 1978.
40 Michel Morineau, *Les Faux-semblants d'un démarrage économique: agriculture et démographie en France au XVIIIe siècle*, Paris, Colin, 'Cahier des Annales', no. 30, 1971.
41 Charles Parain, *Outils, Ethnies et Développement historique*, Paris, Ed. Sociales, 1979.
42 Jean-Robert Pitte, *Histoire du paysage français*, vol. II, *Le Profane: du XVIe siècle à nos jours*, Paris, Taillandier, 1983.
43 Anthony Rowley, *Evolution économique de la France du milieu du XIXe siècle à 1914*, Paris, SEDES-CDU, 1982.
44 Jean-Claude Toutain, *Le produit de l'agriculture française de 1700 à 1958*, Paris, 'Cahier de l'ISEA', no. 115, 1961.
45 Françoise Zonabend, *La Mémoire longue. Temps et histoire au village*, Paris, PUF, 1980.

The political context

46 Pierre Barral, *Les Agrariens français de Méline à Pisani*, Paris, Colin, 'Cahiers de la FNSP', 1968.

47 Philippe Gratton, *Les Luttes de classe dans les campagnes*, Paris, Anthropos, 1971.

48 Philippe Gratton, *Les Paysans contre l'agrarisme*, Paris, Maspero, 1972.

49 Hervé Le Bras, *Les Trois France*, Paris, Ed. Odile Jacob-Seuil, 1986.

50 Hervé Le Bras and Emmanuel Todd, *L'Invention de la France. Atlas anthropologique et politique*, Paris, Le Livre de Poche, 1981.

51 *Les Nostalgies des Français*, special number, *Histoire*, no. 5, June 1980.

52 *Les Maires en France du Consulat à nos jours*, Paris, Publications de la Sorbonne, 1987.

53 'Les paysans et la politique (1750–1850)', colloquium at Rennes, 21–2 May 1981, *Annales de Bretagne et des pays de l'Ouest*, vol. LXXXIX, 1982, no. 2, pp. 141–265.

54 'Mouvements populaires et conscience sociale, XVe–XIXe siècle', *Actes du colloque de Paris, 24–26 mai 1984*, Paris, Maloine, 1985.

Regional monographs (history)

55 Pierre Barral, *Le Département de l'Isère sous la IIIe République (1870–1940)*, Paris, Colin, 1962.

56 Paul Bois, *Paysans de l'Ouest. Des structures économiques et sociales aux options politiques depuis l'époque révolutionnaire dans la Sarthe*, Le Mans, Vilaine, 1960; abridged edn, Paris, Flammarion, 1971.

57 Alain Corbin, *Archaisme et Modernité en Limousin au XIXe siècle (1845–1880)*, 2 vols., Paris, Marcel Rivière, 1975.

58 Michel Denis, *Les Royalistes de la Mayenne et le Monde moderne (XIXe–XXe siècle)*, Paris, Klincksieck, 1977.

59 Gabriel Désert, *Une société rurale au XIXe siècle. Les Paysans du Calvados (1815–1895)*, 3 vols., Lille, Atelier de reproduction des thèses, 1975.

60 Georges Dupeux, *Aspects de l'histoire sociale et politique du Loir-et-Cher*, La Haye-Paris, Mouton, 1962.

61 Jean-Claude Farcy, *Les Paysans beaucerons de la fin de l'Ancien Régime au lendemain de la Première Guerre mondiale*, 3 vols., Paris X-Nanterre, 1985 (mimeographed thesis).

62 Gilbert Garrier, *Paysans du Beaujolais et du Lyonnais (1800–1970)*, 2 vols., Grenoble, Presses universitaires de Grenoble, 1973; summarised and complemented in *Vignerons du Beaujolais au siècle dernier*, Roanne, Horvath, 1984.

63 Geneviève Gavignaud, *Propriétaires-viticulteurs en Roussillon. Structures. Conjoncture. Société (XVIIe–XXe siècle)*, 2 vols., Paris, Publications de la Sorbonne, 1983.

64 Michel Hau, *La Croissance économique de la Champagne de 1810 à 1869*, Paris, Ophrys, 1976.

65 Ronald Hubscher, *L'Agriculture et la société rurale dans le Pas-de-Calais du milieu du XIXe siècle à 1914*, 2 vols., Arras, Mémoires de la Commission départementale des monuments historiques du Pas-de-Calais, 1980.

66 Jean-Pierre Jessenne, *Pouvoir au village et Révolution. Artois (1760–1848)*, Lille, Presses universitaires de Lille, 1987.

67 Pierre Lévêque, *Une société provinciale: la Bourgogne sous la monarchie de Juillet*, Paris, EHESS, 1983.

68 Pierre Lévêque, *Une société en crise: la Bourgogne au milieu du XIXe siècle (1846–1852)*, Paris, EHESS, 1983.

69 Jean Merley, *La Haute-Loire de la fin de l'Ancien Régime aux débuts de la IIIe République (1776–1886)*, 2 vols., Le Puy, Ed. des Cahiers de la Haute-Loire, 1974.

70 Claude Mesliand, *Paysans du Vaucluse (1860–1939)*, 5 vols., Paris X-Nanterre, 1980 (mimeographed thesis).

71 Yves Rinaudo, *Les Paysans du Var (fin XIXe siècle–début XXe siècle)*, 3 vols., Lille, Atelier de reproduction des thèses, 1982; abridged edn, *Les Vendanges de la République. Les Paysans du Var à la fin du XIXe siècle*, Lyon, Presses universitaires de Lyon, 1982.

Regional monographs (geography)

The opening chapters often contain valuable material on the evolution of rural life since the nineteenth century. A selected list would include:

72 Jean Boichard, *L'Elevage bovin, ses structures et ses produits en Franche-Comté*, 2 vols., Paris, Les Belles Lettres, 1977.

73 Pierre Brunet, *Structure agraire et économie rurale des plateaux tertiaires entre la Seine et l'Oise*, Caen, Caron et Cie, 1960.

74 Max Derruau, *La Grande Limagne auvergnate et bourbonnaise*, Clermont-Ferrand, Delaunay, 1949.

75 Roger Dugrand, *Villes et Campagnes en bas Languedoc. Le Réseau urbain du bas Languedoc méditerranéen*, Paris, PUF, 1963.

76 André Fel, *Les Hautes Terres du Massif central. Trdition paysanne et économie agricole*, Clermont-Ferrand, Publications de la faculté des Lettres, 1962.

77 Etienne Juillard, *La Vie rurale en basse Alsace*, Paris, Les Belles Lettres, 1953.

78 René Pijassou, *Un grand vignoble de qualité: le Médoc*, 4 vols., Bordeaux, Taillandier, 1978.

2. The peasantry at the end of the ancien régime

Economic and legal context

79 Georges Durand, *Vin, Vigne et Vignerons en Lyonnais et Beaujolais (XVIe–XVIIIe siècle)*, Lyon, Presses universitaires de Lyon, 1979.

80 Pierre Goubert, *L'Ancien Régime*, Paris, Colin, 1969.

81 *La France d'ancien régime. Etudes réunies en l'honneur de Pierre Goubert*, Toulouse, Privat, 1984.

82 Ernest Labrousse, *La Crise de l'économie française à la fin de l'ancien régime et au début de la Révolution*, Paris, PUF, 1944.

83 Marcel Lachiver, *Vin, Vigne et Vignerons en région parisienne du XVIIe au XIXe siècles*, Pontoise, Société historique et archéologique de Pontoise, 1982.

84 Jean Nicolas, *La Savoie au XVIIIe siècle, noblesse et bourgeoisie*, Paris, Maloine, 1978.

85 Jacques Péret, *Seigneurs et Seigneuries en Gâtine poitevine, le duché de la Meilleraye (XVIIe–XVIIIe siècle)*, Poitiers, Société des Antiquaires de l'Ouest, 1976.

86 Abel Poitrineau, *La Vie rurale en basse Auvergne au XVIIIe siècle (1726–1789)*, 2 vols., Paris, PUF, 1965.

87 Pierre de Saint-Jacob, *Les Paysans de la Burgogne du Nord au dernier siècle de l'ancien régime*, Paris, 1964.

88 Jean-Michel Sallmann, 'Le partage des biens communaux en Artois, 1770–1789', *Etudes rurales*, July–December 1977, pp. 71–84.

89 Alexis de Tocqueville, *L'Ancien Régime et la Révolution, 1789–1848*, 1856; new edn, Paris, Maspero, 1976.

Demography, family structures

90 Philippe Ariès, *L'Enfant et la vie familiale sous l'ancien régime*, Paris, Ed. du Seuil, 1973.

91 Philippe Ariès, *L'Homme devant la mort*, Paris, Ed. du Seuil, 1977.

92 Louis Assier-Andrieu, 'La communauté villageoise. Objet historique. Enjeu théorique', *Ethnologie française*, no. 4, 1986, pp. 351–60.

93 Alain Collomp, *La Maison du père. Famille et village en Haute-Provence au XVIIe et XVIIIe siècles*, Paris, PUF, 1983.

94 Bernard Derouet, 'Familles, ménage paysan et mobilité de la terre et des personnes en Thimerais au XVIIIe siècle', *Etudes rurales*, no. 86, April–June 1982.

95 Jean-Louis Flandrin, *Familles, parenté, maison, sexualité dans l'ancienne société*, Paris, 1976; new edn, Paris, Ed. du Seuil, 1984.

96 *Parenté et Alliance dans les sociétés paysannes*, special number of *Ethnologie française*, no. 4, 1981.

97 Abel Poitrineau, *Remues d'hommes, les migrations montagnardes en France (XVIIe–XVIIIe siècle)*, Paris, Aubier-Montaigne, 1983.

Social and political relations

98 Yves-Marie Bercé, *Croquants et Nu-Pieds. Les soulèvements paysans en France du XVI au XIX siècle*, Paris, Gallimard, 1974.

99 Yves-Marie Bercé, *Fête et Révolte. Essai sur la disparition des fêtes populaires du XVIe au XVIIIe siècle*, Paris, Hachette, 1975.

100 Jean-Michel Boehler, 'Communauté villageoise et contrastes sociaux: laboureurs et manouvriers dans la campagne strasbourgeoise de la fin du XVIIe au début du XIXe siècle', *Etudes rurales*, July–December, 1976, pp. 93–116.

101 Elisabeth Claverie and Pierre Lamaison, *L'Impossible Mariage. Violence et parenté en Gévaudan (XVIIe–XVIII siècle)*, Paris, Hachette, 1982.
102 Jean-Louis Flandrin, *Les Amours paysannes. Amour et Sexualité dans les campagnes de l'ancienne France (XVIe–XIXe siècle)*, Paris, Julliard, coll. 'Archives', 1975.
103 Bernard Grosperrin, *Les Petites Ecoles sous l'ancien régime*, Rennes, Ouest-France, 1984.
104 Jean-Pierre Gutton, *La Sociabilité villageoise dans l'ancienne France*, Paris, Hachette, 1979.
105 Olwen H. Hufton, 'Le paysan et la loi en France', *Annales ESC*, May–June 1983, pp. 679–701.
106 Nicole Pellegrin, *Les Bachelleries. Organisation et fêtes de la jeunesse dans le Centre-Ouest, XVe–XVIIe siècle*, Poitiers, Mémoires de la Société des antiquaires de l'Ouest, 1982.
107 Martine Segalen, *Amours et Mariages de l'ancienne France*, Paris, Berger-Levrault, 1981.
108 Michel Vovelle, *Les Métamorphoses de la fête en Provence de 1750 à 1820*, Paris, Aubier-Flammarion, 1976.
109 Michel Vovelle, *Ville et Campagne au XVIIIe siècle (Chartres et la Beauce)*, Paris, Ed. Sociales, 1980.

3. Revolution and empire

The peasantry during the Revolution

110 Paul Bois, 'La Vendée contre la République", *L'Histoire*, no. 27, October 1980, pp. 10–17.
111 Roger Chartier, 'Cultures, lumières, doléances: les cahiers de 1789', *Revue d'histoire moderne et contemporaine*, vol. XXVIII, 1981, pp. 68–93.
112 Roger Dupuy, 'La Contre-Révolution (1780–1802): éléments d'un chantier', *Bulletin de la Société d'histoire moderne*, no. 3, 1986, pp. 16–20.
113 Jacques Godechot, *La Révolution française dans le Midi toulousain*, Toulouse, Privat, 1986.
114 Jean-Pierre Jessenne, 'Le pouvoir des fermiers dans les villages d'Artois (1770–1848)', *Annales ESC*, May–June 1983, pp. 702–34.
115 Georges Lefebvre, *Les Paysans du Nord pendant la Révolution française*, 1st edn, 1924; new edn, Paris, Colin, 1972.
116 Georges Lefebvre, *Questions agraires au temps de la Terreur*, Strasbourg, Lenig, 1932.
117 Guy Lemarchand, 'La féodalité et la Révolution française: seigneurie et communauté paysanne", *Annales historiques de la Révolution française*, October–December 1980, pp. 536–58.
118 *Les Résistances à la Révolution. Actes du colloque de Rennes (17–21 septembre 1985)*, Paris, Imago, 1987.
119 Jean-Noël Luc, *Paysans et Droits féodaux en Charente-Inférieure pendant la*

Révolution, Paris, Commission d'histoire de la Révolution française, 1984.

120 Jean-Clément Martin, *La Vendée et la France*, Paris, Ed. du Seuil, 1987.

121 Jean Nicolas, 'Les mouvements populaires dans le monde rural sous la Révolution française: état de la question', *Bulletin de la Société d'histoire moderne*, no. 3, 1986, pp. 20–9.

122 Claude Petitfrère, *Blancs et Bleus d'Anjou (1789–1793)*, Lille, Atelier de reproduction de thèses, 1979.

123 Claude Petitfrère, *La Vendée et les Vendéens*, Paris, Gallimard, coll. 'Archives', 1981.

124 Claude Petitfrère, 'Le peuple contre la Révolution française', *l'Histoire*, no. 53, February 1983, pp. 34–43.

125 Reynald Secher, *La Chapelle-Basse-Mer, village vendéen. Révolution et contrerévolution*, Paris, Perrin, 1986.

126 Reynald Secher, *Le Génocide franco-français, La Vendée-Vengé*, Paris, PUF, 1986.

127 Albert Soboul, *Problèmes paysans de la Révolution*, Paris, Maspero, 1976; new edn, 1983.

128 Albert Soboul, 'Les paysans "partageux" et la Révolution française', *L'Histoire*, no. 26, September 1980, pp. 30–7.

The new institutional framework

129 Louis Bergeron, *L'Episode napoléonien*, vol. IV of *Nouvelle histoire de la France contemporaine*, Paris, Ed. du Seuil, 1972.

130 Jacques Godechot, *Les Institutions de la France sous la Révolution et l'Empire*, Paris, PUF, 1951; new edn, 1985.

131 Roland Marx, *La Révolution et les classes sociales en basse Alsace. Structures agraires et vente des biens nationaux*, Paris, BN, 1974.

132 *La France sous le premier Empire*, special number of *Revue d'histoire moderne et contemporaine*, July–September 1970.

133 Xavier Martin, 'Anthropologie et Code Napoléon', *Bulletin de la Société française d'histoire des idées et d'histoire religieuse*, no. 1, 1984, pp. 39–62.

4. Works on the nineteenth century

The economic environment

134 Marie-Louise Aubry-Lebreton, 'La floraison des foires et des marchés au XIXe siècle. L'exemple d'un département breton: l'Ille-et-Vilaine', *Etudes rurales*, April–December 1980, pp. 169–74.

135 Maurice Aymard, 'Autoconsommation et marchés: Chayanov, Labrousse ou Le Roy Ladurie?', *Annales ESC*, no. 6, November–December 1983, pp. 1392–410.

136 Hugh Clout, *French Agriculture on the Eve of the Railway Age*, London, Croom Helm, 1980.

137 Jean-Claude Farcy, 'Le monde rural face au changement technique: le cas de la Beauce au XIXe siècle', *Histoire, économie et société*, no. 1, 1983, pp. 161–80.

138 Jean-Michel Gaillard and André Lespagnol, *Les Mutations économiques et sociales au XIXe siècle (1780–1880)*, Paris, Nathan, 1984.

139 Bernard Garnier, 'Comptabilité agricole et système de production: l'embouche bas-normande au début du XIXe siècle', *Annales ESC*, no. 2, March–April 1982, pp. 320–43.

140 André Gueslin, *Le Crédit mutuel. De la caisse rurale à la banque sociale*, Strasbourg, Coprur, 1982.

141 André Gueslin, *Les Origines du Crédit agricole (1840–1914)*, Nancy, Université de Nancy II, 1978.

142 André Gueslin, *L'Invention de l'économie sociale. Le XIXe siècle français*, Paris, Economica, 1987.

143 Jean Heffer, Jacques Mairesse, Jean-Marie Chanut, 'La culture du blé au milieu du XIXe siècle: rendement, prix, salaires et antres coûts', *Annales ESC*, November–December 1986, pp. 1273–302.

144 Bernard Lepetit, *Chemins de terre et Voies d'eau. Réseau de transports et organisation de l'espace en France (1740–1840)*, Paris, EHESS, 1984.

145 Jacques Mulliez, 'Du blé, "mal nécessaire". Réflexions sur les progrès de l'agriculture de 1750 à 1850', *Revue d'histoire moderne et contemporaine*, January–March 1979, pp. 3–47.

146 Rémy Pech, *Entreprise viticole et Capitalisme en Languedoc-Roussillon*, Toulouse, Publications de l'université de Toulouse-le-Mirail, 1975.

147 Yves Rinaudo, 'Voir et entendre: le progrès dans le vignoble varois à la fin du XIXe siècle', *Bulletin du Centre Pierre Léon*, no. 1–2, 1983, pp. 59–74.

148 François Sigaut, 'Pour une cartographie des assolements en France au début du XIXe siècle', *Annales ESC*, no. 3, May–June 1976, pp. 631–43.

149 Jacques Valette and Alfred Wahl, *Les Français et la France (1859–1899)*, 2 vols., Paris, SEDES, 1986.

150 Christine Veauvy, *Le Marché en région méditerranéenne. Propriétaires fonciers et paysans du pays d'Apt en Vaucluse (1815–1865)*, 2 vols., Paris V, 1981 (thèse de troisième cycle).

Peasants and the land

151 Michel Aubrun, 'La terre et les hommes d'une paroisse. Essai d'histoire régressive', *Etudes rurales*, no. 89–91, 1983, pp. 247–57.

152 Jean Bastier, 'Les paysans de Balzac et l'histoire du droit rural', *Revue d'histoire moderne et contemporaine*, July–September 1978, pp. 396–418,

153 Gabriel Désert, 'Propriétaires et propriété dans le bocage normand au XIXe siècle', in *Problèmes agraires et Société rurale*, issue of *Cahiers des Annales de Normandie*, 1979, pp. 139–73.

154 Alain Guillemin, 'Rente, famille, innovation. Contribution à la sociologie

du grand domaine noble au XIXe siècle', *Annales ESC*, no. 1, January–February 1985, pp. 54–70.

155 Ronald Hubscher, 'La petite exploitation en France: reproduction et compétitivité (fin XIXe–début XXe siècle)', *Annales ESC*, no. 1, January–February 1985, pp. 3–34.

156 Gilles Postel-Vinay, *La Rente foncière dans le capitalisme agricole*, Paris, Maspero, 1974.

157 Gilles Postel-Vinay, 'Pour une apologie du rentier, ou: que font les propriétaires fonciers?', *Le Mouvement social*, no. 115, April–June 1981, pp. 27–50.

158 Philippe Vigier, *Essai sur la répartition de la propriété foncière dans la région alpine*, Paris, SEVPEN, 1963.

Demography, family structures

159 André Armengaud, *La Population française au XIXe siècle*, Paris, PUF, 1976.

160 Georges Augustin, Rolande Bonnain, Yves Péron et Gilles Sauter, *Les Barronies des Pyrénées*, vol. II, *Maisons-Espace-Famille*, Paris, EHESS, 1986.

161 Patrice Bourdelais, 'Vieillir en famille dans la France des ménages complexes (l'exemple de Prayssas, 1836–1911)', *Annales de démographie historique*, 1985, pp. 21–38.

162 Jacques Bourdin, 'Note sur la structure des familles dans la Limagne d'Issoire et sur ses bordures montagneuses (1836–1856)', *Cahiers d'histoire*, no. 3, 1978. pp. 349–53.

163 Agnès Fine-Souriac, 'La famille-souche pyrénéenne au XIXe siècle: quelques réflexions de méthode', *Annales ESC*, no. 3, May–June 1977, pp. 478–87.

164 James R. Lehning, 'Développement économique et mutation familiale. Le ménage paysan dans un village de la région stéphanoise au XIXe siècle', *Cahiers d'histoire*, no. 3, 1978, pp. 275–91.

165 Francklin F. Mendels, 'La composition du ménage paysan en France au XIXe siècle: une analyse économique du mode de production domestique', *Annales ESC*, no. 4, July–August 1978, pp. 780–802.

166 Jean-Claude Peyronnet, 'Famille élargie ou famille nucléaire? L'exemple du Limousin au début du XIXe siècle', *Revue d'histoire moderne et contemporaine*, vol. XXII, October–December 1975, pp. 568–82.

167 Roland Schwab, *De la cellule rurale à la région. L'Alsace (1825–1960)*, Paris, Ophrys, 1980.

168 Elisabeth Thibault, *Quatre Villages du Beauvaisis en 1831*, Paris I, n.d. (mimeographed thèse de troisième cycle).

Migrations, multiple occupations

169 *Aux origines de la révolution industrielle*, special number of the *Revue du Nord*, January–March 1979 and 1981.

170 Abel Châtelain, *Les Migrants temporaires en France de 1800 à 1914*, 2 vols., Lille, Presses universitaires de Lille, 1976.

171 Jean-Claude Farcy, 'L'artisanat rural dans la Beauce au XIXe siècle', *Histoire, économie et société*, no. 4, 1986, pp. 573–90.

172 Ronald Hubscher, 'Société globale et population agricole: un essai de classification des catégories socioprofessionnelles non agricoles', *Revue d'histoire moderne et contemporaine*, April–June 1980, pp. 312–19.

173 Yves Lamy, *Travail du fer, propriété foncière, sociétés paysannes en Périgord (1789–1930). L'exemple de la forge de Savignac-Lédrier*, 2 vols., Paris X-Nanterre, 1984 (thèse de troisième cycle).

174 *La Pluriactivité dans les familles agricoles*, Paris, Association des ruralistes français, 1984.

175 Gérard Noiriel, *Les Ouvriers dans la société française, XIXe–XXe siècle*, Paris, Ed. du Seuil, 1986.

176 Yves Rinaudo, 'Un travail en plus: les paysans d'un métier à l'autre (vers 1830–vers 1950)', *Annales ESC*, no. 2, March–April 1987, pp. 283–302.

Rural society, daily life

177 Yves-Marie Bercé, *Le Chaudron et la Lancette. Croyances populaires et médecine préventive (1798–1830)*, Paris, Presses de la Renaissance, 1984.

178 Ariane Bruneton-Governatori, 'Alimentation et idéologie: le cas de la châtaigne', *Annales ESC*, no. 6, November–December 1984, pp. 1161–89.

179 Françoise Dubost, 'L'usage social du passé. Les maisons anciennes dans un village beaujolais", *Ethnologie française*, no. 1, 1982, pp. 45–60.

180 Thierry Fillaut, *L'Alcoolisme dans l'Ouest de la France pendant la seconde moitié du XIXe siècle*, Paris, La Documentation française, 1983 (thèse de troisième cycle).

181 Thierry Fillaut, 'Manières de boire et alcoolisme dans l'Ouest de la France au XIXe siècle', *Ethnologie française*, no. 4, 1984, pp. 377–86.

182 Jean-Pierre Goubert, *La Conquête de l'eau*, Paris, Laffont, coll. 'Pluriel', 1986.

183 Ronald Hubscher, *La Française au quotidien*, Paris, Colin, 1986 (collection of postcards).

184 Marie-Thérèse Larroque, 'Le linge de maison dans le trousseaux du Pays d'Orthe au XIXe siècle', *Ethnologie française*, no. 3, 1986, pp. 261–72.

185 Marie-Thérèse Larroque, 'Meubles et trousseau en pays d'Orthe entre 1816 et 1914', *Ethnologie française*, no. 3, 1985, pp. 275–84.

186 Jacques Léonard, *La Médecine entre les savoirs et les pouvoirs*, Paris, Aubier-Montaigne, 1981.

187 Jacques Léonard, 'Les guérisseurs en France au XIXe siècle', *Revue d'histoire moderne et contemporaine*, July–September 1980, pp. 501–16.

188 Les gens de Cherves (GRCP Poitiers), 'Contribution à l'étude des costumes paysans en Mirabelais (haut Poitou)', *Ethnologie francaise*, no. 1, 1978, pp. 63–70.

189 Nicole Pellegrin, 'Chemises et chiffons. Le vieux et le neuf en Poitou et Limousin (XVIIIe–XIXe siècle)', *Ethnologie française*, no. 3, 1986.

190 Matthew Ramsey, 'Sur le régime de la législation de 1803: trois enquêtes sur les charlatans au XIXe siècle', *Revue d'histoire moderne et contemporaine*, July–September 1980, pp. 485–500.

191 Guy Thuillier, *L'Imaginaire quotidien au XIXe siècle*, Paris, Economica, 1977.

192 Guy Thuillier, *Pour une histoire du quotidien au XIXe siècle en Nivernais*, La Haye-Paris, Mouton, 1977.

193 Guy Thuillier, 'Pour une histoire du temps en Nivernais au XIXe siècle', *Ethnologie française*, no. 2, 1976, pp. 149–62.

194 *Usages alimentaires des Français*, special number of *Ethnologie française*, no. 3, 1980.

Social relations, ethnology

195 Maurice Agulhon and Maryvonne Bodiguel, *Les Associations au village*, Marseille, Actes/Sud, 1981.

196 Maurice Agulhon, *La Vie sociale en Provence intérieure au lendemain de la Révolution*, Paris, Société des études robespierristes, 1970.

197 Rolande Bonnain-Moerdyk and Donald Moerdyk, 'A propos du charivari: discours bourgeois et coutumes populaires', *Annales ESC*, no. 2, March–April 1977, pp. 381–98.

198 Jean-Marc Chouraqui, 'Le combat de Carnaval et de Carême en Provence (XVIe–XIXe siècle)', *Revue d'histoire moderne et contemporaine*, January–March 1985, pp. 114–24.

199 Paul Gerbod, 'L'institution orphéonique en France du XIXe au XXe siècle', *Ethnologie française*, no. 1, 1980, pp. 27–44.

200 Pierre Goujon, 'Associations et vie associative dans les campagnes au XIXe siècle: le cas du vignoble de Saône-et-Loire', *Cahiers d'histoire*, no. 2, 1981, pp. 107–50.

201 Martine Segalen, *Mari et Femme dans la société paysanne*, Paris, Flammarion, 1980.

202 Arnold Van Gennep, *Manuel du folklore français contemporain*, 9 vols. Paris, A. and J. Picard, 1937–8; new edn, 1981.

Cultural life

203 François Furet and Jacques Ozouf, *Lire et écrire. L'alphabétisation des Français de Calvin à Jules Ferry*, 2 vols., Paris, Ed. de Minuit, 1977.

204 François Furet and Jacques Ozouf, 'L'alphabétisation des Français, trois siècles de métissage culturel', *Annales ESC*, no. 3, May–June 1977, pp. 488–502.

205 *Intermédiaires économiques, sociaux et culturels au village. Colloque ruraliste du 22 mars 1986*, special number of *Bulletin du Centre Pierre Léon*, 1986.

206 Emmanuel Le Roy Ladurie and André Zysberg, 'Anthropologie des conscrits français (1868–1887)', *Ethnologie française*, no. 1, 1979, pp. 47–68.
207 *Léonard, Marie Jean et les autres. Les prénoms en Limousin depuis un millénaire*, Paris, Ed. du CNRS, 1984.
208 Jean-Noël Luc, 'La scolarisation en France au XIXe siècle: l'illusion statistique', *Annales ESC*, no. 4, July–August, 1986, pp. 887–911.
209 François Muel, 'Les instituteurs, les paysans et l'ordre républicain', *Actes de la recherche en sciences sociales*, no. 17–18, November 1977, pp. 37–61.
210 Jacques Ozouf, *Nous les Maîtres d'école. Autobiographies d'instituteurs de la Belle Epoque*, Paris, Julliard, coll. 'Archives', 1973.
211 Rémy Ponton, 'L'éducation morale des ruraux. Tu seras agriculteur. Un manuel de lecture de l'école rurale', *Actes de la recherche en sciences sociales*, no. 57–8, June 1985, pp. 103–17.

Religious life

212 Philippe Boutry, *Prêtres et paroisses au pays du curé d'Ars*, Paris, Ed. du Cerf, 1986.
213 Philippe Boutry, 'Les mutations du paysage paroissial. Reconstruction d'églises et translation de cimetières dans les campagnes de l'Ain au XIXe siècle', *Ethnologie française*, no. 1, 1985, pp. 7–34.
214 Alain Croix and Fanch Roudault, *Les Bretons, la mort et Dieu de 1600 à nos jours*, Paris, Messidor, 1984.
215 Yves-Marie Hilaire, *Une chrétienté au XIXe siècle? La vie religieuse des populations du diocèse d'Arras (1840–1914)*, 2 vols., Lille, Presses universitaires de Lille, 1977.
216 Peter M. Jones, 'Quelques formes élémentaires de la vie religieuse dans la France rurale (fin XVIIIe et XIXe siécle)', *Annales ESC*, no. 1, January–February 1987, pp. 91–116.
217 Marcel Lagrée, *Mentalités, religion et histoire en haute Bretagne au XIXe siècle. Le diocèse de Rennes (1815–1848)*, Rennes, Université de haute Bretagne, 1978.
218 Marcel Launay, *Le Bon Prêtre. Le clergé rural au XIXe siècle*, Paris, Aubier, 1986.
219 *La Religion populaire. Colloque du 17–19 octobre 1977*, Paris, CNRS, 1979.
220 Louis Pérouas, *Refus d'une religion, Religion d'un refus en Limousin rural (1880–1940)*, Paris, EHESS, 1985.
221 Pierre Pierrard, *Histoire des curés de campagne de 1789 à nos jours*, Paris, Plon, 1986.

Politics and syndicalism

222 Maurice Agulhon, *La République au village*, Paris, Ed. du Seuil, 1979.
223 Maurice Agulhon, *Marianne au combat. L'imagerie et la symbolique républicaines de 1789 à 1880*, Paris, Flammarion, 1979.
224 Jean-Claude Bontron, 'Transformations et permanences des pouvoirs dans

une société rurale. A propos du sud de Morvan', *Etudes rurales*, no. 63–4, July–December 1976, pp. 141–51.

225 Michael Burns, *French Politics, Boulangism and the Dreyfus Affair (1886–1900)*, Princeton University Press, 1984.

226 Gilbert Garrier, 'L'Union de Sud-Est des syndicats agricoles de 1888 à 1939', *Bulletin du Centre Pierre Léon*, no. 1–2, 1981, pp. 27–30.

227 Raymond Huard, *La Préhistoire des partis. Le mouvement républicain en bas Languedoc, 1848–1881*, Paris, Presses de la FNSP, 1982.

228 Jean-Luc Mayaud, *Les Secondes Républiques du Doubs*, Paris, Les belles Lettres, 1986.

229 Claude Mesliand, 'Gauche et droite dans les campagnes provençales sous la IIIe république', *Etudes rurales*, no. 63–4, July–December 1976, pp. 207–34.

230 Félix Napo, *1970, La Révolte des vignerons*, Toulouse, Privat, 1971; new edn, 1982.

231 Pierre Nora (directed by), *La République. Les lieux de mémoire*, vol. I, Paris, Gallimard, 1984.

232 Danielle Ponchelet, *Ouvriers nomades et Patrons briards. Les grandes exploitations agricoles dans la Brie (1848–1938)*, 2 vols., Paris X-Nanterre, 1987 (thèse de troisième cycle).

233 Yves Rinaudo, 'Syndicalisme agricole de base: l'exemple du Var au début de XXe siècle', *Le Mouvement social*, July–September 1980, pp. 79–95.

234 Jean Sagnes, *Le Midi rouge. Mythe et réalité*, Paris, Anthropos, 1982.

235 Jean Sagnes, 'Le mouvement de 1907 en Languedoc-Roussillon: de la révolte viticole à la révolte régionale', *Le Mouvement social*, July–September 1978, pp. 4–30.

236 André Siegfried, *Tableau politique de la France de l'Ouest sous la IIIe République*, Paris, Armand Colin, 1913.

237 Pierre Vallin, *Paysans rouges du Limousin: mentalités et comportement politique à Compreignac et dans le nord de la Haute-Vienne (1870–1914)*, Paris, L'Harmattan, 1985.

238 Philippe Vigier, *La Seconde République dans la région alpine*, 2 vols., Paris, PUF, 1963.

239 Marcel Vigreux, 'Les paysans républicains à la fin du second Empire: les élections de 1869 dans le Morvan nivernais', *Revue d'histoire moderne et contemporaine*, July–September 1978, pp. 443–69.

Images of the peasantry

240 Caroline and Richard Brettell, *Les Peintres et le Paysan au XIXe siècle*, Geneva, Skira, 1983.

241 Marie-Thérèse Caille, *Images des paysans*, Paris, Ed. de la Réunion des musées nationaux, 1986.

242 Jean-Claude Chamboredon, 'Peinture des rapports sociaux et invention de l'éternel paysan: les deux manières de Jean-François Millet', *Actes de la recherche en sciences sociales*, no. 17–18, November 1977.

243 Rémy Ponton, 'Les images de la paysannerie dans le roman rural à la fin du XIXe siècle', *Actes de la recherche en sciences sociales*, no. 17–18, November 1977, pp. 62–71.
244 *Roman et Société au XIXe siècle*, Paris, La Documentation française, 1979.
245 Paul Vernois, *Le Roman rustique de G. Sand à Ramuz*, Paris, Nizet, 1963.

5. From one war to another

The peasantry during the First World War

246 Stéphane Audoin-Rouzeau, *14–18. Les Combattants des tranchées*, Paris, Colin, 1986.
247 Michel Augé-Laribé, *L'Agriculture française pendant la guerre*, Paris, PUF, 1925.
248 Gérard Baconnier, André Minet, Louis Soler, *La Plume au fusil. Les poilus du Midi à travers leur correspondance*, Toulouse, Privat, 1985.
249 Jean-Jacques Becker, *1914: comment les Français sont entrés dans la guerre*, Paris, Presses de la FNSP, 1977.
250 Jean-Jacques Becker, *Les Français et la Grande Guerre*, Paris, Laffont, 1980.
251 Annick Cochet, 'Les paysans sur le front en 1916', *Bulletin du Centre d'histoire de la France contemporaine*, no. 3, 1982, pp. 37–48.
252 Patrick Festy, 'Effets et répercussion de la Première Guerre mondiale sur la fécondité française', *Population*, November–December 1984, pp. 977–1010.
253 Henry Gerest, *Les Populations rurales du Montbrisonnais et la Grande Guerre*, Saint-Etienne, Centre d'études foréziennes, 1977.
254 Antoine Prost, *Les Anciens Combattants et la Société française, 1914–1939*, 3 vols., Paris, Presses de la FNSP, 1973.
255 Paul Faybaut, *Les raisins sont bien beaux. Correspondance de guerre d'un rural (1914–1917)*, Paris, Fayard, 1977.

The inter-war years

256 Suzanne Berger, *Peasants against Politics*, Harvard University Press, 1972.
257 *La France et les Français en 1938–1939*, Paris, Presses de la FNSP, 1978.
258 Monique Luirard, *La Région stéphanoise dans la guerre et dans la paix (1936–1951)*, Saint-Etienne, Centre d'études foréziennes, 1980.
259 Patrick Prado, 'La va-et-vient. Migrants bretons à Paris", *Ethnologie française*, no. 2, 1980, pp. 191–6.
260 Alfred Sauvy, *Histoire économique et sociale de la France entre les deux guerres*, 4 vols., Paris, Economica, 1984.
261 Gordon Wright, *La Révolution rurale en France*, Paris, Ed. de l'Epi, 1967.

The Second World War

262 Isabel Boussard, *Vichy et la Corporation paysanne*, Paris, Presses de la FNSP, 1980.

263 Michel Cépède, *Agriculture et Alimentation en France durant la Seconde Guerre mondiale*, Paris, Génin, 1961.
264 *Etudes sur la France de 1939 à nos jours*, Paris, Ed. du Seuil, 1985.
265 Gilbert Garrier, 'La Corporation paysanne en France (1941–1944)', *Bulletin du Centre Pierre Léon*, 1981, pp. 37–40.
266 Richard R. Kuisel, 'Vichy et les origines de la planification économique (1940–1946)', *Le Mouvement social*, no. 98, January–March, 1977, pp. 77–102.
267 Elisabeth Morfin, 'La Corporation paysanne dans le Rhône', *Bulletin du Centre Pierre Léon*, 1981, pp. 41–4.

6. The peasantry after 1945

The agricultural revolution

268 Jean Chombart de Lauwe, *L'Aventure agricole de la France de 1945 à nos jours*, Paris, PUF, 1979.
269 Daniel Faucher, *Le Paysan et la Machine*, Paris, Ed. de Minuit, 1954.
270 André Fel, 'L'agriculture française en mouvement', *Annales de géographie*, no. 517, May–June 1984, pp. 303–25.
271 Gérard Gouzes, *Tradition et Modernité de l'agriculture française. Rapport au Premier ministre*, Paris, Ministère de l'Agriculture, 1985.
272 Joseph Klatzmann, *L'Agriculture française*, Paris, Ed. du Seuil, 1978.
273 Paul Maclouf, 'L'après-crise, une troisième "fin des terroirs"?', *Economie rurale*, no. 166, March–April 1985, pp. 29–32.
274 Henri Mendras, *La Fin des paysans. Innovation et changement dans l'agriculture française*, Paris, Sédéis, 1967; new edn, Actes/Sud, 1984.
275 Violette Rey and Roger Calmès (under the general editorship of), *L'Agriculture française*, Paris, La Documentation française, 1986.
276 Philippe Roudié, *La France, agriculture, forêt, pêche*, Paris, Sirey, 1983.
277 Michael Tracy, *L'Etat et l'Agriculture en Europe occidentale. Crises et réponses au cours d'un siècle*, Paris, Economica, 1986.

Agricultural policies: changing farm structures

278 Jean Astruc, 'La politique des structures a-t-elle évolué depuis 1960?', *Economie rurale*, no. 171, January–February 1986, pp. 27–31.
279 François Bloch-Lainé and Jean Bouvier, *La France restaurée (1944–1954). Dialogue sur les choix d'une modernisation*, Paris, Rayard, 1986.
280 René Groussard, 'Vingt ans de politique des structures: une aide au financement de l'agriculture', *Economie rurale*, no. 181, September–October 1987, pp. 5–10.
281 François Houillier, 'Structures foncières et exploitations agricoles', *Notes et études documentaires*, no. 4655–6, 10 February 1982.
282 Pierre Muller, *Le Technocrate et le Paysan. Essai sur la politique française de modernisation de l'agriculture de 1945 à nos jours*, Paris, Ed. Ouvrières, 1984.

283 Edgard Pisani, *L'Utopie foncière*, Paris, Gallimard, 1977.

284 Guy Barbichon, 'Ruralité citadine et spécificité urbaine', *Ethnologie française*, no. 2, 1982, pp. 217–22.

Peasants in the rural world

285 Gérard Bauer and Jean-Michel Roux, *La Rurbanisation ou la Ville éparpillée*, Paris, Ed. du Seuil, 1976.

286 Roger Béteille, *La France du vide*, Paris, Litec, 1981.

287 Maryvonne Bodiguel, *Le Rural en question*, Paris, L'Harmattan, 1986.

288 Patrick Champagne, 'La restructuration de l'espace villageois', *Actes de la recherche en sciences sociales*, no. 3–4, May 1975, pp. 43–54.

289 Robert Chapuis, *Les Ruraux français*, Paris, Masson, 1986.

290 Philippe Collomp, *La Mort de l'orme séculaire. Crise agricole et migration dans l'Ouest audois des années cinquante*, 2 vols., Paris, PUF, 1984.

291 Philippe Collomp, 'Les émigrants de l'Ouest audois dix-neuf ans après', articles I–IV, *Population*, 1979, pp. 65–90; 1981, pp. 93–122 and 845–82; 1982, pp. 75–112, 837–903 and 1065–98.

292 André Fel, 'Les révolutions vertes de la campagne française, 1955–1985', *Vingtième siècle, revue d'histoire*, no. 8, October–December 1985, pp. 3–18.

293 Bernard Kayser, 'Subversion des villages français', *Etudes rurales*, no. 93–4, June 1984, pp. 295–324.

Social relations within the peasantry

294 Thiphaine Barthélémy de Saizieu, 'Les formes actuelles de l'entraide agricole dans une commune de basse-Bretagne', *Ethnologie française*, no. 4, 1984, pp. 362–76.

295 Patrick Champagne, 'La reproduction de l'identité', *Actes de la recherche en sciences sociales*, November 1986, pp. 41–64.

296 Marie-Claude Pingaud, *Paysans en Bourgogne. Les gens de Minot*, Paris, Flammarion, 1978.

297 Michèle Salitot and Pierre Labat, 'Rapports de production et parenté dans un village du Bassin parisien', *Ethnologie française*, no. 1, 1986, pp. 77–91.

298 Claude Thélot, *Tel père, tel fils*,Paris, Dunod, 1982.

Quality of life

299 'Avec nos sabots . . . La campagne rêvée et convoitée', *Autrement*, dossier no. 14, June 1978.

300 Patrick Champagne, 'Jeunes agriculteurs et vieux paysans. Crise de la succession et apparition du "troisième âge"', *Actes de la recherche en sciences sociales*, no. 26–7, March–April 1979, pp., 83–108.

301 Henri Mendras, *Etudes de sociologie rurale, Novis et Virgin*, Paris, Colin, 'Cahiers de la FNSP', no. 40, 1953.

302 Edgar Morin, *Commune en France, la métamorphose de Plodemet*, Paris, Fayard, 1967; new edn, 1971.
303 Laurence Wylie, *Un village du Vaucluse*, Paris, Gallimard, 1968 and 1979.

Agricultural organisations

304 Pierre Barral, 'L'agrarisme en France depuis 1945', *Bulletin du Centre Pierre Léon*, 1981, pp. 47–52.
305 Daniel Barres, François Colson and Henry Nallet, *La JAC et la Modernisation de l'agriculture*, Paris, INRA, 1980.
306 René Colson, *Un paysan face a l'avenir. La JAC et la modernisation de l'agriculture*. Text collected and edited by N. and F. Colson, H. Nallet, Paris, Ed. de l'Epi, 1976.
307 Sylvain Maresca, *Les Dirigeants paysans*, Paris, Ed. de Minuit, 1983.
308 Sylvain Maresca, 'Grandeur et permanence des grandes familles paysannes. L'essor des organisations agricoles en Meurthe-et-Moselle', *Actes de la recherche en sciences sociales*, no. 31, January 1980, pp. 35–61.
309 Sylvain Maresca, 'La représentation de la paysannerie. Remarques ethnographiques sur le travail de représentation des dirigeants agricoles', *Actes de la recherche en sciences sociales*, no. 38, May 1981, pp. 3–18.

Peasants and politics

310 Gilles Allaire and Michel Blanc, *Politiques agricoles et Paysanneries*, Paris, Le Sycomore, 1982.
311 Isabel Boussard, 'Le comportement électoral des agriculteurs français', *Economie rurale*, no. 149, May–June 1982, pp. 3–11.
312 Patrick Champagne, 'La manifestation. La production de l'événement politique', *Actes de la recherche en sciences sociales*, no. 52–3, June 1984, pp. 9–41.
313 Alain Guillemin, 'Doucement, c'est tout de même une femme. Remarques sur le statut de la violence dans les manifestations paysannes', *Actes de la recherche en sciences sociales*, no. 52–3, June 1984, pp. 42–8.
314 Marcel Jollivet (directed by), *Sociétés paysannes ou la Lutte des classes au village*, Paris, Colin, 1974.
315 Marc Pinol, 'Dix ans de manifestations agricoles sous la Ve République', *Revue de géographie de Lyon*, 1975, pp. 111–26.
316 Yves Tavernier, Michel Gervais and Claude Servolin, *L'Univers politique des paysans*, Paris, Colin, 1972.

7. Novels, biographies, memoirs

The nineteenth century

317 Honoré de Balzac, *Les Paysans*, 1835; new edn, Paris, Gallimard, coll. 'Folio', 1975.

318 Emile Guillaumin, *La Vie d'un simple*, 1904; new edn, Paris, Garnier-Flammarion, 1977.

319 Frédéric Le Play, *Les Ouvriers européens*, Paris, Mame et fils, 1877–9.

320 Roger Thabault, *Mon village, ses gens, ses routes, son école*, Paris, Delagrave, 1943; new edn, Paris, Presses de la FNSP, 1982.

321 Emile Zola, *La Terre*, 1887; new edn, Paris, Gallimard, coll. 'Folio', 1980.

The twentieth century

322 Marcel Chaulanges, *La Terre des autres*, 2 vols., Paris, Delagrave, 1970–2.

323 Michel Debatisse, *La Révolution silencieuse. Le combat des paysans*, Paris, Calmann-Lévy, 1963.

324 Lucien Gachon, *Jean-Marie, homme de la terre*, Paris, Valois, 1932; new edn, Geneva-Paris, Slatkine, 1981.

325 Ephraïm Grenadou and Alain Prévost, *Grenadou, paysan français*, Paris, Ed. du Seuil, 1966.

326 Emile Guillaumin, *Paysans par eux-mêmes*, Paris, Stock, 1935.

327 Daniel Halévy, *Visites aux paysans du Centre*, Paris, Grasset, 1934; new edn, Paris, Le Livre de Poche, coll. 'Pluriel', 1978.

328 Pierre Jakez-Hélias, *Le Cheval d'orgueil. Mémoires d'un Breton du pays bigouden*, Paris, Plon, 1979.

329 Ernest Pérochon, *Les Gardiennes*, Paris, Plon, 1924.

330 Antoine Sylvère, *Toinou, Le cri d'un enfant auvergnat*, Paris, Plon, 1980.

Guide to further reading in English

An increasing amount of literature is available in English either as translations or original work. Reference should be made to journals such as *French History* or *European History Quarterly* for recent publications. An outline of work in both French and English is given in:

M. C. Cleary, 'French Agrarian History after 1750: A Review and Bibliography', *Agricultural History Review*, vol. 37, 1989, pp. 65–74.

An introduction to the place of the peasantry in French history is given in:

M. Bloch, *French Rural History*, London, trans. 1966.

G. Dupeux, *French Society, 1789–1970*, London, 1976.

R. Magraw, *France 1815–1914: The Bourgeois Century*, Oxford, 1983.

R. Price, *A Social History of Nineteenth-Century France*, London, 1987.

T. Zeldin, *France, 1848–1945*, 2 vols., Oxford, 1973–7.

More specific themes such as regional case studies, the impact of the Revolution, the nature of agricultural modernisation or the place of agricultural associations can be found in:

S. Berger, *Peasants Against Politics: Rural Organisation in Brittany*, Cambridge, Mass., 1972.

M. C. Cleary, *Peasants, Politicians and Producers: The Organisation of Agriculture in France since 1918*, Cambridge, 1989.

H. D. Clout, *The Land of France 1815–1914*, London, 1983.

P. M. Jones, *Politics and Rural Society: The Southern Massif Central c. 1750–1880*, Cambridge, 1985.

   The Peasantry in the French Revolution, Cambridge, 1988.

R. Price, *The Modernization of Rural France: Communications Networks and Agricultural Market Structures in Nineteenth-Century France*, London, 1983.

M. Segalen, *Love and Power in the Peasant Family*, Oxford, 1983.

R. Thabault, *Education and Change in a Village Community*, London, 1971.

E. Weber, *Peasants into Frenchmen: The Modernization of Rural France 1870–1914*, London, 1977.

G. Wright, *Rural Revolution in France*, Stanford, 1964.

Index